Theories & Concepts for Football Coaching & Management

Table of Contents

Managing Staff & Players

Player Performance

Training Session Design & Execution

Preface

The initial objective of this book was to consolidate knowledge which can be used as a reference throughout my coaching and management journey. During the process of writing, many discussions, debates and conversations were had in relation to deeper insight into the science, principles, psychology and concepts that could enhance football coaching and management. As a result of this, it became apparent that many more people were interested in these topics than previously thought. As you read the books in this series, you may find yourself asking more questions than finding answers, but this is the exact purpose of the book. To allow you to think, consider and implement what you feel is right for the environment you are working in. Football, much like life, is constantly changing and evolving with various challenges and adaptations that need to be made. No one situation is the same as the next, and it is in those moments that our knowledge base and experiences help us navigate and strategize, in order to achieve success. We often read books that share session plans and training principles, but the role of a coach, reaches far beyond this. In many world industries, the expectation of staff is that they need to be educated, creative, dedicated, understanding, and experienced. It is a standard! Why should coaching be any different? The intention of this book by no means takes away from what has already been taught, learnt, and demonstrated and neither does it imply that there is only one correct way to coach. What it does do is present a broader range of knowledge which can be applied, to increase our probability of achievement in the football environment. I hope this book provides insight in reference to those topics that we as coaches are not always taught but are expected to understand. If it provides a different perspective or activates your thought process in regards to the way you view coaching or implement your skills, sharing this knowledge has been a success.

The Author

Born and raised in London, I completed FA and UEFA qualifications up to my UEFA A License and FA Youth Award, as well as Bachelor's and Master's Degrees in Sports Science, specialising in psychology, pedagogy, and a wide range of topics including elite performance, skill development, sports nutrition, sociology and culture. While completing these qualifications, I worked across various levels of sport and football, including time at Watford F.C. as a Sports Scientist, Tottenham Hotspur F.C. as a Development Coach, Dagenham & Redbridge in various lead academy roles across the club, and Hainault F.C's amateur Sunday League Senior team. Most importantly, over a six year period I worked as a Sports Teacher in over twenty schools across London and Essex, educating thousands of children. During this period I worked with players and students aged from three-years-old to thirty-eight-years-old, some of which have gone on to play professional and even international football. After this period, I left the UK to chase the dream of becoming a professional head coach working with first team footballers on a full-time basis. This led me to Zambia where I became Head Coach of Lusaka Dynamos, in the Zambian Premier League. This gave me an invaluable experience developing an understanding of skills such as dealing with the media, managing a high pressure dressing room, and working with senior management of a professional football club. From Zambia I moved straight to South Africa, where I worked as a Technical Director of one of the largest youth clubs in the country, and now work with the First Team at Orlando Pirates, one of the biggest clubs on the African continent. The education and experience I have gathered has led to speaking at numerous conferences including the Powerade Performance Academy and the Psychology Summit in Johannesburg. Sharing knowledge and learning from coaches has become a passion, writing this series has become a way of fulfilling this desire.

Book Overview

This book focuses on coach development across a wide range of topics to support us in becoming the best coaches we can be. In order to achieve this, we need an understanding of what abilities great coaches should have.

When trying to identify great coaches, society tends to lean towards a few basic criteria: Trophies won, win percentages, and media spotlight (1). The challenge with this criteria is that they focus on outcomes of being a great coach and not processes of becoming a great coach, leaving us questioning, what exactly do we need to do to become great coaches? In the football industry, coaches are often categorised using terms such as tacticians, technicians, and motivators, but can we really just have one strength? Or is there an array of skills we need to have the level of success we desire? While working our way through coaching qualifications, we learn how to deliver technical training drills and tactical team sessions while touching on aspects such as performance analysis and mental strength (2). More recently, English FA Youth courses have started to focus on theory-based approaches to player development and environment design. While these courses have been fundamental for many of our coaching journeys, the knowledge base of the current and future coach will far surpass the knowledge shared on these coaching courses. The intention of this book is to open our minds as coaches to the width and depth of knowledge we can absorb, to support us in being great coaches. Some of the knowledge in this book may crossover with the topics on coaching courses, however many of the theories, principles, and concepts may be unique from current course content. The topics stem from a range of approaches, including psychology, pedagogy, biology, sociology, and even business. Other topics and concepts stem from discussions, interviews, and experiences from a wide range of coaches working across many different levels of football.

Julian Nagelsman, the thirty-two-year-old Head Coach of Red Bull Leipzig, recently said, "As a coach you are almost a psychologist. The mental side of it makes up about seventy percent of the job. If you know everything about tactics, but are an idiot socially, then you'll never be successful" (3). There are many books that focus on the thirty percent. Tactical approaches, session plans, physical programs, coach biographies etc. While these are often extremely insightful, this book intends to focus on the seventy percent, while still covering topics within the thirty percent that are less commonly discussed on coaching courses. With a better understanding of the variety of coaching responsibilities we have, we can better support our players, clubs, colleagues, and the game of football. I have therefore attempted to develop a framework which describes many of the key roles which can support us in becoming better coaches and managers. This framework starts by stating that if a coach wants to achieve holistic success, they must achieve the three following objectives.

Happiness: Players and staff must thoroughly enjoy working and performing in the football environment

Development: Players and staff must continuously develop towards their maximum potential

Performance: The team must achieve results that surpass expectations based on the available resources

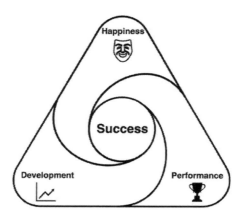

Figure 1: *A framework for enhancing holistic success*

Three Life Beliefs

So where do these objectives stem from? I have three key beliefs about life, which can certainly be applied to coaching environments.

First belief: Everyone deserves happiness and has the right to do what they love and love what they do. Philosopher Allan Watts asked the key question, "What would you do if money were no object?" (4). Many football players and staff already know the answer to that question and are working hard to maintain this. As coaches we should not be the people that ruin this experience. We should be the people enhancing the experience to maximise the experience for all players and staff involved. Liverpool, under Jurgen Klopp, appear to be an example of a club with a heavy emphasis on making football an amazing experience for the players and staff, with the team often reported to be "one big happy family" (6).

Second Belief: Everyone should strive to be the best version of themselves. This does not mean developing players and staff the way we want them to be developed, but rather developing players and staff to ensure they meet their potential as individuals, in the way they wish to develop. This refers to both on the field and off the field. "As we let our light shine, we unconsciously give others permission to do the same" (5). The impact we can have on the players and staff we are working with, can impact the world on a scale greater than we often imagine. While Cristiano Ronaldo has dedicated himself to being the best player in the world, he has made a huge impact both on the field and off of the field. While millions of people idolise him and dream of living the life he lives, his fame, fortune and success has enabled him to become one of the most charitable sports stars in the world, through his ambassadorship, donations, and various other causes he has been involved in (7). As coaches, we can have a significant role in guiding players to having a positive impact both inside and outside of football

Third belief: We only live on this earth once. While we are here, we should have the most amazing, positive experience possible. In the football industry, some of these experiences include winning matches, competitions, and trophies. As coaches there are certain positive highlights of our careers that we will not forget. These often include winning football matches with unbelievable performances, in particular, when the results have surpassed expectations. In the recent era of football, experiences such as Liverpool's 2005 Champions League final win, or Arsenal's unbeaten Premier League season, must be two of the most unbelievable football experiences, both far surpassing any expectations. Not only are they unbelievable experiences for the coaches, they are unique experiences for everyone involved, including players, fans, and families. Regardless of religion, culture, or location, high performance experiences that surpass expectations can bring moments that people cherish forever.

In summary, these three beliefs imply that we should ensure our players and our colleagues are happy doing what they love, are developing towards the best version of themselves, while providing the greatest performances possible to surpass expectations. Depending on the environment we are working in, we may find that one of the three beliefs is more essential than the others. For example, if coaching the under-fives in a little league, it is hopefully clear that happiness of the players is far more important than getting results that surpass the expectations. In a Senior National Team role, it is far more important that results surpass expectations, than having players develop towards their potential. Finding the right balance for the environment is key. We often hear stories of coaches who repeat lines such as 'there is no time to develop players when we have games to win on the weekend', or 'I don't need players to be happy, I need them to win'. However, the belief that one must happen in isolation, is the belief that limits us as coaches. In contrast, we should believe that all three can be achieved, giving us a challenging but rewarding target to meet. But how do we achieve all three? This chapter covers seven topics which we can understand and apply to improve our coaching and management skills within our club environments. Each football environment is unique, meaning there is no 'right way' or 'wrong way', but there are concepts and principles that we can apply to achieve the outcomes we are looking for. Below are the seven key topics:

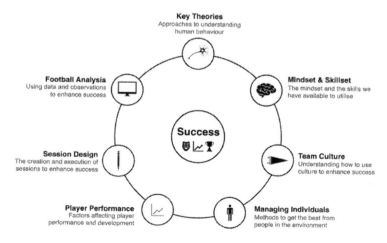

Figure 2: Topics for Improved Coaching & Management

References

1. Becker, J. (2009). 'It is not what they do, it is how they do it: Athlete experiences of great coaching', *International journal of sports science & coaching* 4(1), p93-119.

2. The FA. (2016). Discover the coaching pathway from grassroots to elite level [Online]. Available at http://www.thefa.com/news/2016/oct/07/discover-the-coaching-pathway (Accessed 1 March 2020)

3. Nagelsmann, J. (2016). *Hoffenheim's high-flying boss Julian Nagelsmann is just 29... but who is the 'Baby Mourinho' who turned down a job at Bayern Munich to reach the top* [Online]. Available at https://www.dailymail.co.uk/sport/football/article-3923064/Hoffenheim-s-high-flying-boss-Julian-Nagelsmann-just-29-Baby-Mourinho-turned-job-Bayern-Munich-reach-top.html (Accessed 3 March 2020)

4. Watts, A. (2013). *If money were no object* [Online]. Available at https://zenpencils.com/comic/98-alan-watts-what-if-money-was-no-object/] (Accessed 1 March 2020)

5. Williamson, M. (1992) A return to love: reflections on the principles of "a course in miracles". Revised: Harper Collins

6. Thomas, P. (2020). LOVERPOOL: Klopp has changed Liverpool into LOVErpool as stars want to join his happy family... and stay there. Available at https://www.thesun.co.uk/sport/football/11021012/jurgen-klopp-liverpool-happy-family-phil-thomas/ (Accessed 8 July 2020)

7. Lines, O. (2020). Cristiano Ronaldo philanthropy: What charities is the Juventus star involved in for giving and raising money? Available at https://www.goal.com/en/news/cristiano-ronaldo-philanthropy-what-charities-is-the/zp2qhbgp16ef133rt9t8zx1eu (Accessed 8 July 2020)

"

UNDERSTANDING
BEHAVIOUR

UNDERSTANDING BRINGS AWARENESS, AND AWARENESS ENABLES TRUE INFLUENCE.

"

Introduction

Chapter Objective: The objective of this chapter is to discuss concepts and principles that explain human behaviour. These concepts and principles create a basis for enhancing happiness, development, and performance in our football environments.

Regardless of the objective, the ability of the coach to influence the behaviour of people is at the core of a coach's success. As much as we would like to, as coaches we cannot step on the pitch ourselves, so this means we need to influence others to execute the behaviours that help the players and the team develop and win. Having a better understanding of people will go a long way to helping us get the best out of those we are working with. The people in our environment may range from the players we are working with, the colleagues supporting us, and the senior management who hire and fire us. Influencing these people helps us meet the three objectives of enhancing happiness, development, and performance, within our coaching environments. Another important benefit of understanding people is that we can start to better understand ourselves. How do we grow and evolve if we do not understand what motivates us? Why we do what we do? And why we believe what we believe?

Many of the psychology books in the football coaching industry, are focused on mental toughness and achieving goals. Before setting goals with players and expecting them to be mentally tough, surely we should build an understanding of why people do what they do and why people want what they want. This chapter is focused on a variety of theories which attempt to explain why humans are the way they are, and why we behave the way we behave. The theories discussed stem from a range of scientific approaches, which together form the human formula. Fundamentally, if we can understand people we can have more success influencing people, which is a core role as a football coach.

The Human Formula

After eight years studying psychology from a number of different perspectives, I developed the Human Formula, which is a concept that explains the variety of factors which influence our beliefs, desires, and actions. The objective of this formula is to enhance our understanding of people, to then improve our decision-making within our coaching environments. An improved understanding creates an improved ability to influence. An improved ability to influence enables us to develop our environment towards achieving increased success (1). Below is a diagram illustrating how seven key factors combine and interact to produce a specific state and situation, which then dictates a particular behaviour. This meaning all behaviour can be traced back through the state and situation a human finds themselves in, to gain an understanding of why the behaviour occurred.

Every human action is dictated by their state, and the situation they are in, both which are determined by the following seven factors:

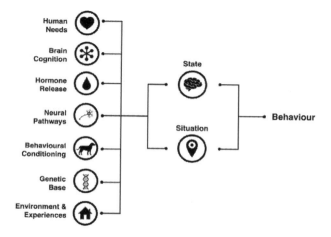

Figure 3: *Causes and factors dictating behaviour*

Human behaviour

The first step to understanding the human formula is understanding behaviour. Behaviour refers to any action that is taken in relation to a situation or stimulus. Therefore every action that a player or colleague takes on or off the field, is a behaviour in relation to the environment that we create. There are two levels of thinking which produce two types of behaviours. The difference in the types of behaviour is based on the level of thought and consideration prior to the execution of the behaviour. Below is an overview of these two types of behaviours.

Conscious behaviours: All decisions that have had a level of consideration of available options and alternatives prior to executing the action. There are several life, training, and match situations that require players and staff to make the best decisions after evaluating a range of alternatives (2). A typical action within a football match would be taking a penalty. With the build-up to the penalty, and the opportunity to think about which direction to shoot and which way the goalkeeper is likely to go, it is a conscious decision with a consideration of options and alternatives.

Subconscious behaviours: All decisions without conscious thinking prior to the action, would be described as subconscious behaviours. This is where there is no conscious analysis of options and alternatives, just an impulsive action with a level of certainty (2). Examples of this would be a goalkeeper's reaction to a deflection or a striker's reaction to a rebound. These are often decisions without a consideration of options and alternatives prior to executing an action. In fact, due to the speed and repetition of actions in football matches and training, most decisions are subconscious habits. For example, a senior centre back has jumped to head the ball so many times that they do not consciously think about which foot to jump off of and which part of their head to use.

State and Situation

Both conscious and subconscious behaviours are a product of state and situation. This meaning the state of the human and the situation they are in, will interact and dictate behaviour. As coaches it is an expected skill to influence the situation our players and colleagues are in, as well as the state they are in when making decisions in these situations. Once we can influence both human state and the situations they are in, we have a great chance of influencing behaviour towards the direction of happiness, development, and performance.

State: Human state refers to someone's feelings at the point of making a decision. It is a combination of all the factors that affect how they feel such as their hormones, thoughts, and desires. For example, at the point of taking a penalty, it would include a player's feelings about taking the penalty, what they are thinking about before taking the penalty, what experience they have in taking penalties, what information they have been given prior to taking the penalty, what beliefs they have about penalties, and many other factors.

Situation: This refers to the full context of the situation at the point of making a decision. This involves a large amount of data for someone to be aware of, including what can be seen, heard, and touched. For example, before taking a penalty, it would include the number of fans watching, the position of the goalkeeper, the state of the game, etc. It is key to understand that situational affects are heavily dependent on perception. For us taking a penalty in front of fifty-thousand people may be pressure, but for another player it may not be. Therefore, we must understand the situation from the persons perspective and not our own.

Factors affecting Human Behaviour

There are seven factors that can influence human behaviour. These seven the...
influence the two factors which are responsible for human decision-making. Sta...
situational perspective (perspective of a situation). Every state we are in and every situati...
perception are influenced by the following theories:

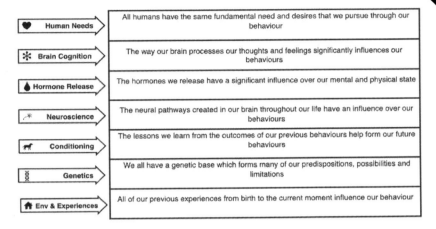

♥ Human Needs	All humans have the same fundamental need and desires that we pursue through our behaviour
✳ Brain Cognition	The way our brain processes our thoughts and feelings significantly influences our behaviours
⬧ Hormone Release	The hormones we release have a significant influence over our mental and physical state
✻ Neuroscience	The neural pathways created in our brain throughout our life have an influence over our behaviours
🐕 Conditioning	The lessons we learn from the outcomes of our previous behaviours help form our future behaviours
⣿ Genetics	We all have a genetic base which forms many of our predispositions, possibilities and limitations
🏠 Env & Experiences	All of our previous experiences from birth to the current moment influence our behaviour

Figure 4: Factors Influencing State & Situational Perspective

All the above factors interact with each other to influence our situational perspective and current state. To give an example of how these interact, picture a striker who has just received a red card for elbowing an opponent. If we analyse the state and the situation, we are better able to understand why they did it. A typical situation may be, the team is losing, they have had no supply of the ball from their teammates, and the opponent has been fouling them all game. As a result of the player's previous experiences in life, they struggle with self-esteem, meaning when someone takes advantage of them, they feel angry, as though they must retaliate to show their strength. They have a genetic predisposition to anger, their neural pathways dealing with this anger are heavily myelinated (strong), and in previous similar situations retaliation made them feel better. This therefore triggers the release of hormones such as cortisol, adrenaline, and testosterone, which are likely to lead to an angry reaction. All these state and situational factors lead the player to elbow the opponent. This may be an extreme case; however, this is an ongoing process affecting all decisions people make throughout the day. Understanding these factors enables us to intervene at numerous stages prior to the behaviour. In relation to the previous example, if we understand these factors, one method of intervention could be substituting the player before the situation arises so that they do not end up elbowing the opponent. Another method may be calling the player over to calm them down by giving them positive words that rebuilds their self-esteem and focus. Alternatively, we could support the player's cognitive processes as soon as we identify them in the season. This may mean teaching the player self-regulation techniques to manage their thoughts and emotions in difficult situations. These are just a few of the possible interventions, there are many more. The key principle to take away, is that by understanding these factors we can better identify and influence behaviour to positively influence happiness, development, and performance.

…ctor 1: Human Needs

…hers have suggested that all humans have the same
…rstand the mechanics of such frameworks, we can increase
…d behaviours of players and colleagues in our environment.
…nfluence behaviour towards the direction we desire and
…meworks for understanding human needs was constructed
…erarchy of Needs' is a positive psychological theory which
…ehaviour based on a pyramid of set criteria (3). The pyramid
…contains five stages of human needs that must be achieved to reach the pinnacle of human state, which he called, self-actualisation. Once meeting this fifth stage of the hierarchy, people can then reach their full potential in relation to happiness, development, and performance.

Figure 5: A Hierarchy of Human Needs

The five levels within the hierarchy represent the different human needs. Maslow suggested that all humans desire these needs in a sequence. First are our basic physiological needs, followed by safety, social, self-esteem and finally self-actualisation needs. The needs at the bottom of the pyramid need to be met to at least a certain standard (Stage 1: 85%, 2: 70%, 3: 50%, 4: 40%, 5: 10%) to increase the likeliness that a human will desire the needs higher up in the pyramid (4). For example, someone who has not eaten for days will most likely prioritise eating over finding love, but someone who is nourished, safe, belongs, and feels confident, is more likely to desire the final needs for fulfilment. Fortunately, football is an amazing tool for fulfilling many of the human needs, and in the right environment with the right coach and culture, it can meet all five, therefore supporting players and staff in reaching self-actualisation. Below is a breakdown with more detail explaining how we can utilise the stages to ensure each player makes it to the pinnacle of self-actualisation.

Level 1. Physiological Needs: This base stage focuses on our immediate needs which keep us alive, functioning, and physiologically developing. This includes aspects such as breathing, nutrition, water, and sleep. Ideally at this level, a player is balanced with the right level of each need. The desire for food, water, and sleep when it is not needed by the body, does not fit into this stage of the hierarchy. In the football industry across most of the world it is more than likely that all players participating or working have these needs met already. However, within our environment, we can still monitor the state of our players in relation to these needs and manage any declines. Can we ensure all players have the optimum levels of hydration, food, sleep, recovery, and rest to fulfil their physiological needs? Players who are not physiologically fulfilled will often have less desire than other players to meet and achieve the needs higher up in the pyramid.

Level 2. Safety Needs: This stage includes the security of our resources such as housing, money, and job. Depending on the environment we are working in, some of these factors may be challenges. Can we ensure players feel safe in the environment, where they know that if they align with the culture, they will not be punished, released, or removed from the team or environment? Threats of releasing players without fair reason and fair warning can often cause players to feel unsafe in the environment. For example, if releasing a player because of mistakes they have made on the pitch, we may find other players start to fear making mistakes because they are worried about losing their security of a contract or the financial benefit they are receiving. This suggests that an increase in the feeling of security from the player should increase their long-term performance if they are striving to achieve full potential. Sometimes players feeling safe may be heavily linked to knowing that they have a support system if something is to go wrong, in both their personal and professional lives.

Level 3: Belongingness: This middle stage is based on the relationships humans have in their environments. It has a heavy reliance on family relationships, however, also relates to relationships in the work and day to day environment outside of the family, such as clubs, schools, religious groups, and societies. Only once players have their physiological and safety needs met, are they then likely to crave this feeling of belongingness. Most players will desire the feeling of trust, acceptance and friendship with teammates and staff. This heavily links to creating the 'family' environment where players want to fight for each other and protect one another, both on and off the pitch. Building this culture is a critical part of a player's journey to maximising their potential and a team having long term success.

Level 4: Esteem Needs: This stage is critical for football players. It is focused on the players feeling significant and confident. With players performing in front of others on a regular basis, self-esteem is a critical aspect for getting the best performances from players. There is no doubt that players perform better when they have high self-esteem as opposed to when they have low self-esteem. The two types of self-esteem humans seek are internal self-esteem, and external self-esteem. We can build internal self-esteem in our players by reminding them of their achievements, ensuring they are successful in training when they are struggling, and helping them achieve regular goals. External self-esteem is based on the opinion of other people. Modern players, particularly at the senior end of football can be extremely sensitive to the opinions of others. With social media allowing everyone to voice their opinion publicly, it is not uncommon to find players darting straight to social media after a game to see what people think of their performance. Managing players self-esteem is key to unlocking the final aspects at the top of the pyramid.

Level 5: Self Actualisation Needs: This is where maximal performance lives. Players who have the previous four needs met and realise their current and potential ability, are the ones who can become everything that they are capable of being. This desire is filled with significance, purpose, growth, problem solving, responsibility, creativity, and accountability, which are all key components of elite sports performance. Once players reach this point, there must be a continued need for growth in the environment in order to keep them there. Often players who achieve this feeling in one environment then seek a new environment or a new challenge so they can maintain the feeling of self-actualisation. If a player feels the club does not match their potential level of growth, the club becomes a limitation for the player, meaning self-actualisation will be limited or sought externally. At this point, if a player is not allowed to move on, their search for self-actualisation somewhere else may become detrimental to our environment. Sir Alex Ferguson has spoken many times of the importance of letting players leave at the right time, as he did with many world class players. "The minute a Manchester United player thought he was bigger than the manager, he had to go," he wrote. "David thought he was bigger than Alex Ferguson (46). For some players, one club will never meet their ambition. Below is a simplification of the hierarchy of needs into five key feelings that players and the team must reach to fulfil their maximal potential. These feelings contribute to the happiness, development, and performance of the players, and therefore the team

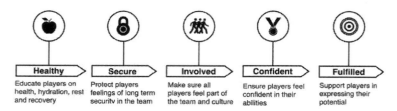

Healthy	Secure	Involved	Confident	Fulfilled
Educate players on health, hydration, rest and recovery	Protect players feelings of long term security in the team	Make sure all players feel part of the team and culture	Ensure players feel confident in their abilities	Support players in expressing their potential

Figure 6: Key Feelings Framework

Factor 2: Brain Cognition

Brain cognition put simply, is a reference to the way the brain 'thinks'. This approach to understanding behaviour focuses on how the way people think, influences what they do. A key framework to understanding this process is the cognitive triangle. The cognitive triangle is a theory that stems from the cognitive behavioural therapy (CBT) approach to psychology (5). As coaches, we can use it to educate players on how to manage their cognitive processes, and we can also use it to have a direct impact on players' cognitive processes through our behaviours, communication, and environment. The basic principle is that our thoughts, emotions, and behaviours are all connected and should not be understood in isolation. This triangle works in continuous cycles where one affects the other. Thoughts affect how we feel, how we feel affects how we behave, how we behave affects how we think, which in turn affects how we feel, and the cycle continues. In summary the cognitive approach pushes the importance of identifying the thoughts and feelings of a person in attempt to understand their behaviour. By analysing this we should have a better idea of why players may demonstrate the behaviours that they do, and we can then intervene to influence their thoughts, emotions, and behaviours.

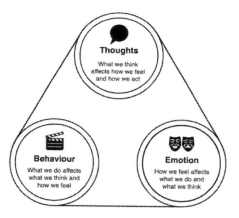

Figure 7: The Cognitive Triangle

Analysing Behaviour

Over my years of coaching I have seen hundreds of situations where we as coaches have not correctly identified how a player feels or what they are thinking but have judged them based on an action. A typical example has been working with coaches who believe a player is arrogant when in fact they are insecure in the environment and have excellent ability. One of the key principles to understand in this cycle, is that there are no set actions that relate to a feeling or thought one-hundred percent of the time. For example, there can be two players who are extremely greedy in possession of the ball, one may think they are the best player, feeling extremely arrogant, where the other may think that no one believes they are good enough, and feels they must change peoples' minds to prove themselves. Same action, two different feelings and thought processes. With a deeper understanding of human behaviour, the coach would have realised that the player was struggling socially and needed support to build their confidence and self-esteem. It is important that we take time to understand what the actions of people really mean, and not to jump to conclusions based on the experiences we have been limited to. Questioning and digging deeper enables us to get a better understanding of our player's thoughts, feelings, and behaviours.

Self-Fulfilling Prophecy

"The self-fulfilling prophecy is, in the beginning, a false definition of the situation evoking a new behaviour which makes the originally false conception come true" (6). To put it more simply, our beliefs will eventually become reality because our actions will lead us in that direction. Therefore, what we believe is a powerful tool in dictating our reality. With an appreciation of how our thoughts, feelings and actions work we can better understand how this process works, with thoughts influencing feelings and feelings influencing actions. If we have players that think they are not good enough, the self-fulfilling prophecy tells us their actions will not be good enough. In relation to our role as coaches, if we can ensure players have a positive mindset and positive beliefs, we can increase the probability that they will have positive feelings and therefore demonstrate positive actions that lead towards improved happiness, development, and performance. It all starts with our thoughts.

Pygmalion Effect

Another theory to understand in relation to the cognitive triangle is called 'The Pygmalion Effect'. This theory is similar to the self-fulfilling prophecy; however, it is based on how the thoughts and beliefs of one person can affect the reality of another person (7). In 1984, research found that when teachers were led to expect enhanced performance from children, the performance of the children was enhanced. (8). This suggests that when we have thoughts based on high expectations of others, it is more probable that our feelings around that person and therefore our actions will change towards them, which therefore impacts their thoughts feelings and behaviour. High expectations equal higher performance. Once we are aware of how our own opinions of people affect their actions, we can take more control of the way we think about players and staff that we are working with. The better we think of them, the better we act towards them, and the better the actions they execute.

A practical example

The thoughts that a player or staff member has when coming to training or matches will have a direct impact on the way they feel when they are there and in turn the way they behave when they are there. This cycle will then continue as the behaviours they demonstrate, and the response they get, will then influence what they think:

Thoughts: Player A comes to training believing that he is not liked by the staff and players. (This may or not be true).

Feelings: When they arrive, they feel insecure and paranoid about what people are saying about them and how people are going to treat them.

Actions: They stay out of players' and staff members' way and only greet when they must. When they are on the pitch they do not communicate with players and do not express themselves or take any risks. As a result of the lack of communication, they receive the ball less and because they are playing simple, players do not want to pass to them as much.

Thoughts: The idea that players and staff do not like them is now reinforced even more with thoughts such as, 'hardly anyone greets me', 'no one passes me the ball'.

Feelings: They now feel even more insecure about themselves and feel like they are not worthy or not good enough.

Actions: More isolation and more mistakes and lack of contribution on the pitch.

Of course, this is an extreme example however it paints the picture of how the process works. There may be less dramatic examples occurring every day in coaching environments across all levels. It could be the player who does not contribute much, but it could also be the greedy player, or the player who misbehaves, or the player who bosses everyone around. The first key is to understand the process as a coach so that these situations can be observed and analysed.

Influencing the Cognitive Triangle

Once behaviour is analysed and understood from a cognitive standpoint, there are several interventions we can use to manage the behaviour of players and colleagues. When dealing with players who are struggling from a 'life' perspective, it is critical that we contact a psychologist or follow club protocol to ensure the health of the player is always put first. However, when they are struggling within the football environment but are managing life well outside, it falls on us as coaches to help develop players psychologically, unless we are fortunate enough to be dealing with sports psychologists.

Environment Management: The easiest intervention for a coach with less psychological understanding is to manage the environment to support the thoughts of a player being more positive. For example, with the player who feels he is disliked, the key would be to increase his communication and positive relationships in the environment to adapt their thought pattern from 'I am disliked', to 'some players like me', to 'I am liked in this environment'. There are many ways to achieve this, some of which may be putting them in groups or pairs for a task, or utilising a 2v2, 3v3 tournament, and putting them with players who we can instruct to communicate with them and offer the player support. We could also simply request all staff to make a conscious effort to greet the player and make conversation. Providing these interventions allow the player to feel genuinely liked with the player's thoughts positively impacted. The principle is the same across all situations, how can we use the environment to turn a player's negative thoughts into positive thoughts? Aspects of the environment that can be utilised can range from personnel (staff and players) to training session design, and even structure design (changing rooms, dining areas etc.)

Framing Perception: As the leader in the environment, our response to actions will heavily dictate how people feel about what happened. From the minute we enter the environment to the minute we leave the environment, it is key we are aware of our communication, including body language. For example, if a player laughs at another player for making a mistake, we have a moment to impact how the player perceives what just happened. The moment the mistake has been made, we could comment with 'that was an excellent idea', or 'that was fantastic determination to try that' or 'great attempt, keep trying that when the time is right'. We can have a significant impact on how the player perceives what they have done. Instead of the thought process being 'I am useless', 'I cannot execute that skill, everyone thinks I am rubbish' we can change the thinking to 'I made the right decision', 'I can execute it next time'. The principle illustrates that communication used in the moment, in order to interrupt the cycle, alters the perception of an action and therefore positively affects the thoughts, feelings and actions that follow.

Educating: A more challenging way of dealing with players struggling with the cycle, is to educate players in reference to framing their own thoughts. While this may seem like the role of a psychologist, there are certainly things we can do within the scope of coaching that can have a positive impact. This education process may start with explaining how the thoughts-feelings-action-perception cycle works. Doing this in a group environment may make individuals feel less targeted. We can encourage individuals to try controlling one of the aspects in the cycle and test its effects on the rest of the cycle. For example, challenging a player to act like everybody likes them by smiling, being friendly and communicating throughout the day on and off the pitch. Providing there is no real issue between the players, the likely outcome of this behaviour is a more engaging response from some of the players and staff, and an increase in communication which would increase the positivity in relationships. Once they understand the process, the next step is for players to be able to identify when they are having negative thoughts and feelings or are demonstrating negative behaviours. Self-interventions only work when players can identify the problem as it is occurring. Educating the players on this process of how they can influence their thoughts, emotions and actions is more likely to work for those who already have a level of emotional intelligence. More time and perseverance may be needed when educating those with less of an understanding of themselves.

Factor 3: Hormone Release

Behavioural endocrinology is the scientific study of interactions between hormones and behaviour. These interactions are a two-way process meaning hormones influence our behaviour, and our behaviour influences our hormone levels (9). Understanding the relationship between hormones and behaviour gives us another method of identifying why players and staff may behave in certain ways. It also enables us to utilise methods of influencing hormone levels and therefore influencing behaviour. This approach to motivating human behaviour suggests that as humans we are consistently searching for the next hormone release through our environment. Examples of these are, the food we eat, the shows we watch, the people we see or the activities we partake in. We are consistently searching for the best hormonal balance and the next great hormone release. The implication being, we are creatures on a never-ending hormone hunt. Within the football industry hormones are very rarely mentioned, with exception to stories such as Lionel Messi and his growth hormone deficiency. However, they play a far bigger role than we think in any working environment. Hormones are in fact a critical component to high performance. There are many research projects that have investigated the impact hormones have on sports performance, and there are several rules and tests to prevent players from enhancing performance through hormone therapy such as testosterone abuse. Through our scientific understanding and coaching skills, we can naturally influence key hormones and sports performance.

To get to grips with this theory, a simple understanding of the functions of hormones within the endocrine system is needed. The endocrine system is an organisation of glands that are responsible for secreting chemical messengers (hormones) which influence the cells and organs throughout the whole body (10). These hormones have an impact on three key systems that can affect our behaviour. These are the sensory system (what we hear, see, touch, smell and taste), our nervous system (the messages that are sent through the brain and the body), and output systems (the components used for action such as muscles). In summary hormones influence what we sense, what we think and what we do. These interactions between hormones and our body's systems can have both a positive and negative affect on behaviour. A typical example explaining this process would be someone staring at us with an angry gaze from across the street. In a calm balanced hormonal state we may not even notice the person staring (sensory system), if we do notice them we are more likely to process it as something we can ignore (nervous system), and if we decide to act we may act with a calm question such as 'is everything okay?' (output system). In an unbalanced abrupt state, we are more likely to notice a potential threat (sensory), process it as a problem to deal with (nervous system), and aggressively confront the person (output system). To demonstrate how behaviour influences hormones, after aggressively confronting the person, there will be a hormonal reaction to the confrontation, which has an impact on our bodies hormonal balance, which will then affect our systems and behaviour. The hormonal process continues until the body finds its balance again. Each individual's balance can control their day to day cycle. There are several different hormones which we can influence through our behaviours and impacts on the environment. Each hormone has a different role within the body and therefore impacts the probability of different behaviours in different ways. The hormone we want players to secrete will depend on the players current state, the actions we want them to take and the environment or situation the players find themselves in. Below are brief explanations of seven of the key hormones which we can impact to enhance happiness, development, and performance:

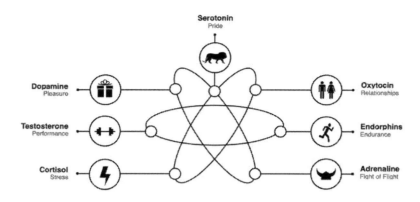

Figure 8: Key Hormones

Dopamine is one of the most well-known human hormones and is often correlated with happiness. Research has demonstrated that it has an impact on far more than just happiness. Correlations have been found between dopamine and motor skills, learning, motivation, sleep, and many other psychological and physiological aspects (11). In the football environment, dopamine can be a powerful hormone. If we can build a relationship between success and dopamine, we can support the process of players craving and giving extra effort in order to succeed. When people have increased levels of dopamine, we will find they are likely to have an increased focus for learning, as well as an increased motivation to meet their goals or objectives. An increase in dopamine will improve the level of enjoyment within the environment, increase learning capacity for development, and increase the desire to win. Research has suggested that elite athletes have higher levels of dopamine transporters than normal athletes, demonstrating the important role dopamine plays in elite performance.

Tip: Provide regular dopamine boosts to create a continuous desire for success by:

1. Ensuring all players have regular achievable goals set, and rewarding these achievements

2. Ensuring all football activities are as active and enjoyable as possible

3. Prioritising high quality sleep, a balanced diet and sunlight for players where possible

Serotonin is the key hormone for feelings of pride, confidence, and self-esteem. Also often described as a 'happy hormone', serotonin significantly increases when players feel that they are respected by people they respect. The high from serotonin is what causes our desire for external self-esteem. People with higher levels of serotonin feel more confident in their abilities and are therefore more likely to demonstrate them. Serotonin also decreases the probability of players making impulsive decisions (12). We as coaches also get a serotonin boost when our players and colleagues are successful, due to us feeling that we played some part in their success. If the right culture is created and all players feel involved, all players will experience a serotonin boost when the team is successful. If everybody feels involved, then everybody feels significant.

Tip: Ensure high serotonin levels to keep high leadership, pride, and confidence by:

1. Regularly showing recognition to players and staff for their efforts

2. Reminding all players and staff of their significance within the team

3. Finding ways for all players and staff to contribute to ensure they feel proud of other's successes

Oxytocin is the 'relationship' hormone. It is the hormone most critical to creating a team culture. As we build relationships with colleagues and teammates, we increase their oxytocin, and in return oxytocin increases a players desire to build stronger relationships and form a stronger group (13). Research has shown that people with higher levels of oxytocin are more likely to trust others around them, and more likely to invest into something they deem important (14). It is critical that oxytocin is kept high within the group. When players feel like they are not part of the group or they are not given the respect they deserve within the group, they will use their energy to create their own group. This group will compete with the rest of the team to fulfil their own desires. This is often why subgroups are formed within a larger group and also why smaller groups find it easier to stick together. The bigger the group, the harder it is to ensure everyone feels valued and part of the group. Increased oxytocin levels have also been linked to increases in problem solving skills and creativity. Players who feel valued are more likely to solve problems themselves and risk being creative for the benefit of the group. Building oxytocin levels among players is a continuous process that takes time, energy, and investment. Once there is a strong family feeling within the group, people outside of the family become enemies and threats which can be advantageous when competing with opponents on matchday.

Tip: Increase individual and group oxytocin levels in order to increase loyalty and commitment from players by:

1. Reducing unnecessary stress in the environment (stress caused by striving for team achievement is fine as it supports oxytocin release)

2. Supporting relationship building for everyone in the team

3. Showing vulnerability by asking for ideas and input in order to make players feel trusted

4. Communicating frequently, both verbally and physically with greetings and celebrations

Endorphins are the 'endurance' hormones. They induce a feeling of euphoria which enables us to mask physical pain. One of the examples of this euphoria is the feeling of a 'runners high' (15). Their role in masking pain is critical for us as physical beings and can be critical in sport to maximise performance when under physical stress. Research suggests that a healthy level of endorphins supports prolonged physical exercise, mood management, self-esteem, and general well-being post exercise (16). It is another example of a hormone that has a two-way relationship. Increased endorphins equal increased duration of potential exercise, and an increase in exercise equals an increase in endorphin secretion. One of the key affects endorphins have on the brain is a reduction in stress and therefore an increased potential for brain development (neurogenesis). According to research there are relationships between endorphins and pleasurable activities such as music and meditation. (Reference)

Tip: Increase individual endorphin levels to improve resilience and mask pain by:

1. Encouraging frequent prolonged exercise for part-time players or full-time players during off season or in season breaks.

2. Ensuring players engage in activities that are pleasurable but not detrimental to themselves as an athlete or person.

Adrenaline is one of two hormones released in reaction to a stressful or arousing situation. It is likely to increase pre-match for many players, particularly before and during high pressure games. Once adrenaline is released, it creates an increase of energy that is sent to the muscle groups, an increase in pain threshold, an enhanced alertness due to arousal of the central nervous system, increased sweating to prepare the body to manage body temperature, and an increase in pupil dilation to improve environmental observations (17). With adrenaline release being heavily related to emotion and testosterone increase, there is a clear benefit to increasing adrenaline in the environment prior to training or performance. Similarly, there is a correlation between adrenaline and exercise. We should use the right exercises with the right intensity and length to promote adrenaline prior to training and performance. However, when adrenaline is too high, it can cause extreme arousal or anxiety, and therefore a decrease in composure and ability to make decisions which is likely to cause difficulty in many aspects of football performance.

Tip: Manage adrenaline to ensure arousal at the right times and right levels by:

1. Increasing pressure on the process but decreasing pressure on the occasion

2. Encouraging positive visualisation of the realistic processes being successful

3. Ensuring caffeine limitation prior to or during adrenaline spikes.

Cortisol is the second of two key hormones released in reaction to a stressful and arousing situation. Cortisol increases the glucose levels available for the muscles to create energy, however, it also inhibits other systems of the body to allow full focus on performance (18). If too stressed, cortisol levels can rise so significantly, that it has a detrimental effect on performance. The key is to prepare the players to have the right balance between arousal and anxiety by managing their stress levels. Too much anxiety or too much arousal, and performance is likely to decrease. Each player may have a balance for optimum performance, whereby they are 'stressed' enough that they have a huge desire to succeed, but not 'stressed' so much that they want to avoid the performance or start worrying about the outcome. A critical fact to understand in relation to team environments is that when one player demonstrates high stress levels, they can create an increase in cortisol in other players, meaning stress can be passed between players. Similarly, it can be passed from coach to players and players to coach. This tells us how important it is to monitor our stress and our body language during stressful situations. Much research has demonstrated the negative impact cortisol can have on decision-making, problem solving, cognitive development, physical development, immune function, injury frequency and happiness (18). This makes it a key hormone to manage to ensure players are happy, developing, and performing. Once players are aware of the balance they need, they can control their balance with behaviours such as music and motivational videos. Once we are aware of our players ideal balance, it should impact how we manage them prior to performance.

Which players need us to stress them? Which ones need us to help them relax? And for which games may stress need to be increased vs decreased?

Tips: Manage cortisol to improve all round brain & body function by:

1. Managing communication with players to increase stress only when beneficial for performance

2. Educating players on the importance of a balanced lifestyle, particularly including nutrition

3. Creating hobbies and activities for use before or after training such as football tennis and games

4. Encouraging a healthy sleep routine, avoiding sleeping late at night or sleeping in for long periods

Testosterone is a hormone that has a heavy relationship with performance. Research has demonstrated its importance in relation to muscle development, spatial abilities, physical exercise, aggression, and competition (19). The influence can be so large that certain testosterone boosting substances have been banned by international governing bodies. Though it is produced in a larger quantity in men, women also produce it and can be affected by any significant increases. Increasing testosterone naturally prior to training and competition can significantly increase the potential of development and performance. In sports such as rugby it is common for teams to use testosterone boosting exercises prior to performance, to improve aggression, focus and the execution of actions during competition. Research papers have suggested there is a correlation between rugby victory and pre-match testosterone levels (20). Even more interestingly, winning further increases testosterone levels, creating a nudge in the probability of future high performance. In the inverse situation, research has found that losing decreases testosterone (21). This then decreasing the probability of future high performance.

Tip: Manage testosterone to enhance development and performance by:

1. Using short high intensity exercises for a testosterone boost

2. Utilising morning sessions to utilise the testosterone peak (which happens in the morning).

3. Using priming sessions prior to afternoon or evening competitions, to delay testosterone decline (which happens later in the day)

4. Using competitive concepts and exercises with winners and losers to increase motivation and testosterone

Key Concepts

Hormone Interaction: One hormone can cause an increase or decrease in other hormones. For example, serotonin hyperfunction (levels below normal) equals dopamine hyperfunction (levels above normal). Research suggests this causes an increased probability of impulsive behaviour. A good serotonin balance causes a decreased probability of impulsive behaviour. The more important someone feels the less they search for impulsive rewards (22). It is key to understand that as we observe and influence hormonal changes it is possible that there may be changes in a range of behaviours. Cortisol is a particularly interactive hormone which limits the release of serotonin and oxytocin.

Hormones & Injury: In a 2005 study, research into psychological measurements and injury found a small but significant correlation (23). This correlation suggested that measures of mood and life stress can be an indication of injury risk. Although they cannot be the only method used to measure injury probability as there are many physiological measurements such as training load which have a higher correlation. Therefore, psychological measurements should be used to supplement physiological methods when predicting injury risks. Williams & Anderson created a stress-injury model that suggests three categories which can influence an athlete's likelihood of injury. This being the athlete's personality, history of stress, and coping resources (24). By integrating a psychological perspective into the sport injury area, it is hopefully possible to help even more players to participate continuously (25)

Hormone Cycles: When following a well-designed training program hormones such as cortisol can be removed from the body within 24 hours. However, during stressful periods cortisol may become accumulated creating a continuous problem. Research has reported that players were found to have significantly higher levels of cortisol during the middle of the season than at the start or end of the season. At the end of the season once all games were finished, players' cortisol levels significantly dropped (26). Utilisation of a training program that offers enough breaks and recovery days in an environment that is conducive to relieve stress, may be a critical aspect to sustaining performance throughout the season.

Factor 4: Neuroscience

We spend hours, days, weeks, months, and years in the football industry attempting to mould players' physical ability, hiring teams of conditioning coaches focusing on a range of elements such as strength, speed, flexibility, and injury prevention. While this is undoubtedly a critical aspect of elite performance and development, I am sure that part of the reason why we invest so heavily in the field is because we can visually see and measure the benefits of the work. We see a player develop bigger thighs and biceps, we can measure their number of training days vs days out injured and we can visually see someone compete with an opponent in a 1v1 duel and link their success or failure back to their training. The fact that we can see and measure these aspects leads us to have full belief in the effect of training on the body, but does this same mindset that we must see it to believe it limit us in understanding the effects that training can have on the brain? Many coaches in elite sport, particularly senior elite sport believe "you are who you are", and that while we can adapt the body, we cannot adapt the mind. The theory of neuroplasticity paints a vastly different picture.

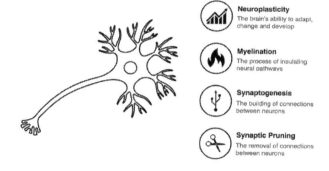

Neuroplasticity
The brain's ability to adapt, change and develop

Myelination
The process of insulating neural pathways

Synaptogenesis
The building of connections between neurons

Synaptic Pruning
The removal of connections between neurons

Figure 9: Key Neuroscience Terminology

Neuroplasticity

"Everything that is to do with human training and education must be re-examined in light of neuroplasticity" (27). Neuroplasticity is a neuroscience approach to the brain and behaviour. It can be defined as "the brains ability to change", and therefore presents the concept that the human brain develops and changes throughout our whole life, rather than only during childhood and adolescence. The changes the brain makes are significantly related to the environment the person finds themselves in and the behaviours they carry out on a day to day basis. A more in-depth definition from Dr Campbell is; "Neuroplasticity refers to the physiological changes in the brain that happen as a result of our interaction with our environment. From the time the brain begins to develop in utero until the day we die, the connections among the cells in our brain reorganise in response to our changing needs. This dynamic process allows us to learn from and adapt to different experiences" (28). Once we enter adulthood it has been suggested that this process slows down, however it does not stop completely. There are many different physiological brain changes that fall under the neuroplasticity umbrella. The key changes to consider in relation to coaching are:

Neural changes: The brain is able to rewire current connections to adapt beliefs and behaviours that are already present in the brain.

Neural growth: The brain is able to grow new structures to learn and develop beliefs and behaviours that are not already present in the brain.

This means we have two roles as coaches when utilising the potential of neuroplasticity:

Firstly, framing and reframing knowledge players already have, to build and adapt connections between information. An example of this would be using analogies around techniques such as 'creating a cushion' for controlling the ball with the chest. The player already understands the characteristics of a cushion and can now link that with the behaviour of chesting the ball. Any previous techniques for chesting the ball can be adapted based on these characteristics.

Also, teaching new knowledge to players will help them build new neurons and can also be framed during teaching, to give the players a specific place to store the information. For example, teaching a player about the phase 'counter pressing' and linking it to the phase 'in possession', so that 'counter pressing' can be connected to 'in possession' in the mind.

The level of neuroplasticity that can take place will be dependent on the mindset of the individual. For us as coaches, with the right mindset we can make drastic physiological changes in the brain which can make significant changes in our lives. Similarly, with players, if educated and supported they can do the same. Here are some key tips to increase the ability for the brain to develop and grow closer to its full potential.

1. Keep players learning on a frequent basis to make growth and development a continuous process

2. When we are teaching something new, decrease stress levels for the players for increased neuroplasticity
3. Educate players on the brain's potential to learn so they believe in the learning experience

4. Let players know the beliefs and behaviours that limit their happiness, development, and performance

In essence, our brain will be directly affected by the environment we are in. The phrase 'you are a product of your environment' is starting to look more like a scientific truth than a philosophical quote. In the Ted Talk 'After watching this your brain will not be the same' Lara Boyd explains the neuroplasticity process in more detail and focuses on the different types of changes including chemical, functional, and structural changes that occur (29).

Myelination

Myelination is a fantastic example of the brain and body's adaptation to training. As players develop their motor skills, (precision of technical actions) do we understand what is happening? If we can understand what is happening, we can enhance training to increase the speed and quality of the development. It is clear that repetition is one of the keys for developing new skills and maintaining current skills (30). All human motor skills are a product of the brain's pathways and brain to body pathways. Once we have initially understood a skill and can execute it the first time, we can then start fine tuning the skill and strengthen our ability to execute it more frequently and accurately. This process of repetition and fine-tuning triggers the process of myelination to start. Myelination is the process of myelin (a fatty substance made of water, proteins, and lipids) insulating the nerves and neural wiring to ensure efficient electrical transfers in the brain itself, and throughout the brain and body (31). As players start to identify skills that they need to repeat to get a specific outcome, the myelin sheath grows thicker to further increase the efficiency. A more efficient neural pathway means less energy and focus is required to execute the skill, therefore focus and energy can be put into other areas. The best example to think about when trying to understand the importance of myelination, is to try and teach a player to cross with their stronger foot, then trying to teach them to execute the same cross with their weaker foot. For the high majority of players there is a clear difference in quality. One of the key explanations for this is the difference in neural pathways and myelination between the left foot, the body and the brain, and the right foot, the body, and the brain. The more a skill is practiced with intent and focus, the more efficiently and accurately the skill can be performed, and the more focus and energy can be placed on other factors such as awareness and decision-making. On a wider scale, research has also suggested that intelligent level of myelination is an indicator of intellectual performance. "The thicker the myelin, the better the brain" (31). Of course, thicker myelin is key in relation to effective motor skills and effective decision-making, however thick myelination for ineffective decision-making and ineffective motor skills can cause challenges.

Principles to increase myelination:

Visualisation: Before executing a skill, visualisation can help with triggering neurons in the brain which need myelination to improve the motor skill.

Self-focus: Player focus and understanding can ensure the correct hormone balance and neural pathway activation to enhance the myelination process.

Player state: The player's mindset regarding how much of a desire they have to learn, and how important the action is to their development, can enhance myelination.

Meaning: Inform or ask the player about what the action means for them in the long term, e.g. relating penalty practice to a cup final they may find themselves in.

Environment: Creating an environment with positivity during the learning experience will have an impact on the hormones released during the repetitions, with clear relationships found between testosterone levels and myelination.

Lifestyle: Sleep and diet have had clear correlations with myelination, suggesting that sleep and specific nutrients such as Vitamin D can also enhance the myelination process.

Synaptogenesis & Synaptic Pruning

It is clear that because of neuroplasticity the brain can change, adapt, and develop its neural pathways. A result of myelination is that we can strengthen our neural pathways, but the questions is, how exactly do we build new pathways and clear unwanted pathways? With the brain developing hundreds of billions of neurons throughout our life, there are two critical synaptic processes. Synaptogenesis which is the process of building connections between neurons, and synaptic pruning which is the process of removing connections between the neurons. A synapse is the junction between nerve cells which allows for impulses to move across and create thoughts, emotions, and behaviours. It is the connection of numerous nerve cells which is critical for human activity. Synaptogenesis is fundamental in the role of learning and developing, which is why it starts weeks before birth and continues throughout childhood and adulthood (32). While synaptogenesis occurs, synaptic pruning manages the development of the neural structures to control what pathways we keep and what pathways we remove. With billions of synapses, there are going to be connections which are not as beneficial as others. Only in recent years have they delved deeper into the realm of synaptic pruning, with studies finding that there are cells and proteins with a specific function of clearing unwanted cells. The process of breaking synapses is crucial to the learning process. Though it is unclear exactly how the synapses are selected for removal, some research has suggested that those that are used frequently or are critical for thriving and surviving in our environment are unlikely to be pruned, whereas those that are used less frequently and not critical are more likely to be pruned (33).

What does this mean for us as coaches? It means that all the key aspects of the game for our teams and players must be regularly practised in training with buy-in from the players to avoid pruning of the aspects players have been taught. Buy-in brings a level of importance on the connection to avoid pruning. This also supports the idea of periodisation to ensure that all important topics are covered throughout the training schedule. From a development standpoint, it also suggests that as players move clubs and encounter coach transitions, new learning can potentially replace old learning.

Key Neuroscience takeaway messages:

1. Players are capable of growth and development throughout their whole career

2. Abilities can be both developed, improved and removed

3. The environment and coaching strategies can enhance or limit player development

4. The thoughts of staff and players will impact their team's reality.

Factor 5: Behavioural Conditioning

Psychological conditioning is the process by which the behaviour of a person can be controlled, affected, and/or modified by someone or something. It can be divided into two key categories. Classical Conditioning and Operant Conditioning. While both result in change and learning, the processes are quite different (34).

Classical Conditioning was first described by Ivan Pavlov through the 'Pavlov's Dog' experiment. It is the theory that the mind can create biological responses to an external stimulus via association (35). For example, if a person listens to new music when on an amazing holiday, which brings them feelings of joy and happiness and the same music is played years later, biological responses will occur from that moment which can replicate those feelings of happiness and joy. After the initial moment, the brain created a psychological link between the music and the feeling. This demonstrates the process which has been labelled the 'Pavlov's Dog' experiment. After ringing a bell and presenting food for a dog, he noticed that the bell triggered the dog to salivate, even when there was no food present. The association between the sound of a bell and food, created a biological response of salivating in response to the sound of the bell. In football, classical conditioning can be used to ensure players associate football, and more specifically the team, with the desired feelings, such as happiness, excitement, and focus. If this association can be made, then players should biologically start releasing the right hormones on arrival and throughout training and matches. Other theories arguably use terminology based around 'energy' and the 'vibe' they get when being around certain people, or in an environment. The theory of classical conditioning would suggest that the triggers in the environment are what release certain hormones or chemicals in the brain, which would then go on to create the feeling (vibe or energy).

Tip: Keys to creating the right biological response within the football environment

1. Ensure consistent positive greetings on players' arrival

2. Immediately deal with negative body language and conversations

3. Create challenging enjoyable activities throughout the day

4. Ensure players leave with positive feelings, players must leave associating football with happiness

"Imagine your football environment like a restaurant, if you were to go for dinner where you were greeted positively, all the people in the restaurant were positive and friendly, the food was enjoyable and any issues were dealt with before leaving, how do these factors increase the likeliness of you being excited to come back"

Operant Conditioning was developed by B.F Skinner. This theory focuses on using either positive or negative reinforcement (rewards or punishments) to increase or decrease a behaviour (36). Through this reinforcement an association is created between the specific behaviour and the consequence of this behaviour. Imagine that we are trying to increase the amount of times our players complete extra training at home. If we set a punishment such as 'no small sided games at training' for those who do not complete the extra training and then criticise players who did not complete extra training, the amount of completed extra training should increase. Players should start to complete their extra training for the enjoyment of being involved in the small sided games, while also being safe from criticism. If we were to create a reward for when extra training is completed such as giving them a financial bonus and a lot of praise, there should be a further increase in extra training completion, as they now associate extra training with financial rewards and praise. Overall there should be a significant increase in extra training completed. It is important when using reinforcement as a conditioning technique that we get the balance right between positive reinforcement (praise and rewards) and negative reinforcement (criticism and punishment). Of course, the success of this method is also dependent on selecting the right punishments and rewards for the environment and the individual. Different individuals respond to different rewards and punishments. Similarly, in different environments some reinforcement methods will be more successful than others. Factors such as age group will heavily dictate the success of reinforcement methods.

Reinforcement can also be extremely powerful when influencing decision-making on the pitch. If a player needs to improve their ball retention, giving the player a lot of praise after a successful pass can create an association between ball retention, and praise from the coach. If after praise the player's overall ball retention does not improve, critiquing the individual player may be a key to improving the player, especially if it can be supported by video footage demonstrating the decision-making.

One of the potential risks of using too much operant conditioning is that players start to behave based on external motivations (rewards and punishments) and less on internal motivations such as meeting their potential. This often means that when a player moves to an environment where there are no rewards and punishments, they are likely to be less motivated as they await a reward or punishment to push them.

Keys to using Operant Conditioning

1. Only use negative criticism for behaviours players can control (not technical errors)

2. Negative reinforcement is most powerful when dealing with behaviour which breaks the behavioural expectations

3. Performing in front of people is a brave experience, public positive reinforcement is immensely powerful

4. Positive reinforcement must far outweigh negative reinforcement to keep a positive association

Factor 6: The Genetic Base

The nature vs nurture argument is one of the most common debates across several subjects and sports. There is no argument that both play their part in relation to human behaviour, however, the extent to which one is more dominant is arguable. At one extreme we have studies that have focused on twins that were separated from birth. These studies allowed the assessment of behaviour in adult twins who had completely different environments. In these studies, there have been some similarities found between behaviours which the researchers attributed to genetic influences. The challenge with some of these studies is that confirmation bias (people looking to confirm their hypothesis) would mean it is possible that these similarities are present, but the many differences were not reported. There is also research which contradicts the idea that genetics heavily influence behaviour, such as studies using separated twins where one develops mental health issues and the other does not. When finding that only one has a mental health challenge such as schizophrenia, it suggests that genetics play a less significant role in influencing behaviour than what is often suggested. Robert Plomin, a leading expert in genetics is the author of the book 'Blueprint: How DNA Makes Us Who We Are'. He suggests that our genetics account for roughly half of the differences between us, and that the rest is mostly attributable to life experiences (37). If the experts are telling us that genes have this level of influence, one of the key questions we must try to answer is, are there 'elite athlete genes'?

Performance Genes

Are there genes that will make players elite athletes? The answer is still blurry. Many of the physical traits such as muscle fibres, muscle mass, strength, flexibility, and aerobic capacity have a clear effect on sports performance, some of which have been linked to specific genetic markers (38). The idea that there is a specific gene that guarantees a performance factor seems to be extremely unlikely. A more likely situation is that a combination of many genes may increase the probability of someone being stronger, quicker, or having an increased aerobic capacity for example. There are examples of specific genes which have been frequently studied such as ACTN3 and ACE (39). According to research, these genes can influence the fibre type that makes up muscles and have been linked to both strength and endurance. Other genes have been linked to having slow twitch muscle fibres, increased energy production and more efficient nerve cell communication. There has also been research that has found a link between genes and hormone release. For example, research has found genetic markers which increase the likeliness of having higher testosterone levels (40). With the clear knowledge regarding testosterone and enhanced performance, it would suggest that genes can have a further indirect role in sports performance. With many genome projects under way it is likely that future research will reveal the relevant genes influencing performance, as well as the interaction between those genes and environmental factors (41). What is currently clear is that both genetics and environmental factors play a significant role in both developing elite athletes and maximising elite player performance. The common middle ground in the nature nurture argument suggests that the genetic foundations can create predispositions for certain behaviours, however their life experiences will dictate if and when these behaviours are carried out. Our height is one example where genetic predispositions exist but lifestyle factors such as nutrition significantly impacts how a person's development can be enhanced or held back (42). Here are two explanations which provide further understanding on how this may be possible.

Gene Regulation

The idea that we were given a set of genes at conception and this foundation will stay the same through our life is gradually being dis-proven. Gene regulation is the process of human development where genes are 'turned on and off' (43). This process is critical for the process of the body having to adapt to environmental changes. While scientists are now sure that this process frequently occurs, there is much research required to further understand the full process and exactly when and why the process occurs. This is however another argument to support the fact that "we are not always who we were yesterday". Our genes do not completely limit us as coaches, and do not completely limit our players from developing and changing their behaviours and capabilities. While our genes can bring limitations, they can also bring opportunities. The excuse of "it is just the way I am", or "it is just the way they are" is gradually becoming a weaker argument that we should avoid as coaches.

Gene-environment interaction

The relationship between a player's genetics and their environment may be the most valuable scientific principle to understand as coaches. Research has demonstrated how life events within the environment may impact people differently based on the individual's genetic susceptibility (44). This means that in a football environment, genetics may play a role in explaining why players respond to situations differently. Two players may both be out of the squad on a match day but may react completely differently. In more serious situations, two players may lose family members but have contrasting reactions in how they deal with the situation. Understanding that genetics may be an influence in a player's reaction to situations, tells us that all players cannot be treated in the same way, and our expectations of them to act in a certain way, may cause friction and tension in difficult situations.

Key messages:

Understanding the depth of genetics is not necessarily going to improve our coaching ability. However, understanding the basic principles can support our knowledge of how a player's genetic base may impact their happiness, development, and performance.

1. At any given time genetics may play a role in a player's behaviour

2. There is currently no 'elite performance gene', however, genetics may influence specific physical abilities.

3. Genes can be 'turned on and off', which can influence long term behaviour

4. Our environment and behaviours will influence genetic regulation and therefore future behaviour.

Factor 7: Environment and Experiences

The other side to the genetic (nature) argument is the life experiences (nurture) argument. This is often referred to as environment, however I think it far extends the definition of environment and is more about what is personally experienced. Two players can go through the same academy system but have completely different experiences within it which are often dependent on relationships, how they perceive events, and social or group dynamics. There is much psychological research which demonstrates how a wide variety of experiences and environmental changes can have a significant influence on human behaviour. Whilst there are an infinite number of experiences that can influence behaviour, some are discussed below to give an insight into factors to consider. It is key to understand that one factor does not directly determine a behaviour, however, correlations are found between experiences and behaviours which suggests at least an increased probability. Some of the best sporting examples can be found in the book 'The Goldmine Effect' by Rasmus Enkersen (45). Rasmus travelled the world to crack the codes of what makes a world class athlete. While accepting genetic influences on athletes, he was searching for the environmental factors that meant that so many world class athletes could stem from specific locations. One of the greatest examples he found was in Ethiopia. Whilst the general belief is that Ethiopians are genetically better suited for endurance running events, Rasmus Enkersen found that athletes from one village named 'Bekoji', which only has thirty-thousand people, had achieved ten gold medals, broken ten world records, and held thirty-two world championships. How can such a small village create so many world class athletes in comparison to the rest of the country? Environment. Yet not everyone from that village makes it to the Olympics? Experiences. Below are just a few of the environments and experiences that we must consider when understanding behaviour:

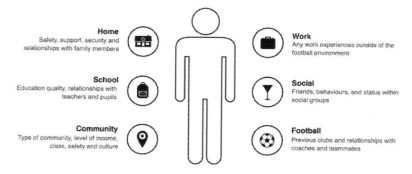

Home
Safety, support, security and relationships with family members

Work
Any work experiences outside of the football environment

School
Education quality, relationships with teachers and pupils

Social
Friends, behaviours, and status within social groups

Community
Type of community, level of income, class, safety and culture

Football
Previous clubs and relationships with coaches and teammates

Figure 10: Key Environments & Experiences

The challenge when discussing environments and experiences, is that the formula to understanding behaviour becomes extraordinarily complex. For example, poverty as an experience, can have many different effects on human behaviour. Some become motivated to work harder to break out of poverty, some struggle mentally to deal with poverty and never make it out. Some are accepting of poverty and do not demonstrate any kind of behaviour outside of 'normal'. The reason for these differences is the relationships between the experiences one has. The combination of experiences and environments eventually ends with specific outcomes. The more experiences we have with athletes from varying backgrounds, the easier it becomes to link experiences to behaviours. When working with players, one of the principles I have come to understand is that the more extreme the behaviour of a player, the more extreme experiences they have had. Behaviour should be seen as a message that indicates previous experiences. A player who is extremely arrogant is likely to have had more extreme experiences than the player who fits normally into the group. This is often similar for any players who show behaviour outside of the norm such as consistent sadness, avoidance, addiction, or consistent anger. Analysing behaviour in relation to experiences and environments becomes more difficult as players get older. The formula becomes more complicated. If we really take the time, we can certainly take huge strides in understanding. To paint the picture, I always compare the build-up of experiences and environments to maths formulas. This is simply a concept to demonstrate the principle of life experiences affecting behaviour.

$2 + 2 = 4$ = A baby cries when they are hungry. The formula is simple as it only has hunger and crying.

$2 + 2 + 8 + 15 + 12$ = A six-year-old who has parents that fight at home and goes to a school with large classes and limited staff. At football training this child kicks other players and does not accept punishment.

$6 + 4 + 9 + 15 + 12 + 28 + 21 + 32 + 49$ = A sixteen-year-old who is bullied at school, has two parents who are always working, is in a team where they have no friends, has no similar interests to the players in the group, has bad eye sight so wears glasses that people laugh at, is forced to go to training by their Dad as his dad tells him that he must be a football player, and is no longer picked for his school football team. This player is extremely quiet at football training and avoids challenging situations and confrontation at all costs.

$6 + 4 + 9 + 15 + 12 + 28 + 21 + 32 + 49 + 90$ = The same sixteen-year-old, but who now has an extremely supportive best friend who joins the club, and they both play in midfield together, the outcome may be completely different based on the addition of one factor.

The numbers of course do not mean anything. They are visual representations of how different experiences and environments combining together can create different behavioural outcomes. Once we understand this, we can see the importance of building relationships with players where they can openly tell us things about themselves that will help us indicate why a player behaves the way they do.

Key Messages:

1. Take the time to understand players life experiences to better understand their behaviour

2. Support players in framing their life experiences to develop positive outcomes

3. Positively influence life experiences through the football environment

Summary

To summarise, understanding these seven factors gives us an advantage in understanding and influencing behaviour to enhance happiness, development, and performances. If we can influence and manage the environment to effect these seven factors, we are far more likely to positively influence happiness, development and performance. Here are some key points to summarise how we can understand and apply this knowledge in our coaching environments:

1. Ensure people's physiological, social, and psychological needs are met before expecting them to demonstrate elite performance. When people have voids in their desires, they will search for fulfilment of these voids before searching for the optimal needs including problem solving, creativity, and maximising potential.

2. Educate and support players to adapt their thoughts, feelings, and actions to encourage personal and professional positivity. It is unlikely players are aware of how much their thoughts and feelings influence their behaviour. Educating the players and managing the environment can bring the positive influence to change how the players think and feel when they are training and performing.

3. When we are struggling to influence behaviour, we should identify positive and negative reinforcement methods that may support the process. These methods should be made clear and fair to ensure players react with the behaviours we are looking for.

4. Create a positive environment full of positive experiences and manage individuals to optimise hormonal balance in all the players and staff we are working with. Remembering that each individual has unique methods of achieving their optimal balance for happiness, development and performance.

5. Whilst genes do have an influence over behaviour, genes can be switched on and off and there are several influences over behaviour such as the other six factors discussed. This means we should not believe someone cannot and will not change, grow, and develop.

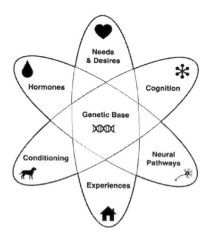

References

1. Adling, R. B. (2017). 'Importance of sports psychology in physical education and sports: *International journal of yoga, physiotherapy and physical education* 2(5), p215-218

2. Benedetti, F. (2014). *Placebo Effects*. Revised. Oxford: Oxford University Press.

3. Maslow, A. H. (1970). *Motivation and Personality*. Revised. US. Harper Collins Publishers

4. Uysal, T. H., Aydemir, S., Genc, G. (2017). 'Maslow's hierarchy of needs in the 21st century: *The examination of vocational differences. Research on science and art in 21st century Turkey*, p211 – 227.

5. Gavrilova, Y., Donohue, B., Galante, M. (2017). Mental health and sport performance programming in athletes who present without pathology: A case examination supporting optimization. *Clinical case studies*. 16(157), p1-20.

6. Merton, R. K. (1948). 'The self-fulfilling prophecy'. *The Antioch reviews*. 8(2), p193-210

7. Raudenbush, S. W., Stephen, W. (1984). 'Magnitude of teacher expectancy effects on pupil IQ as a function of the credibility of expectancy induction: A synthesis of findings from 18 experiments. *Journal of Educational Psychology*. 76. p85-97

8. Niari, M. Manousou, E., Lionarakis, A. (2016). The pygmalion effect in distance learning: A case study at the Hellenic Open University. *European journal of open, distance and e-learning*. 19. p37-52

9. Nelson, R. J. (2010). Hormones and behaviour: Basic concepts. *In Encyclopedia of Animal Behaviour*. New York: Academic Press

10. Matthew Neal, J. (2016). *How the endocrine system works*. Revised. New York: John Wiley & Sons

11. 2014. *Catecholamine Research in the 21st century* [Online]. Available at https://www.sciencedirect.com/topics/medicine-and-dentistry/dopamine (Accessed 9 March 2020)

12. Rogers, R. D. (2011). The roles of dopamine and serotonin in decision-making evidence from pharmacological experiments in humans. *Neuropsychopharmacology: official publication of the American College of Neuropsychopharmacology,* 36(1), p114-132.

13. Pepping, G. J., & Timmermans, E. J. (2012). Oxytocin and the biopsychology of performance in team sports. *The Scientific World Journal, 2012*, 567363.

14. Levin, M. (2017). *8 ways to build a culture of trust based on Harvard's neuroscience research* [Online]. Available at https://www.inc.com/marissa-levin/harvard-neuroscience-research-reveals-8-ways-to-build-a-culture-of-trust.html (Accessed 7 March 2020).

15. Leuenberger, A. (2006). Endorphins, exercise, and addictions: A review of exercise dependence. *The premier journal of undergraduate publications in the neurosciences,* p1-9.

16. Rokade, P. B. (2011). Release of endomorphin hormone and its effects on our body and moods. *International conference on chemical, biological and environment sciences,* p436-438.

17. Samuels, E. R., & Szabadi, E. (2008). Functional neuroanatomy of the noradrenergic locus coeruleus: its roles in the regulation of arousal and autonomic function part II: physiological and pharmacological manipulations and pathological alterations of locus coeruleus activity in humans. *Current neuropharmacology, 6*(3), p254–285.

18. Van Paridon, K. N., Timmis, M. A., Nevison, C. M., & Bristow, M. (2017). The anticipatory stress response to sport competition; a systematic review with meta-analysis of cortisol reactivity. *BMJ open sport & exercise medicine, 3*(1), p1-23

19. Archer, J. (1991). The influence of testosterone on human aggression. *British Journal of Psychology,* 82, p1-28.

20. Gaviglio, C., Crewther, B., Kilduff, L., Stoke, K., Cook, C. (2013). Relationship between pre-game free testosterone concentrations and outcome in rugby union. *International journal of sports physiology and performance.* 9(2), p324-331.

21. Booth, A., Shelley, G., Mazur, A., Tharp, G., Kittok, R. (1989). Testosterone, and winning and losing in human competition. *Hormonal behaviour,* 23(4), p556-571.

22. Seo, D., Patrick, C. J., Kennealy, P. J. (2008). Role of serotonin and dopamine system interactions in the neurobiology of impulsive aggression and its comorbidity with other clinical disorders. *Aggression and violent behaviour,* 13(5), p383-395.

23. Michailidis, Y. (2014). Stress hormonal analysis in elite soccer players during a season. *Journal of sport and health science,* 3(4), p279-283.

24. Williams, J. M., & Andersen, M. B. (1998). Psychosocial antecedents of sport injury: Review and critique of the stress and injury model. *Journal of Applied Sports Psychology,* 10(1), p5-25.

25. Tranaeus, U., Ivarsson, A., Johnson, U. (2018). Stress and injuries in elite sport. *In Handbook of stress regulation and sport.* Berlin: Springer-Verlag Berlin and Heidelberg GmbH & Co. KG, P451-466

26. Galambos, S. A., Terry, P., Moyle, G., Locke, S.A., Lane, A. (2005). Psychological predictors of injury among elite athletes. *British journal of sports medicine.* 39(6), p51-354

27. Doidge, N. (2008). *The brain that changes itself: Stories of personal triumph from the frontiers of brain science.* London: Penguin Books.

28. Campbell, C. (2009). *What is neuroplasticity?* [Online]. Available at https://www.brainline.org/author/celeste-campbell/qa/what-neuroplasticity (Accessed 4 April 2020)

29. Boyd, L. (2015). After watching this your brain will never be the same again [Online]. Available at https://www.youtube.com/watch?v=LNHBMFCzznE (Accessed 19 March 2020).

30. Farrow, D., Baker, J., Macmahon, C. (2007). *Developing sport expertise: research and coaches put theory into practice.* London: Taylor & Francis Ltd.

31. Sands, R. R., Sands, L. R. (2013). *The anthropology of sport and human movement: a biocultural perspective.* Lanham: Lexington Books.

32. Tau, G. Z., & Peterson, B. S. (2010). Normal development of brain circuits. *Neuropsychopharmacology: official publication of the American College of Neuropsychopharmacology, 35*(1), 147–168.

33. Benson, J. B., Haith, M. M. (2009). *Diseases and disorders in infancy and early childhood.* San Diego: Elsevier Science Publishing Co.

34. McSweeney, F. K., Murphy, E. S. (2014). *The wiley blackwell handbook of operant and classical conditioning.* New York: John Wiley & Sons.

35. Gormezano, I., Prokasy, W. F., Thompson, R. F. (1987). *Classical Conditioning.* US: Taylor & Francis.

36. Catania, C. A., Harnad, S. (1988). *The selection of behaviour: the operant behaviourism of B.F. Skinner: comments and consequences.* Cambridge: Cambridge University Press.

37. Timsit, A. (2018). *A leading genetic expert tackles the nature vs. nurture debate.* [Online] Available at https://qz.com/1443795/a-genetic-expert-tackles-the-nature-vs-nurture-debate/ (Accessed 21 April 2020)

38. Ahmetoc, I, I., Fedotovskaya, O. N. (2015). Current progress in sports genomics. *Advances in clinical chemistry,* 70, p247-314.

39. Guth, L. M., Roth, S. M. (2013). Genetic influence on athletic performance. *Current opinion in paediatrics,* 25(6), p653-658.

40. Harden, K. P., Kretsch, N., Tackett, J. L., & Tucker-Drob, E. M. (2014). Genetic and environmental influences on testosterone in adolescents: evidence for sex differences. *Developmental psychobiology, 56*(6), 1278–1289.

41. Yan, X., Papadimitrious, I., Lidor, R., Eynon, N. (2016). Nature vs nurture in determining athletic ability. *Medicine and Sports Science,* 61, p15-28.

42. Bonjour, J. P (2011). Protein intake and bone health. *International journal for vitamin and nutrition research, 81(2-3), p134-142.*

43. (2020) *Can genes be turned on and off in cells?* [Online]. Available at https://ghr.nlm.nih.gov/primer/howgeneswork/geneonoff (Accessed 6 April 2020)

44. Silberg, J., Rutter, M., Neale, M. & Eaves, L. (2001). Genetic moderation of environment risk for depression and anxiety in adolescent girls. *British Journal of Psychiatry,* 179, p116–21.

45. Ankersen, R. (2013). *The Goldmine Effect.* London: Icon Books

46. Ferguson, A. (2013). *ALEX FERGUSON My Autobiography: The autobiography of the legendary Manchester United manager*. Hodder & Stoughton.

"

COACHING MINDSET
& SKILLSETS

BEFORE YOU CAN
COACH OTHERS
YOU MUST LEARN
TO COACH
YOURSELF

Johan Cruyff

,,

Introduction

Objective: The objective of this chapter is to increase our awareness of areas in which we can develop as coaches to increase our probability of success in our environments. The topics cover both our mindset (the way we think), and our skill set (the actions we execute) we can use to enhance happiness, development, and performance.

When Sir Alex Ferguson was asked "What is the most important aspect to becoming a successful manager", he answered, "The most important thing is to be consistent, don't change". Consistency is one of the most important aspects when working in a high-pressure coaching role. Players and staff have an expectation that we know what we are doing and know what we believe in. We do not have the opportunity to change our rules each week, change our style of training every day, or change the way we treat players every month. This meaning the best time to develop new beliefs and new ways of working is when we are in low pressure coaching roles or in between coaching roles. When we do enter a high pressure coaching or management role, we should have a clear idea of the environment, culture, and style that we want to implement and maintain. This starts with us. The mindset of the leader will lead the decision-making of the led. Our mindset and skillsets have a direct influence on every aspect of our coaching ability and will significantly impact the happiness, development, and performance of the groups we are working with. Our mindset gives us the quality of thinking while the skill set enables us to execute our ideas. When going through the following topics it is imperative that we try to identify where our strengths and weaknesses lie. Honest reflection will enable us to place focus on the areas where we have room for improvement.

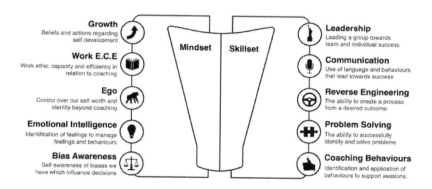

Figure 11: Mindset and Skillset

Growth Mindset

If our mindset leads the decisions of those, we are leading, our mindset should reflect our desires for our players. This means that for our players to be happy, developing, and performing, we should be happy, developing, and performing as well. One of the key factors in achieving these objectives is having a growth mindset. Leading mindset psychologists have cited polls whereby hundreds of creativity researchers have stated that the number-one trait underpinning creative achievement is precisely the kind of resilience and fail-forward perseverance attributed to the growth mindset (1). Our belief regarding growth and fixed mindsets will have a huge baring on the work we execute and the relationships we have with our players. A 'fixed mindset' is the more common mindset. It is the mindset where people believe that their characteristics such as skill, intelligence, and creativity are given to us through our genes or religion and that we are unable to change them. Therefore, our potential for achievement is limited to the traits that have been passed down or given to us. In context, a 'growth mindset' is less common, and is based on the belief that we can develop characteristics through learning and discovery. We can significantly change and influence our brain's structures, thoughts, feelings, and behaviours, making a growth mindset very achievable for all of us. With this being the case, why would we not want to grow and develop? Below are the key beliefs associated with the growth mindset that enable us to develop and deal with failure:

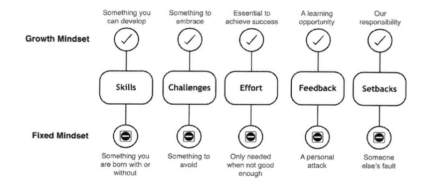

Figure 12: Growth Mindset Characteristics

People that have a fixed mindset often believe that they must prove what they currently have as opposed to improving what they currently have. For example, two coaches with similar abilities, in terms of implementing coaching sessions, can often end up heading in different directions. One may focus on showing everyone their current level of ability by repeating the same sessions with the same information and behaviours, while the other focuses on developing their sessions to take them to the next level. One fears appearing deficient (fixed mindset); the other fears staying stagnant (growth mindset). A fear of staying stagnant will take us further long term than a fear of appearing deficient. A second important reason for having a growth mindset is the important role it plays in dealing with the failures that we all encounter. Our reaction to failures is heavily dictated by the mindset we have. If we can frame our failures as growth opportunities, we are far more likely to learn, develop and bounce back. For someone searching for growth, failure is a beneficial component to our long-term development. Of course, at some point in football, success must outweigh failure, but even when we make it to this point, there will still be moments that we will initially perceive as failure. A growth mindset will utilise these opportunities to take us even further. Once we have decided we want to have a growth mindset, the biggest challenge is transitioning it into habitual thoughts and actions. What does someone with a growth mindset do differently to someone with a fixed mindset?

Skill Development: Coaches with a growth mindset actively look for opportunities to develop their knowledge and skills. When working with youth players this may be identifying new skills to teach the players and practising them to ensure we have the best demonstrations possible. At senior level this may be developing our match observation skills by watching a variety of games and trying to identify formations and strategies earlier and quicker. A coach with a fixed mindset will be more likely to spend their time utilising the same skills to ensure they always appear competent. How we intentionally look for skills we can develop, and how often we practice these skills, will determine how skilful we can become as practitioners.

Challenge acceptance: Throughout our coaching journey we are certain to encounter challenges. To ensure growth we must perceive challenges as positive experiences regardless of the outcome. This meaning that whether we succeed or fail in the challenge, we will learn from it. Coaches with a fixed mindset will avoid challenges, and when challenges arise which they cannot avoid, they will tend to pass responsibility and blame to others in order to protect their image and insecurity. Coaches with a growth mindset will actively search for challenging situations to ensure they are continuously experiencing new opportunities for growth. This may mean coaching new age groups, working in new environments or attempting to use new coaching methods. The more challenges we can experience and learn from, the higher our long-term growth will be. A great method for taking this growth to the next level is to search for challenges that align with our weaknesses and fears. If we are unsure of our ability when coaching senior players, we should throw ourselves in to the deep end and learn wherever possible. When I was twenty-one, I took the challenge of coaching a senior Sunday league team with players aged between eighteen and thirty-six. Although there were many hiccups, it resulted in several learning experiences, placing me in a confident position to coach senior players a few years later, under far higher pressures with far higher expectations.

Effort through challenge: When we do come up against challenges that will require effort to succeed, it is easy to put minimal work into them so that if we fail, we can always blame our lack of effort. "I wasn't that bothered", "I didn't take it seriously". It takes a strong person to put in a high amount of effort knowing that they may not succeed. In the early moments of attempting new things we are likely to struggle. Our first session working with a group of three-year-old children, is never going to be as successful as our tenth. However, working hard and putting in a lot of effort from the first session will increase the level of success and give us a better platform to build upon. Therefore, by our tenth session we are likely to be at a higher level than we would be if we put in minimal effort in the initial sessions. Failing after investing high amounts of effort must become a positive process with a feeling of opportunity to grow as opposed to an opportunity to fail.

Search for feedback: Coaching with several people observing can be a daunting task. As we walk off the training pitch, we have two options. One is avoiding feedback. The other is to seek feedback. While taking feedback from others can be a difficult process, it can be a great method of growth. It is good to believe our training sessions, video sessions and team meetings were perfect, but in reality, this is rarely the case as there is always room for improvement. If we have people around us who can deliver constructive feedback at the right level, the feedback process may be as simple as having a discussion with those around us, including players at times. If we are not as fortunate, then it may be a case of inviting a specific person to observe our work, or even recording our work and sending it to others to provide feedback. At times most of the feedback may not align with the improvements we are looking for, however with a growth mindset, we must be searching for that one detail that may increase our ability. Even if it is by one-percent.

Pushing through setbacks: Fortunately, or unfortunately (depending on our perspective) the coaching journey is often full of setbacks. This can be in the form of losing matches, getting fired or even periods of unemployment. How we deal with these setbacks is what defines how our journey is going to look. During times of unemployment how do we react? With a growth mindset unemployment is a great opportunity to develop and utilise the freedom to search for the next best opportunity. With a fixed mindset it can be a depressing period which turns us towards leaving the industry. After financial challenges with my head coach role in Zambia I decided to sell all my furniture in one weekend and book a flight to move to a new country in search of new opportunities. This included sleeping on a mattress a neighbour lent me, with only my MacBook, suitcases of clothes and a fan in a corridor in my apartment, to avoid being bitten by mosquitoes. This was followed by months of unemployment with a daily hustle to arrange meetings with agents and coaches. While there were many moments of struggle, stress, and disappointment, a few days before my visa was due to expire, a phone call came through with a job opportunity. Years later I am still in the country coaching with the first team for one of the biggest clubs on the continent. It is our mindset during these moments, that will shape our coaching careers.

Work Ethic, Work Capacity and Work Efficiency (ECE)

Some of the mindset principles take some time to fully understand and master. Other principles are far easier to develop. This is one of the latter. We have complete control over our work ethic, capacity, and efficiency, and this can start today.

Work ethic: How many hours do we put in to perfecting the craft of coaching? This can mean formal education, informal studying, study trips, use of mentors, use of networking, the list goes on. Throughout our coaching journey we will encounter hundreds of coaches with dreams of working at different levels within the football industry. The key question we must ask is, does the current work ethic correlate with the challenge faced in getting to this level? If we want to win the Champions League as a coach with no senior playing experience or having never worked in a professional football environment, the amount of work that needs to be put into it as well as your attitude towards the level of work, needs to be tremendous. When evaluating our work ethic, it cannot be comparable with anyone else, only comparable with our objectives. For others, who may have international playing experience and want to coach at any full-time academy in the world, it is likely they will be able to meet their objective with less of a work ethic. If we are not yet where we want to be as coaches, when we reflect over our journey so far, could we have increased our work ethic? An increase in work ethic will certainly mean an increase in development and over a long-term period, an increase in our coaching performance. Having a high work ethic also sets the tone for players in our environment. We can all expect and ask players to work hard, but can we take it to the next level and inspire players to work hard through their observation of our hard work?

Work capacity: Our work capacity is based on the width and depth of knowledge and experiences we obtain during our coaching journey. For some coaches, understanding football tactics and strategies is enough for them to work at the level they want to, however for others there may be an immense width and depth of knowledge required. Twenty years ago, coaches in the premier league required an understanding of football and managing a team, now the level of knowledge ranges from psychology to physiology to cultural anthropology and much more. This is normal like any industry; the expectations of knowledge and experience increase as the industry moves forward. If we can understand this principle, how can we as coaches apply it, in relation to developing it? First off, we should certainly not be focused on understanding one element of our coaching role. A high percentage of conversations between coaches are focused on tactics and sessions. If we delve deeper into topics, this may give us an improved depth. Only once we look outside of these topics will we gain more width. With an increased width and depth of knowledge we can contribute a wider range of attributes to our environments which supports the happiness, development and performance of our players and teams.

Work efficiency: Do we know what needs to be learnt and what can be disposed of? Do we know where we can learn what we need to learn? Often, we expect a significant amount of learning to come from coach education courses and conferences. As great as these opportunities are, with the power of the internet we have learning available to us all day every day, with the ability to search for specific topics that relate to the environments we are working in. Work efficiency is the component of our mindset that ensures we develop in the areas that are going to have the greatest impact on us meeting our objectives. If working in an environment where the team requires more cohesion, we should spend our time developing our understanding of team cohesion rather than learning about new tactics and formations. When we want to be an expert foundation phase coach, we could be developing our understanding on child development rather than reading a tactical coaching book. Can we ensure that we are learning the information that is going to best support our personal development, professional development, and long-term coaching success?

Tips:

1. Identify the knowledge and skills we will require to meet our long-term objectives
2. Identify where and how we can acquire the knowledge and skills
3. Prioritise knowledge and skills that we need in our current role
4. Use available time to develop other areas
5. Do not follow the crowd, if we learn what everyone else is learning we will be the same as everyone else

Ego

One of the gross mistakes we can make as coaches, is believing that our achievements as a coach define who we are. While football coaching is certainly a passion for most of us, it must not define us as a person. To understand why this is so important, we must develop an understanding of how our ego works. There have been numerous definitions by psychologists and philosophers to explain how ego is relevant to our thinking and our behaviour. One concept is that our ego is our protection system working to maintain our identity. This suggests that when our identity is threatened, our ego kicks in to alert us of danger. This can be useful in many areas of life especially when in leadership positions. For example, how would we feel if moments before a big game the physio came over to offer a motivational team talk just before we were about to give our speech? This feeling is hard to explain, but it is certainly an egotistical feeling that takes over that may make us act aggressively and emotionally. Someone has challenged our identity as the leader in the group. This is an important feeling to have as a coach, however, we must learn how to manage our ego for us not to be misled by it, causing us to overreact in challenging situations. Research has found that athletes who are trained by low ego-orientated coaches show a higher intrinsic motivation and higher goal orientation, whereas athletes trained by high ego-orientated coaches were less intrinsically motivated and less goal orientated (2). Therefore, managing our ego is not only important for managing ourselves, but also important when managing players. Research has also shown a clear relationship between testosterone and ego-centred decision-making. Studies have been conducted to test the likeliness of collaboration when people were induced with higher levels of testosterone. They found that when those with higher levels of testosterone were asked to make the decision whether to collaborate or run with their own beliefs, they were more likely to choose the egocentric decision and made their own choices (3). This is a dangerous trait to have when working with other staff members or within a technical team. When working with other staff we must be able to effectively collaborate and ensure everybody feels a level of importance. How do we manage our ego to be collaborative with others and share the spotlight without losing our identity as the coach or the leader within the environment?

Increasing personal self-worth: A great lesson to learn during our coaching journey is regarding how we define ourselves as people. Generally, in society when we meet someone for the first time, one of the first questions we normally lean towards asking is what they do for a living. This gives us a perspective on who the person is and what they are going to be like. It helps us identify who they are and helps others identify who we are. After discovering that this does not occur all over the world it can make us wonder how important this aspect of our identity is. In the Maori culture which is the culture of the indigenous people of New Zealand, they have a different method of identifying themselves. This is called Pepeha. Pepeha is the process where people are identified based on their name, place of upbringing, a special mountain, or a special body of water closest to them (5). Most of us would never think to identify ourselves with use of mountains or water. However, what this does point out is that we should not be defined by our job role. There are far more important attributes about us than the job we do. As coaches how can we ensure we focus on building our identity as people and place a heavier emphasis on what we do as a person than what we do as a coach? The higher our self-worth is as a person, the less vulnerable we are to our ego being bruised as coaches. The less vulnerable we are to people affecting our ego, the calmer and more in control we will be during challenging situations.

Aligning identity with behaviours: A common reason why our ego is hurt is because others do not perceive us as we believe we should be perceived. We are therefore not treated as we believe we should be treated. At times this may be due to people intentionally challenging us or disliking us due to their own issues. In a lot of cases however, it is because our behaviours do not align with our identity. There are two aspects of 'us' that we can control, 'who we are' and 'how we act'. For example, if we want to be seen and treated as a leader then we must demonstrate behaviours that reflect a leader. When we demonstrate behaviours that do not align with leadership but expect to be perceived as a leader, we are certainly going to have our ego bruised on a regular basis. Often in these situations, we blame the person challenging our identity as opposed to reflecting on ourselves and identifying how we can better influence people's perceptions and behaviours, so that we are then perceived and treated as we believe we should be. We must align 'who we are' with 'how we act'.

Managing moments: Once we have increased our self-worth and aligned our behaviours with our identity, there are still going to be moments where our role as a coach or leader will be challenged and our ego kicks in to alert us. How we manage these moments will have a significant influence on our survival within the football industry. At times it may be our Academy Manager who takes over our session mid-way through, to adjust it to what they want, or it may be a parent who attempts to coach players during the match. At senior level it could be a player who criticises us in front of the team. In all these moments we may find our ego bruised, and we must make two decisions. One is whether we should react to the moment and the second is how to react to the moment. There is no fixed answer, as the outcome is completely dependent on several factors such as the situation that has occurred, our personal and professional circumstances, as well as the environments we are working in. For example, a parent who gives their child a few words of encouragement could be dealt with completely differently to a parent who starts telling the whole team what to do. An Academy Manager who politely steps in to adjust the session, can be dealt with differently to one who steps in and humiliates us by telling us what we are doing wrong. Furthermore, our job security and dependence on income would further affect what we should do, as we have children and bills to pay. We may have to tolerate more than we would if we were financially comfortable. The one principle that must apply to all situations is to stay assertive and calm with whatever action we take, to ensure we make decisions we will not regret after the fact.

Emotional Intelligence

The ability to understand how we think, and feel is important. In a leadership position it is just as important to understand what other people are thinking and feeling. Leaders in the field of emotional intelligence have suggested that emotional intelligence is at the centre of effective leadership and involves not only recognising emotions in oneself and others, but also knowing how and when emotions unfold and using this to lead accordingly (6). Emotional intelligence has been defined as "the ability to monitor one's own and other's emotions, to discriminate among them, and to use the information to guide one's thinking and actions" (7). Research suggests "it is responsible for as much as eighty-percent of the success in our lives" (8). Emotional intelligence is a growing area of research and discussion that has more recently entered the football coaching industry through conferences and courses. Much of the research has focused on awareness and management of people as individuals with less knowledge surrounding the use of emotional intelligence in group environments. Understanding that we are significantly influenced by our environment suggests that we should also place emphasis on understanding people in relation to the environment they are in. It is crucial that we understand that our emotional state is influenced by our environment, the way we feel in an environment is influenced by other people, and other peoples' state is influenced by our state. It is a complex dynamic working with many people in one environment. Ever identified how players or staff act differently when the environment changes? The difference between how they act when they are one-to-one with you, as opposed to within the group or how a youth team player acts within their age group then how they change when they play up or down with a different age group? These are examples of how ourselves, others, and the environment are all influencing factors in the process of emotionally intelligence. Once we have the level of emotional intelligence where we are aware of these factors, we can then manage a wider range of environments, wider variety of people, and of course better manage ourselves, all with the purpose of enhancing happiness, development, and success.

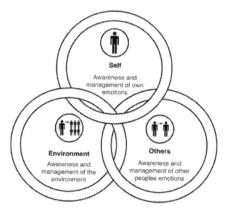

Figure 13: Three factors of Emotional Intelligence

Awareness and management of self: The first step in having emotional intelligence is being able to identify and understand how we think and feel. If we can identify when we feel emotions such as anger, stress, and fear, then we can start to develop an understanding of the triggers that are linked to feelings. Understanding the triggers helps us do three things:

1. Avoid the triggers that create negative feelings
2. Utilise the triggers that create positive feelings

3. Create interventions so we are prepared to deal with negative situations and feelings

For example, if we are aware that we react badly to criticism directly after losing a match, we can use all three strategies to manage our emotion. First would be to ask players and staff to save critical evaluations until the days after the game. Two would be to speak about the positives from the game directly after. Three would be to prepare a calm statement in advance in case a staff member does attempt to critique after the game such as, 'I appreciate your thoughts, however, I think it would be best if we could save our critique for tomorrow'. Through our self-awareness we have avoided a negative situation, encouraged a more positive situation, and utilised an intervention to deal with the negative situation that arose. Not only is this important to manage ourselves, but it also manages the impact that we have on the environment. In some cases where we have a high number of negative feelings to situations, we may need psychological help to develop our confidence, self-esteem, and positive mindset to ensure we are less sensitive to frequently encountered situations. Our coping mechanisms and thought patterns can enhance our management during tough situations to demonstrate personality traits such as restraint, grit, and adaptability.

Only once we can identify and manage our own emotions can we frequently have success identifying and managing the emotions of others. When we attempt to manage others without being in the right state ourselves, it is very possible our emotion will affect what we see in others and how we choose to manage others. For example, if we are angry with the team for losing a game and we see a player laughing with a former team mate from the opposition, we are likely to come to the conclusion that the player does not care about the team and result, which is more likely to lead us to shouting at the player in the dressing room when debriefing. In fact, the player may be extremely disappointed and was solely responding to a joke the opposition player said which was related to something personal, outside of football. By regulating ourselves we may be able to rationalise the situation and understand why the player was laughing and therefore be less likely to criticise the player unjustly. Research has demonstrated that leaders who are capable of managing their emotions are more likely to be adaptive and able to create an environment of trust and fairness (9). People are more likely to trust someone who stays calm and composed in challenging situations than someone who frequently exposes their emotions and acts based on them. Someone who demonstrates calm emotions and behaviour is more likely to be rational, consistent, and fair with their decisions and behaviour.

Awareness and management of others: Identifying the emotional state of those around us is an exceptional skill if we can utilise it, but it can almost feel like a punishment if we do not have the skills to manage people. This skill is most commonly labelled as empathy. Empathy is a soft skill that has been researched through the history of humans and even animals. Much research has found that feeling the emotions of others is a mechanism deep rooted in the brain. Regarding defining empathy, the Cambridge dictionary definition is "the ability to share someone else's feelings or experiences by imagining what it would be like to be in that person's situation" (45). More simply, it can be defined as the "ability to understand and feel the thoughts and emotions of another person". The level of empathetic ability we have will determine our depth in analysis and ability to problem solve. Typical football comments from coaches with a lack of empathy can range from the following, "they just don't want it enough", "they are mentally weak", or "they think they are something special". Phrases such as these can be called lazy deductions. If we can ensure that we are in an empathetic state more often, then we can make fewer lazy deductions and more accurate empathetic deductions. The skill of efficient and accurate empathy makes the process of coaching far easier. Whether we only have one hour per week with a small group of players, or we are full-time, with a squad of forty players and staff to manage, we will not have time to sit down for thirty minutes with everyone, to understand what they are thinking and how they are feeling. Efficient and accurate empathy enables us to identify which players may need our time more than others, meaning we can then manage the limited time we have, to ensure everyone is in the right psychological place to be happy, to develop and to perform. There are two key types of empathy that we must understand:

Cognitive Empathy: Simply understanding what someone is thinking and feeling. The more skilled we are at this the less information we require to gain insights. An example of cognitive empathy would be leaving a player out of the squad, observing their reaction, and identifying that they believe they are not good enough to play for the club.

Affective Empathy: When we feel how someone else feels after observing and listening. For example, if after leaving a player out of the squad and watching their sad reaction, we feel the sadness that they are feeling. Similarly, if someone demonstrates other feelings such as anxiety or anger then we feel the same, this would be affective empathy.

While both forms of empathy can be useful and are often intertwined, as a coach it is critical to be cognitively empathetic but not always affectively empathetic. When dealing with large groups of people on a personal level there are a lot of emotions that we may feel we must deal with. If we allow the emotions of others to change our emotions, our mood and decision-making will then be affected. This can then impair our coaching ability. For example, if dealing with a player who is upset that they have been dropped from the squad, while we must make every effort to understand exactly how they are feeling and what they are thinking, we still have a squad of players that require coaching. It is critical that we stay in the optimal emotional state to execute the session. If we are affectively empathetic to that player, we may then go out on to the pitch feeling sad for the player who has been dropped or frustrated that we had to drop them. It is not always easy, especially when reaching the professional level where we end up responsible for an individual's professional life. When linking this process to psychology, it is an important principle that psychologists must understand their clients, but not become emotionally attached when dealing with them. There are three skills required to use empathy successfully:

1. **Observation:** What do we look and listen for? (tone of voice, body language, behavioural changes)
2. **Deduction:** Can we draw a logical conclusion based on analysis of information and previous experiences?
3. **Action:** How do we respond to the deduction if any action is necessary?

Awareness & management of the environment: Understanding environments enables us to improve our management of the team. The environment is comprised of several factors, including structural aspects such as design and layout, group roles and dynamics, and organisational features such as culture and history (10). Understanding the impact these factors have and managing them for positive outcomes is a key aspect to our emotional intelligence as leaders and coaches. For example, how does the layout of the dining area impact player interaction? How do the number of minutes or hours they spend in the analysis room impact what the players feel and think? How do the group dynamics affect happiness, development, and performance? These are some of the questions that we must ask ourselves as emotionally intelligent coaches. Below are some of the coaching related points that we should remain aware of:

Design: The layout, structure, and image of an environment can influence peoples' thoughts and emotions. Working under a variety of coaches I have seen meeting rooms, offices, and dining areas organised in a variety of ways, which has had varying impacts. Meeting room layouts have had a closer family feel when chairs have been together in one group and closer towards the front of the room where the coach has been speaking, as opposed to having a larger distance between players and the coach. Staff have felt more important when they have had their own designated office space as opposed to working from any space they find. Teams that dine on bigger tables have had increased social interaction as opposed to teams that have dined on smaller tables. How can we best design our environment to maximise happiness, development, and performance?

Time: Understanding that the amount of time players spend in the environment or within a scenario, such as meetings can be crucial. How much time should players spend in the environment to enhance their happiness, development, and performance? There is no right or wrong answer. Some coaches openly report that they keep players at training from morning to evening, where others prefer only a morning session. Regarding components such as meetings, some coaches have regular one-hour meetings, some have fifteen-minute meetings. Of course, the longer the players spend at training and in meetings, the more they could develop. Once the time length starts to decrease their happiness, it can have a detrimental effect on their performance. Being aware of these kind of factors enables us to manage them with more success. The key is finding the right balance for the players and the environment.

Group Dynamics: Environment is often the product of the people within it. Ever walk into a room and get a particular feeling based on the people? Being aware of this feeling and identifying what is going on is also an important aspect of emotional intelligence. The feeling they give you may indicate what management method is required. For example, walking into a room for an analysis meeting with players, excited and eager, may mean we can go straight into the session and sustain their attention for longer. Walking into the room and seeing players that look tired, may mean we must start off with something to engage everyone or keep the meeting short and concise. At times, the dynamics may vary. What is most important may be to align everybody's thoughts, feelings, and mood before starting the meeting. This may mean using methods such as humour, motivation, or empathetic words that demonstrate we understand how they are feeling and why they are feeling the way they do. Emotional intelligence allows us to have a better understanding of what the group and individuals require from us in the particular moment.

Behaviour vs Feelings

One important factor when observing behaviour and events is to understand that feelings and thoughts do not always directly represent behaviour. Someone who is demonstrating behaviours of anger can actually be feeling sad or frustrated. We all have heard of the phrases 'tears of joy' and 'tears of anger'. They are two examples of situations where the behaviour and the feeling may not align. Being aware of this enables us to have more accurate deductions when observing behaviour and events in order to have a better understanding of what is actually being felt and thought. This gives us an advantage if any action is required. Remembering this can help us deal with an argumentative player who may be insecure or feeling like they are not good enough, or a quiet staff member who comes across rude, but is shy and tries to avoid communicating.

Summary of emotional intelligence:

1. Be aware of how we are feeling and how others in our environment are feeling

2. Manage our own feelings first to ensure we are in a positive state and have the right perspective

3. With a positive state and logical perspective, identify and influence the environment, and the feelings of others.

Bias Awareness

As coaches it is our job to analyse and make observations and judgements on players and staff within our teams. How do we ensure our insights are accurate and objective? Often our insights can be heavily influenced based on biases that we have picked up throughout our lives and coaching journeys thus far. A cognitive bias is a mistake in cognitive processes such as reasoning or evaluating, often occurring as a result of holding onto one's preferences and beliefs regardless of contrary information (11). Being unaware of our biases increases the likeliness of us making inaccurate decisions which can be identified by others in the environment. Being aware of our biases enables us to make more accurate decisions which will enhance success. There are many forms of cognitive bias, the following are particularly relevant to the coaching industry:

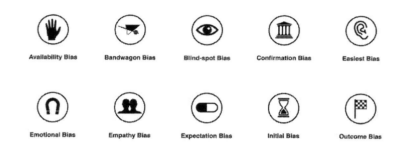

Figure 14: *10 Cognitive Biases for Coaches*

Availability Bias: This occurs when we rely too heavily on the information that we have because it is the only information that is available. For example, if we hear that the next opponent plays a 4-4-2 formation, but we have not been able to see them play, we may rely on that specific piece of information too heavily without being sure of its accuracy. The reliability and accuracy of the information is far more important than the availability of information. Historically newspapers have relied on us having this bias as it was the only method of delivering information regarding what was going on in the world. We would believe everything we were told as it was our only access to information.

Bandwagon Bias: When working within a large technical team this can become a common challenge. Bandwagon bias is when we believe something simply because many people believe it. An increased number of people with a belief does not necessarily make it an accurate belief. Often in meetings when many people have a particular view, others tend to take on that view and start believing the same thing. 'If many people believe it then it must be true'.

Blind-spot Bias: When we are not aware of our biases, it is called blind-spot bias. Being aware of our biases enables us to think more objectively when making judgements on topics that we may have biases towards. When we are unaware of the biases, we have we are more likely to make inaccurate decisions that are concluded, with poor reasoning. An example of this is, if we are aware of our availability bias, we can identify when we are depending on something simply because it is available, and then depend less on the information without being sure of its reliability.

Confirmation Bias: This happens when we seek information that supports our current opinion as opposed to looking for objective information and adjusting our opinion based on facts and fair analysis. Often when judging a football player's ability, we make assumptions based on their race, appearance, football boots and their first few actions on the pitch. Once we have created these opinions, we look to prove ourselves right by taking more notice of the actions that support the opinion and take less notice of the observations that disprove it. The biggest concern with this bias is that once we have formed this opinion and proved it with our own bias judgements, we then treat the player accordingly, which can have negative effects as suggested by the Pygmalion effect.

Easiest Bias: This refers to the point of lazy deductions. We make a judgement based on what is the easiest solution we can find as opposed to taking time to analyse the situation objectively. For example, believing a player has a bad attitude because they are late to training on one of their first day. There are many possible reasons for this, however we often jump to the easiest conclusion which would be that they 'just have a bad attitude'. The actual reason may have been a serious accident on the road, which caused heavy traffic, or a family event that happened at home. These reasons would not necessarily mean someone has a bad attitude, yet we may still prefer to believe the easiest conclusion.

Emotional Bias: When we base our opinion on an emotion over logical thought. For example, playing our favourite player because we like them as opposed to playing the player who is more likely to perform in the upcoming match. When we do this, we often go against the principles that we set verbally, which gives players reasons to feel frustrated when the decisions do not reflect the words. If we say that a player will be dropped for poor performance, then one of our favourite players perform badly, the expectation from all is that he is dropped. If we keep them in the team for an emotional reason that cannot be explained to the team, we are inviting problems into the group.

Empathy Bias: A common bias involved with empathy is believing 'you don't know me, but I know you'. A series of psychological experiments have shown that we tend to think we know people better than we really do. This illusion is called 'asymmetric insight' (12). Of course, we like to think we have superior interpersonal insights. If we intentionally practice observations and deductions, we can improve our insights, however in many cases we do not know people as well as we think. What does this mean for empathy? It means that we should develop a wider range of observations to increase our quality of logical reasoning to make more accurate deductions. Further to this, we should be sure about any deductions before taking any action, this ensures we really do know what someone is thinking and feeling before attempting to manage them.

Expectation Bias: This is when our expectation of what is going to happen influences what we observe. A classic coaching example of this is when we expect a referee to make a number of incorrect decisions, we therefore place heavy emphasis on observing and critiquing every decision they make. In reflection, after the game analysis, what is demonstrated is that the referee did make the right decisions throughout the game. Studies have found that the expectations of people significantly impact their thoughts, feelings, and actions, even to the extent that placebo medication is more effective for those who expect it to work (13).

Initial Bias: When we are over-reliant on the first piece of information we receive and less receptive to new information. For example, if we are told that a potential signing has a poor social life, we use that as a base to make judgements on the player as opposed to having an open neutral mindset. Even after we receive new information, we still place higher importance on the first piece of information because we believe that initial information is more accurate than new information.

Outcome Bias: Outcome bias is a vital bias to be aware of as coaches. An outcome bias is when we use the outcome of an event to create beliefs about the decisions that were made. As coaches this may mean believing that the team played well because they won when in fact the decisions made during the game may normally lead to losing most games. Similarly, when a player makes a decision that does not align with the game model but has success, we can get caught in the trap of believing it was a great decision and praising the player. Pep Guardiola substituted Thierry Henry, after he had scored, for not following the principle of staying wide. This is an example of taking control of outcome bias and focusing on the process and decision-making in line with principles and not outcome (14).

Leadership

When speaking of football coaches who are responsible for a group of players, we are often referred to as managers instead of leaders. Literature will suggest that management and leadership are heavily intertwined. For me, leadership is based on us being an example that inspires others to follow. Whereas management is understanding others and influencing them based on their needs and desires. Both skills are critical for football coaches. If we lead by example to inspire but have some players in our group who are not following us, we may need to use management skills to align their beliefs and behaviour with those in the group, at least temporarily until they leave the group. If we try to manage people without demonstrating an example that inspires, we may find it difficult for players to buy into what we are asking of them. For example, asking players to ensure they are early for training, yet we are not one of the first to arrive ourselves. The importance of setting the example is critical in that we are leaders before we are coaches, and we genuinely live our leadership.

Live your leadership

When leading a group our personality, mindset, beliefs, and values are going to heavily influence those in our environment. Therefore, the first person we must make sure we lead, is our self. Leading our self, starts with identifying our reason for coaching, as this is most likely going to be our biggest influence as it relates to what we believe and how we function within the environment. What is our 'why'? Are we coaching because we enjoy having power? Are we searching for the financial gains? Or do we have more personal reasons? Very few people can clearly articulate why they do what they do. Why do we get out of the bed in the morning and why should anyone care? (16). It is our 'why' that will motivate others to follow us. Once we have identified our 'why', our personality and behaviour will follow. We can then be clear and consistent in our personality, mindset, beliefs, and values in relation to the expectations of those in the group.

How many coaches have we seen who have asked their players to be creative but have showed limited creativity in their session design themselves? Or coaches that have asked their players to stay calm but the next day they are shouting manically from the touchline? It is important that we are clear and consistent with a personality that inspires others to follow. We should think, look, speak, and act as a representation of the group we are leading. Therefore, if we want players and staff who are happy, developing and performing, we should consistently look and sound like someone who is happy, developing, and performing. Generally speaking, any personality that promotes both team and individual happiness, development and performance, will inspire others to follow. Which player would not want to follow a coach who is happy, developing, and performing successfully? What does this mean for us regarding how we look and sound? What does happiness, development and performance look and sound like? It is certainly unique to age, culture, and environment. Some coaches prefer to wear a suit on game day where others prefer a tracksuit. Some coaches speak in a relaxed manner with humour, and others speak very professionally and seriously. The key is relating this to our environment. If we dress in a relaxed style with a relaxed manner and humour, we should be expecting players to feel the same within the environment. If we are extremely focused and attentive during meetings, we can expect the same of others. We should not be laughing and joking in meetings then be angry when someone makes a joke. Our leadership should inspire the behaviour of others. A key question to ask is; when leading a group, would we be successful if we had a group full of people like ourselves? Would the group be happy, developing, and performing?

Value		Actions
⍾	Freedom of Expression	Dress in a relaxed manner Speak about a wider range of topics outside of football Give and ask people for their honest opinions
▭	Work ECE	Early arrival and late exit from training Educate players and staff on a variety of important topics Engage in intelligent and efficient meetings and discussions
👍	Positivity	Frame challenges into positive opportunities Praise players and staff for positive moments Uplift players and staff when they are feeling down
⚡	Discipline	Stick to agreements and promises Use appropriate language Stick to training start time and meeting times

Figure 15: Alignment of values and actions

A key component to living our leadership is to work on our life outside of football. Often when getting to know coaches on a personal level it becomes significantly easier to understand why they are the way they are as coaches. Coaches who are unhappy at work are often unhappy outside of work. Coaches who are developing themselves in the work environment are also developing themselves as people outside work. If our football life reflects our life outside of football, it becomes clear that we should ensure we have a great, personal life. Not only does this help with our leadership, but it also helps us deal with the roller coaster we all experience within the coaching industry.

Fault vs Responsibility

Epictetus; "It is the part of an uneducated person to blame others where he himself fares ill; to blame himself is the part of one whose education has begun; to blame neither another nor his own self is the part of one whose education is already complete" (15). Will Smith gave a short Instagram speech which really changed one of the aspects of coaching we may struggle with. He explained the difference between responsibility and fault. As leaders we must be responsible, however, we can be responsible for everything but at fault for nothing. Responsibility keeps us accountable but does not make us guilty if the outcome is not as expected. This keeps us pushing to achieve without having to feel terrible if we do not. When we think of the word 'fault', it comes with a negative feeling, often described as guilt. With this feeling of guilt comes negative self-talk, and a difficulty in accepting events. However, when thinking of being 'responsible' for improving the situation, it comes with positive words, which help us plan and move forward instead of living in the past. A typical example of this as a coach is dealing with a poor performance and negative result, or a recreational session where the players have clearly not enjoyed or learnt anything. The initial reaction is that it was our fault, we are not good enough, or we pass the blame onto others. 'The support staff didn't do their job', 'the referee cheated us', 'the players were useless'. If we can turn this reaction into a feeling of the result and performance not being our fault, but it being our responsibility to improve them for next time, it enables us to skip the guilt and look forward and think 'what can I do better to prepare next time?'. This enables us to become more self-critical and really evaluate everything we can do to improve. Also, if the referee or support staff, or the players were the issue, it enables us to think of how we can work with them to get more of what we want from them, instead of blaming them for the outcomes. There is no human on earth who feels good being told that something they did, did not go well or was their fault, but many of us are happy to be asked to take responsibility to improve something. This goes far outside of football and sport. Have a look at the two following statements; 'You lot were useless in today's game, what were you doing out there? You cannot play like that again next week'. In comparison to; 'There is a lot we need to improve on from today's game, we all must evaluate and make sure we prepare much better for the next game'. The first phrase puts fault onto the players, which will make them feel defensive and most likely shift that fault onto teammates or back on the coach in their mind. The second phrase puts no fault onto anyone, however, puts the responsibility on everyone to evaluate and improve, to make sure there is progress. Of course, this does not mean that there are not moments where we are going to shout and be critical of players. However, the reason behind the critique should never be to pass fault onto others. As leaders our motivation for communication should always be positive. If that means shouting at a player to push them, this can be achieved without putting blame. Here are two examples which can both push a player who needs it; 'You keep giving the ball away, and you are playing terribly, what are you doing out there?'. In comparison to; 'Your second half must be better; you have a chance to show why you are one of the best players in the league. Use it'.

Attributes of Leadership

Once we have followers, there will be certain expectations of us. Meeting these expectations is critical to keeping them as followers. Followers that we lose, can very quickly become our enemies, which in football can create the situation labelled 'losing the dressing room'.

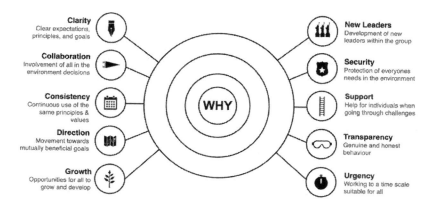

Figure 16: Ten Attributes of Leadership

Clarity: To ensure those following us to develop and perform, we need to ensure we give them clarity on the principles, ideas, and expectations. A common difficulty that players find when dealing with coaches is that they are unsure of what exactly the coach expects from them. It is not rare to hear players say that one of the things they loved about a previous coach is that the coach made it clear exactly what was expected of them and exactly where they stood in the team.

Collaboration: With one of the key desires of people wanting to feel involved in the process, collaborating with players and staff can increase the 'buy-in' we get and increase the investment they make. The investment theory suggests that the more they invest in ideas, the more they will want to see success in the task (43). This meaning if we can get staff and players to share thoughts and ideas that we can utilise, we can increase their investment and therefore increase their desire for success.

Consistency: Trust is a critical component to team success, and a key component of trust within a group is consistency of behaviour. Research has found that consistency in behaviour has a significant influence on levels of trust (17). Consistency makes it easier for others to act in comfort, knowing what type of response will be received. For example, it is easier to make a joke with someone who always laughs than someone who one day laughs but the next day gets angry. Predictability is critical for people to relax under our leadership, unless of course we want an uptight environment based on fear and rigidity.

Direction: Most coaches have a direction they are heading in, however, how many of these directions are mutually beneficial for everyone involved? For example, if working in a team that is fighting relegation, loan players are less likely to be invested in the relegation battle, as they will be returning to their parent club at the end of the season. How can we ensure there are rewards for all if success is reached in the direction we are heading?

Growth: As frequently discussed, development for all is a key component of coaching success. It is also an area that has become an expectation from players in the modern game. Players and staff are always looking for the next step in their journey. If we can create those development opportunities, there will be an increased buy-in and following from players and staff.

New Leaders: One of the roles of leaders is to create new leaders. A football team can be a golden environment to give leadership guidance and opportunities. This may start with staff who are heads of departments or the captain and vice-captain in the team. Further to this we can create leaders across the pitch with players leading their units across different phases of the game. For example, the full backs vocally leading the channels when defending deep, but the wingers vocally leading the channels when pressing. A team with many leaders is more likely to ensure increased success, particularly with achieving long term goals.

Security: When leading at the top of a hierarchy, our role is to protect everyone following us, even if this means sacrificing ourselves. When pressure arises, or a threat approaches the group, as leaders we should be the first ones to deal with it in order to protect the rest of the group. This can be pressure from groups such as opponents, management, or fans. When we do not protect our staff and players there is a significant decrease in trust that occurs, and people then start to look out for themselves as opposed to others in the group. When we do show we are willing to sacrifice ourselves for the team we build a stronger level of trust within the group, and people are therefore more likely to look out for each other and not just themselves.

Support: At some point the players and staff we are working with are going to face adversity. Players who run into financial or family problems will expect support from a leader. These are key moments which can be seen as tests of how genuine the leader is. Often coaches take significant interest in supporting the football aspects and less interest in supporting the personal aspects. In many cases the players do not even report their personal challenges to the coaches they work with. It is our job to monitor players, identify when they are facing problems and support them through these problems, where possible. At times this may mean bringing in external staff to help us in supporting the player. Spending time listening and supporting people, is the most valuable act we can demonstrate. Once we give time to someone, we cannot get it back. It is far easier to support with finances or kind words. Players and staff feel the difference when we invest our time as opposed to investing with other methods, which often significantly strengthens relationships.

Transparency: Research has found that a leader's level of transparency has a significant impact on their followers perceived trust and evaluations of the leader's effectiveness (18). Transparency can be a difficult value to maintain within football. Whether we work in youth or senior football, there will be information that we are expected to keep quiet and not share with other staff or players. This may range from retain or release decisions or incoming and outgoing transfers. In these situations, our transparency may feel compromised. The best method to deal with this may be to declare that we are not comfortable keeping information, and request that the player(s) or staff member(s) involved be informed as soon as possible.

Urgency: In relation to moving in a mutually beneficial direction, there is also a time scale to this based on the individuals. For example, if putting together a three-year plan to gain success but working with players that are in the final year or two of their career, our objectives do not match their urgency. At times we may also have young players that have a desire to move to a bigger club sooner rather than later. If we still attempt to give them a three-year plan, it may not meet the urgency to turn them into a loyal follower. A great method of managing these situations is to give targets that are more urgent for those individuals but explain that there are higher expectations they must meet in order to achieve those targets. For example, giving a three-year plan or a one-year plan alternative if they are willing to commit to the extra work required to meet the plan.

Communication

Communication has been discussed on many coaching courses and workshops and is another topic that is becoming more detailed. There are so many aspects to communication that we can analyse and develop to enhance our coaching success. "Communication is a skill that you can learn. It is like riding a bicycle or typing. If you're willing to work at it, you can rapidly improve the quality of every part of your life" (19). Once we know that we can improve our communication, we should start by trying to understand what exactly communication is. Communication can be defined as the process of transmitting information and common understanding from one person to another (20). It is the exchange of thoughts, ideas, emotions and understanding between sender(s) and receiver(s). The key aspect to understand is that communication only occurs when some kind of information has been received. Simply speaking out loud does not mean communication has taken place unless someone has received something from the message. Therefore, making ourselves understood is an important part of communication. The communication process can be far more complex than we often imagine. When we attempt to transmit information, we must understand those who are going to be receiving the information. How do they think? How will they interpret the information I send? What information will they choose to retain? How will they feel after receiving this information? What impact is this going to have on the individual and the group environment? These are some of the questions we should consider when communicating.

The Communication Process

Understanding the process of communication allows us to identify and develop the areas where we may need to improve, and helps us identify where there may be breakdowns in communication, which we can fix by adjusting aspects of the process. There are ten components of the communication process which can be broken down into two phases. The transmission phase involves the steps from the initial idea of something which should be communicated, to the reception of the communication by the receiver. The feedback phase starts with the reception of the communication through to the reception of the feedback to the sender. This communication process is a continuous loop that often occurs subconsciously, however, once we are aware of the stages of the process, we can then become consciously aware and therefore have more influence over the process.

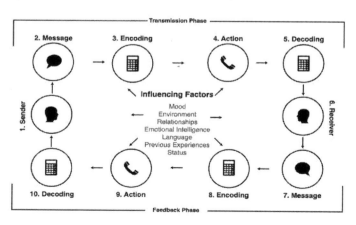

Figure 17: The Communication Process

Sender: This is the initial stage of communication whereby an idea, thought or feeling occurs in the mind of someone.

Message: This is the stage where the sender constructs meaning to their idea, thought, or feeling in a way that they themselves understand. This may also involve setting an objective for the communication we are about to transmit.

Encoding: This is where we process the message into planning a form of action, for example using the objective and meaning to plan a speech (this can be mentally), or send an email, or select a body language action.

Action: This is where the method is executed to transmit the message, this can involve speech, body language, digital messaging, or physical actions. It is also received by someone who becomes the receiver.

Decoding: In this stage the receiver now attempts to break down and understand the communication as it is received.

Receiver: Once broken down and understood the receiver now mentally reacts to the communication with ideas, thoughts, and feelings.

Message: These ideas, thoughts and feelings then become a summarised message that can be transmitted as feedback to the sender.

Encoding: The feedback message is then processed to plan a form of action, to be communicated to the initial sender.

Action: The selected method is then used to transmit the feedback to the initial sender, which is then received.

Decoding: The initial sender has now received the communication and is breaking it down in attempt to understand it.

Sender: The initial sender has now received the feedback which then influences ideas, thoughts, and feelings.

Influencing Factors: There are several factors which influence how we send and receive communication. These factors interact with every stage of the process, from the ideas, thoughts, and feelings of the initial sender, all the way through, until the communication process has finished. The influencing factors range from the way we feel, our relationship with those we are communicating with, the potential language barriers due to vocabulary or fluency, our status and the status of those we are communicating with, the environment we are in, as well as our emotional intelligence to understand both ourselves and those we are communicating with. Understanding these factors and how they impact the sending and receiving of messages can significantly help increase the success of our communication, which can significantly influence the happiness, development, and performance of the players and staff we are working with.

Communication Objectives

One way of categorising communication is to look at the variety of objectives we may be using communication for. This can guide us in the methods we use to communicate and the factors we must consider when communicating. Below are some of the objectives we may have when communicating with players and staff.

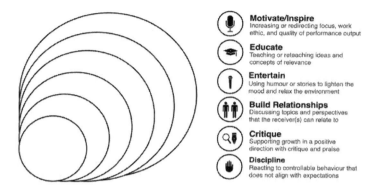

Motivate/Inspire
Increasing or redirecting focus, work ethic, and quality of performance output

Educate
Teaching or reteaching ideas and concepts of relevance

Entertain
Using humour or stories to lighten the mood and relax the environment

Build Relationships
Discussing topics and perspectives that the receiver(s) can relate to

Critique
Supporting growth in a positive direction with critique and praise

Discipline
Reacting to controllable behaviour that does not align with expectations

Figure 18: Communication Objectives

Communicating to Motivate and Inspire

Motivating and inspiring players and teams is one of the most important communication styles for us as coaches. When motivating and inspiring others we are looking to positively influence their future actions. To motivate may be to push someone to achieve something within the realms of what they already believe. To inspire is to change the mindset of what is achievable. Understanding the difference makes it likely that motivation creates a short-term increase in desire, while inspiration creates a medium to long term change in beliefs and desires. Motivation may be more essential in critical moments where you need a short-term boost in desire from players and staff. Inspiring may be more essential at the start of a loop such as pre-season or match block (a set number of fixtures with a start date and finish date). The length of time that is required to change behaviour and desire, should dictate the method used. The outcomes of motivation and inspiration may differ in terms of how they affect time, however, there are principles that can be applied to both. After inspiring or motivating our players, what exactly do we want them to be inspired or motivated to do? This will dictate what communication we deliver and how we deliver the communication. Everything should be guided towards ensuring they want to achieve happiness, development, and performance. The feelings and thoughts we leave them with can dictate their next behaviour patterns. The most famous speeches and teachings tend to have one key message behind them that they build throughout the speech, lecture, or teaching. In following that message, they influence a spiral of new behaviour in some or all the people receiving the communication. Below are some factors for enhancing how we inspire and motivate through communication.

Remove ego: When motivating and inspiring others we should be doing it to impact the receivers for the benefit of them, rather than influencing them purely to change what they think of us. People are far more intelligent when listening than we give them credit for. They will often be very quick to ascertain whether we are speaking to them for the benefit of them or speaking to them for the benefit of ourselves. We must put ourselves last and deliver what is going to have the impact required by them in their journey, as well as the team's journey. We can create a far greater impact when they believe our intentions are pure.

Structure: Structuring what we say enables us to increase the impact of the message. Just like writing a story, having an introduction, a plot and a conclusion is one way of structuring communication to inspire and motivate. Structures such as this often resonate with people as it is the way we are taught during early years of life. Similar structures are present throughout most successful motivational speeches.

Connect: No experience has made me understand this point more than working in different countries and cultures. There have been many moments where coaches have attempted to motivate players using the things that motivate them, which completely misses the point. In order to build motivation and inspiration in others we must understand what type of content inspires and motivates them. Jurgen Klopp humbly told the story which paints a perfect picture of the importance of connecting with players by understanding what they connect with. He shared the story of how he gave a motivational speech at Borussia Dortmund before they played Bayern Munich based on the Rocky movie. After playing scenes from the movie and giving the players analogies, he then realised that only two people were born when the film came out and because of this, the impact of his speech was limited. He recently stated, "My entire speech was nonsense, sometimes as human beings we embarrass ourselves, that's how it is" (21). Because he is a huge Rocky fan, he wanted to use it to motivate players, but he did not take the time to identify what it would mean to them. We must understand what motivates them and not what motivates us.

Relate: As well as using empathy to consider methods that connect with our players, we should also look to relate what we say to situations they have found, currently find, or in the future may find themselves in. For example, if the players are underdogs in an upcoming fixture, sharing stories of underdogs being successful should relate to their current situation. Losing 3-0 at half-time in a cup final, sharing stories of teams that have managed to come back and win the game in the second half may be the required method to ensure they relate to what we are saying when motivating them. If our players are going through a club academy system producing players for the first team, Lionel Messi's story may be more inspirational than Ronaldo's, who has played for many different clubs. The people we often admire are the ones we can relate to. We can use this knowledge to ensure what we are communicating is relatable to those who are receiving it.

Call to Action: After motivating and inspiring our players and colleagues, what are they supposed to do with it? Sometimes we think the players know what to do with it but sometimes the actions that follow are not always what we were looking for. Have you ever seen an extremely motivated player end get a red card or give away a penalty in the first minutes of the game? Once our players are filled with emotion, we must ensure that we push them in the right direction for them to implement the desired actions. If our players are pumped after a great motivational talk before the game, our final message may be, 'Let us go out there and make sure we dominate this game with our pressing and direct football". We must direct the energy into the actions we require from those we are working with.

Communicating to Educate

A great tip to improving our quality of communication used to educate, is to work in a school environment. For five years I worked in schools with children aged between four and nineteen. In this time, experiences included taking groups of twenty children, aged six and seven for P.E lessons, teaching them to throw and catch. The majority of the children wanted to run around and play, while others often would prefer to refrain from being in the lesson. I had to learn methods to get the children to participate and learn in the class when they did not want to be there. This included naughty children who wanted to run around kicking things, and in some cases people. It took two approaches to creating success in the environment. One is lesson design, which is discussed in the session design chapter. The second is the way in which we communicate to educate. After educating children who did not want to be educated, educating football players and staff who love football is a walk in the park. As coaches, speaking to educate is a more unique ability that we can develop expertise in. Our job across all levels of football is to educate the players we are working with. Whether that is teaching three-year olds, how many parts of the foot they can use in football, or teaching the principles of defending against aerial crosses in the box when playing in a back three. Educating is critical for development of the player and person. There are many principles to consider when communicating to educate. Education is not instruction. Players are only better educated when learning takes place that can be executed when we are not present. For true education to take place there must be an understanding of the 'why' and a genuine belief in what they are being taught. Here are some factors to consider:

Engagement Before Teaching: "Teachers have long realised that student engagement is absolutely essential for student learning; if students are not engaged with the content to be mastered, they will not learn" (21). Luckily for football coaches, in the majority of circumstances the players we are coaching, love football. This makes engagement an easier task. Before we start a talk aimed at educating the players, we should first try to gain full attention of the players by engaging with them. This may be by asking a question to get them thinking or conducting a brainstorm and asking them to contribute. It can even be by asking a riddle or telling a story. Something that will successfully ensure that they are fully with us mentally before we start teaching. There is plenty of research that confirms the importance of the link between engagement and learning success, particularly in a technological era where people are engaged in stimulating activities for most of the day (23).

Objective Based: Depending on the generation we attended school in, we may remember teachers always starting the lesson by writing the objective on the chalkboard or whiteboard. Regardless of the generation, there is ample support for the importance of well-designed learning objectives (24). Research has also suggested the benefit of articulating the learning objectives prior to a lesson (25). As coaches, if we can identify exactly what we need the players to learn before educating them, then our decisions on what to say and how to present it are made far simpler. We can even identify when we are going off on a tangent, which is the number one method of creating a decrease in engagement. To create our objectives, we should ask ourselves the question; what must players understand before I finish speaking to them?

Linking: The best teachers and coaches are not the ones who have the most knowledge. The art of educating is being able to transfer knowledge to other people that they can then utilise. One of the best ways to transfer knowledge is by linking new knowledge to old knowledge they already have. For example, if we are teaching a defender how to deal with 1v2 situations and they have already learnt how to deal with 1v1 situations, we can link the two together by explaining what stays the same and what must be different. Although the situations may appear different, depending on the principles we use, we should be able to find some similarities. We may present it as, "when we are looking at 1v2 defending, the principles are similar to 1v1 defending in terms of forcing the opponent to our area of strength and their area of weakness". After this we can go on to explain 1v2 defending in more detail. Just by linking 1v2 defending to 1v1 defending, we have advanced the learning process. They should now have an idea of some of the concepts that may be discussed, and can now store some of the information they are about to learn in relation to the information they already know. This is similar to the benefit of analogies. We often describe passing a coaching assessment in relation to passing a driving test. Why do we do this? It instantly triggers thoughts such as "oh, we should coach how the instructor wants us to coach to ensure we pass the assessment". We have just triggered principles and thoughts without explaining anything.

Framing: When learning new information, the key questions we often ask are how is this information going to help and when do I need to use it? If we can frame our talk well enough, we can answer both questions. After watching Coach Carter, there are a few moments where he speaks to educate players. He does this using framing. "Today's flavour, offence. Now I have a sister. Her name Is Linda. Linda is smart, political, she's radical. She's got a big afro. She's our pick n roll offence" (26). For the first ten times watching the film, I did not think anything of it, however, after reading about framing information, I realised that in this example he framed the pick n roll by explaining that today the topic is offence, and then gave analogies to explain the mindset needed to execute the pick n roll, before even telling them they are working on the pick n roll. Every topic we are trying to educate players on must fit into the full game somewhere. If we are coaching body shape when trying to regain the ball, we can start with, "when we are in transition after losing the ball and we are counter pressing to win it back, we must improve our body shape to increase our regain success". We have just created a clear picture where they can understand how this information is going to help and which situations they are required to use it. This helps with both storing the information and recalling the information to apply it.

Visual and Practical Tools: To further enhance the learning experience we can introduce visual and practical tools. With players having different learning preferences ranging from visual, auditory, reading, writing, or practising, we can use tools such as tactics boards and video footage to support the education process. For players who need more of an interactive approach to learning, we can arrange groups to discuss the concept and give feedback on what they believe. In an ideal situation we should combine a variety of methods into one teaching experience to ensure we maximise the learning for all players and staff involved. Not only does the variety support the different learning preferences of different people, it also consolidates learning in numerous ways for the same person.

Examples and Stories: One of the best methods of painting the 'why' picture is to give them an example or a story of when the lesson was critical. When teaching defenders about the importance of being first to defensive rebounds, we may start with a story of a critical game where we lost due to the defenders reacting too late in getting to the ball. Before we have started educating them on how to ensure they get to defensive rebounds, first we have gained their attention due to the emphasis of how critical this learning moment may be. By going straight into the topic with detail about why what is going to be worked on is important, we may not have complete buy-in from the players and therefore may have a reduced focus from the group. Reduced focus equals reduced learning.

Speed vs Detail: Depending on the environment we are coaching in, we may have either high pressure to teach a lot, in a short space of time, or high pressure to teach in detail. Ideally, we want to have a significant amount of time to coach in detail, which give us the best chance of development and performance. There are, however, many coaching roles where there are high expectations early on. Coaching a team to play in a 3 -5 -2 formation can take one session or can take twenty sessions. Both may be successful, however the team that used twenty sessions will likely execute the formation with more detail. It allows time to go through many different situations and monitor and enhance the knowledge of the players where required. Before educating the players on a specific topic we should consider how long we must teach it and how much detail and experience we want the players to have understood, before moving on. The more efficient we are as a coach the more detail we will be able to teach in a shorter amount of time. If we have a limited amount of time, we are better off teaching a lower amount of detail with high clarity regarding the important components.

Checking for Understanding: What good is education if the learners cannot implement what they have learnt? If we can ensure that our players can implement what they have been taught, we can be sure that we can move on. The key consideration when checking for understanding is asking the question; Do they utilise what they have learnt when they have freedom of choice and the right pictures are present? We can present to the players on the importance of using different parts of the foot when in a rondo and how it will give them an advantage when playing penetrative passes, but if they go on the pitch and play rondos but do not use different parts of the foot when the triggers were present, the education has not been successful yet. Further intervention or education may be needed to modify their understanding or solidify the learning. We should then recheck for understanding at a later point. What is the point in teaching players if they are not able to, or do not choose to implement what they are being taught?

Communicating to Entertain

While I am sure most coaches are not planning on being stand-up comedians, there may be occasions where we need to lighten the mood in the group. There are many ways to do this, one of the ways may be speaking with humour. While I certainly do not classify myself as particularly funny, I have made numerous attempts at being humorous to lighten the mood, which have not always been successful. However, at minimum, it allows people to take us less seriously for that moment and see a more human side to us. This is particularly special when working with younger age groups. When working with the three-to-five-year olds in a development programme at Tottenham Hotspur, one of the most loved coaches was the coach who acted like an entertainer before and after the sessions. He came to the session with all sorts of tricks, and always told an amazing story about superheroes before the session. It had all the children laughing and then listening attentively. Even for coaches working with senior players, Jose Mourinho and Jurgen Klopp have both shared many comedic moments. How frequently they use humour with their players is unknown, however, in front of the media there have been some great moments of communication to entertain. Jose Mourinho told the story of how he spent fourteen of the fifteen minutes during half-time telling Balotelli not to get a second yellow, and in the 46th minute Balotelli was sent off (27). While the story itself was funny, the way the story was delivered gave a clear indication of Mourinho's ability to speak to entertain. The ability to speak to entertain is simply an extra tool we can have in our arsenal in case it is needed.

Communicating to Build Relationships

When we evaluate our relationships, we will often find that those we are closest to are those we can relate to. The basis of a relationship is based on the term 'relate'. Therefore, our relationships with players will likely be built on the number of topics and perspectives we can relate on. If we have a group of players and staff who we cannot relate to, we may need to start trying to understand some of the things they are interested in, or delve deeper in order to find some of the few things we may have in common with them. An easy starting point is normally family; however, topics of interest really range between individuals and environments. If there are no clear initial common interests, then it is a good idea to start asking questions across a wide range of subjects until something clicks. Think religion, music, family, films, hobbies, and if needed football, which should create similar interests. Although, when building personal relationships with players and staff the best topics are normally those outside of the professional remit. If we have a limited number of personal topics in common, the concept of building a relationship refers to building on the areas in which we can relate. A strong personal relationship with a player will be appreciated far more than a professional one. The best investment we can make in building a relationship with players and staff is giving time to understanding and bonding with the person behind the player. Once we do have stronger relationships with players and staff, due to the increase in trust, it then becomes easier to meet the other objectives of communication such as entertaining, inspiring, educating and critiquing.

Communicating to Critique

Whenever critiquing a player to support their growth, the most important factor is having a level of trust where they believe we are critiquing them for their benefit and not simply our own. Without this trust, critiquing others can create tension and a lack of buy-in. When having to go through the critiquing process, the sandwich effect is a fantastic tool which enables us to support the criticism with positive support. The sandwich effect means starting with positive praise before giving the critique, then finishing with further positive praise. The idea behind this is that we can get the message across while supporting the emotional process of digesting the critique, by reminding them of the things they are good at. We may think that players will forget the critique in the middle if it is sandwiched, however, most people remember the negative critique before remembering the positive praise. Harvard research suggests that within high performance teams, there should be a ratio of five or six positive comments to one negative comment (28). This meaning for every comment such as 'I disagree', or 'that's not a good idea', there must be six comments such as 'I agree', or 'that is a great idea'. As well as this coming from us as coaches, we can also monitor this type of communication between players and staff to ensure this kind of ratio is occurring between everyone in the environment. If we can ensure we use a high amount of positive comments then we will have more freedom to critique others when needed, without causing tension or confrontation.

Communicating to Discipline

Whilst the sandwich effect is beneficial for critiquing players to support their growth, it is not required when disciplining players for unacceptable controllable behaviour. If a player is intentionally disrespectful, the more direct we are in dealing with the behaviour the better. A critical aspect of disciplining players is having a reference point as to why what they did was wrong. This reference can be formal, such as a written contract or handbook, or it can be a meeting which explained the expectations of players and staff while playing or working at the club. When there is no reference point, someone can always say they were not aware that the action was a problem. However, when there is previous written or verbal clarity it increases the likeliness that we are disciplining players for reasons that they understand and that they had previous warning of. Where possible, the discipline methods should also be stated within the reference points, such as a deduction of wages or removing them from team training as part of the punishments. Some clubs have a long list of disciplinary actions with consequences, others prefer it to be more culturally based. These points are discussed within the chapter focused on designing a culture. The key to deciding whether a behaviour requires discipline is judging the intention behind the behaviour. If the intentions were based on the expectations within the team, discipline is often not the best option. As they say, we are all human. We all make mistakes, but it is our intentions that must align with the values of the team. All actions can be divided into four categories based on whether the intent and outcome align with the expectations within the environment. The action required as coaches is dependent on the category the action falls in:

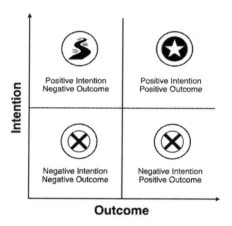

Figure 19: Behavioural Intent vs Outcome

1. Positive Intent and Positive Outcome: This behaviour should be expected, however there is no harm in praising the behaviour to reinforce its importance within the environment. For example, being on time to training every day is an expectation of everyone in the group.

2. Positive Intent and Negative Outcome: This behaviour should be guided. When players or staff have the right intention, but the outcome is not great, support and guidance towards future positive outcomes is often the best solution. For example, a player who tried to block a shot but gave away a penalty after the ball hit their arm. They do not need disciplining, but they may need guiding and educating regarding how to keep their arms close to their sides to prevent similar negative outcomes in the future.

3. Negative Intent and Positive Outcome: This behaviour needs discipline, but it also needs a clear explanation on why they are being disciplined. For example, our player has a fight on the pitch with an opponent where the opponent is sent off, but our player is not. They may think their behaviour was positive because the opponent was sent off, however, it is an opportunity to discipline the player for fighting while explaining that fighting on the pitch does not meet our expectations. It sets a bad example to other players and impacts the club's reputation. Discipline without education may confuse players and staff as they believe they achieved something with the outcome.

4. Negative Intent and Negative Outcome: This behaviour needs discipline, however, does not always need an explanation. For example, a player that deliberately fouls a teammate at training and the teammate ends up injured. Of course, discipline is needed to deal with the player, however an explanation may not be needed as it will be clear for them to identify the negative impact of their behaviour. Of course, support and education to realign their actions may be beneficial at a later point after the discipline has taken place.

Communication Factors

Once we understand the different types of communication based on the objectives, we can also develop a further understanding of other factors which impact the success of our communication. Many of these factors are what differentiate skilled communicators from unskilled communicators.

Vocal Skills

There are a number of vocal skills we can use whether we are in an analysis session or on the training pitch. If we can master these skills, we can enhance the communication of the messages we give to players and colleagues. Use of the right selection and variety of vocal skills increases engagement, understanding and enjoyment from our communication.

Clarity: When referring to clarity we often think of the content we are communicating. However, this can also refer to the clarity in our speech. How clearly do we pronounce words in relation to those who need to receive the message? How we speak with our peer group to ensure clarity and how we speak with players who may not be fluent in our language may need to be quite different. This is particularly important when working with a group of players with a variety of nationalities or languages.

Intonation: This may be the most powerful tool of all when we are communicating. Intonation is the use of tone when speaking, that impacts the feeling the receivers feel. High intonation is a way of creating excitement in our speech, while lowering our tone will help close a point we are making. Being able to utilise a variety of tones can increase engagement and focus.

Pace: The rate at which we speak is often a challenging habit to change, however it can make all the difference for those who are receiving what we are communicating. Pace of speech can also be used to engage those listening in an aspect of what we are saying. For example, using a variety of speeds by slowing down and speeding up the pace can re-engage players and staff for the crucial elements in what we are saying. Our use of pace will always influence our rhythm of speech, which is key to the receivers of our communication understanding of what we are saying.

Pause: Moments of silence can always be extremely powerful when speaking. It creates a moment for those receiving, to think. It can convey emotion after speaking of something powerful and can be used to replace filler words such as 'umm'. If we were to use a strong pause after a statement such as 'tomorrow is a huge, huge game', it can help build emotion around the game.

Volume: What good is communication if not everyone can hear us? Volume is the simplest skill to understand as it simply refers to how loud or soft we speak. If we can use the right volume level, we can ensure all players and staff hear what we are saying clearly throughout the room. We can also use volume variety to increase focus at key points when communicating. For example, if during a presentation we want to emphasise how important it is to start off with a quick tempo, we may raise our volume at this point to ensure we have everybody's full attention.

Group vs Individual Communication

Depending on the communication objective and environment, we must decide on the most suitable audience. Does the message need to be received by everyone? Or is it more suitable for individuals or small groups? This can be critical across all the different communication objectives. Some of the key questions to ask before deciding on the audience we require are; who needs to hear the communication? Which audience will best help meet the objective? Where should this communication take place to best meet the objective? When disciplining a player, if we want to send a message to the rest of the group it may be powerful to do it in front of a larger audience. However, while this may have a positive effect on the others making them scared to use that behaviour, it may create a bigger problem with the player who has been disciplined. Another example is when we must communicate tactical information with the team. Do we need the whole team present? Do we need units, or just particular individuals? Whoever is listening to our communication should feel like they will gain some benefit from it in order to keep them engaged, both in the moment and for future communication. The inverse situation also occurs, where maybe we discuss a key tactical topic with the starting line-up, and do not inform the other players in the group of what we have discussed. Now the gap between the starting players and the other players gets bigger, from both a tactical perspective, and psychological perspective. So before having meetings and group or individual discussions we must think about who needs to be present. Lastly the location of the meeting can also be important, depending on the size of the audience. Individual meetings are often best used in private, so that the player feels like they can be more open and other players are not watching and listening. The exact situation will dictate the best option, and the skill of us as coaches is to understand the situation and understand the effects of group vs individual communication.

Listening

When we think of improving our communication, our first point of call is normally how we can improve what we want to say. Those who we speak to are far more likely to listen to us if we listen to them. Listening is a skill that can be challenging for us to develop, especially as coaches. We are expected to have all the answers and all the solutions; therefore, we spend most of our time demonstrating our knowledge and ability through our speech and behaviour. It is exceedingly rare to hear a parent, academy manager, or CEO comment on how good a listener the coach is. Yet after sitting and investigating what players want from their coach, a large amount of the feedback is based around the desire for their coaches to understand them better. As much as we hope that our deductions through observation help us work with our players, the probability of making correct deductions from observations is still far from one-hundred-percent, even for the best coaches. The best way we can learn to improve our work with our players is to improve our listening skills. "Listening is an art that requires attention over talent, spirit over ego, and others over self" (29). Listening can be divided into five categories. The type that is required is dependent on both what they want us to absorb, and what we need to absorb. Our listening skill level is dependent on how many of the five we can complete, and how often we can identify which listening style(s) is needed for which moment.

Critique: This is the most common type of listening for coaches. We listen to critique what is being said and decide if we agree or disagree. This is a powerful tool for our own development, but it can be a limiting tool for building relationships. It is not often that people speak and want somebody to critique what they are saying, but it can be crucial to be able to do this when in important discussions with players and staff.

Understand: When we are teaching, we are hoping that the knowledge we are sharing is understood. Similarly, when staff, players or management are speaking to us, they are often hoping that we try to understand their perspective and where they are coming from. This type of listener is often labelled a 'good listener', however this is not always the case. There are moments where listening to understand is extremely effective, however there are also moments where other listening skills are more beneficial. Identifying the times when it is important for us to listen to understand is imperative.

Remember: This type of listening is less required in the modern day due to technology. We can Google search many pieces of information that we would have previously been expected to remember. As coaches, there are still situations where we should remember what we are being told. For example, when players and staff are informing us of personal information, such as when they are having baby, when they are sitting exams, or the previous injuries they have had. Remembering some of these details enables us to be more aware of situations that have arisen or may arise in the future and demonstrate their significance to us as people.

Feel: As previously discussed, empathy is one of the most important characteristics of a coach. Listening with empathy allows us to feel the feelings of the person whom we are listening to. This can be beneficial with players who we are trying to get the best out of. Feeling how they feel can help us build stronger relationships and understand exactly what they need. We may initially believe a player is strong and can handle us shouting at them, with added pressure ,but by taking time to listen and understand how they really feel before performing, we may better understand what are sensitive triggers and what requires a different approach to what we believed they needed.

Enjoy: In some cases, people are speaking to us to entertain us. In this case, trying to understand what they are saying may lead us to missing the entertainment. When people are trying to entertain us, we are more likely to be entertained if we understand that, that is their objective. When we go to a comedy show, we do not sit there trying to understand how they feel or learn lessons, we sit and wait to laugh and enjoy the moment. At times this is how comedians get away with so much controversy. We may have people in our environment who are most comfortable communicating through entertainment. By listening to enjoy what they are saying, they are more likely to come and speak to us more often. Every storyteller and comedian loves a good audience. In the right moment we can be that audience.

Responding

Once we are listening using the right method in relation to the objectives of who we are speaking to, the next step is understanding how we can respond. There are several different skills we can use to respond. An example being that when we are listening to critique, we can ask questions, when listening to understand, we can paraphrase. Below are some of the different responding techniques we can use when people are communicating with us. The selection of the method is dependent on the communication style of the person communicating with us, and how we want to deal with the person and communication:

Figure 20: Responding Techniques

As well as responding techniques there are also four different responding styles we should be aware of. It has been suggested that there are four key responding styles based on whether we are active or passive, and constructive or destructive (30). Understanding these styles can assist us in improving our close relationships by enabling us to respond more actively and constructively (31). Active responding is focused on placing importance and genuine interest in the person communicating and what they must say, encouraging them to communicate further. Passive responding involves giving minimal response and interest in the person communicating and what they must say, which encourages them to stop communicating. The constructive-destructive spectrum refers to whether our body language and words are positive and beneficial or negative and critical.

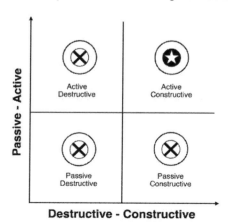

Figure 21: Responding Styles

Here is an example of communication we may receive from a player: "I worked really hard in training yesterday and I feel like I'm getting better every day"

1. **Active Constructive:** This response style is the most powerful method of responding to communication. This means we engage with what they are saying and make them feel important and valued. We can do this by making clear and consistent eye contact, ignoring distractions that occur in the environment, and giving positive responses in relation to what they are communicating. An active constructive response to the example communication would be; 'I agree with you, you were fantastic yesterday and I can see that with time you are getting better and better, I can't wait to see how great you are going to be, how are you finding the workload?'

2. **Active Destructive:** These responses involve actively engaging with the person communicating, while being critical and negative in response to the content they are communicating. It can make someone feel valued as we are giving them our attention, however it may reduce self-esteem if we are critical of what they believe. An active destructive response to the example communication would be; 'I'm not sure I have seen the progress yet, you must work harder if you want to become a better player as you aren't working hard enough yet'

3. **Passive Constructive:** When we respond passively with constructive engagement, we may protect their self-esteem in relation to the content they share. We may also make people feel unimportant as we do not engage with them. This may mean not giving eye contact and being distracted when listening but responding positively. A passive constructive response to the example communication would be, 'yes I agree you are working hard and developing, well done'.

4. **Passive Destructive:** This response style has the most negative effect on the people communicating with us. It suggests both a lack of interest and negative criticism. Often it makes them feel unimportant and undervalued, reducing the quality of relationships and the self-esteem of those we respond to. A passive destructive response to the example communication would be; 'I am not sure if you are working hard enough, you need to work harder'. If we can utilise active constructive responses to players and staff in our environment, we are far more likely to build strong relationships and have success enhancing happiness, development, and performances.

Body Language

When we think of communication, one of the last aspects we often consider is body language. How does our body language impact others? More recently there have been discussions around how our body language influences ourselves. Research at Harvard & Columbia business schools have demonstrated how the use of power poses can increase the levels of testosterone in the body, as well as decrease levels of cortisol which is linked to stress (32). These hormonal boosts can become vital for us as coaches in leadership positions, particularly in challenging environments. Below are some examples of how we can use body language to positively impact ourselves and others:

Demonstrate values: Research has shown that placing our body in a powerful pose, for example with our legs on a desk with hands behind the head (like a CEO) can increase our level of testosterone and bring a feeling of confidence. When talking to players, we should ensure our stance demonstrates confidence and the values we want to present in the environment

Utilise contact: When somebody respects us and believes in our intentions, making physical contact with them through handshakes, hi fives, and hugs creates feelings of appreciation and kindness. These are vital attributes to get maximum performance from players. Studies have found that physical contact in the workplace used with praise and positivity has significant benefits (44). Intelligent use of contact can help us develop the right feelings that we desire within the environment

Facial expression: Studies of the 'facial feedback hypothesis' report that while happiness does make us smile, if we force our face to smile, we will trigger feelings of happiness inside ourselves (33). The movements of the muscles in our face which create the smile, trigger hormones such as dopamine, endorphins, and serotonin to be released which creates a feeling of happiness. This is a way of manipulating our hormonal state suitability for the situation we are about to be in.

Attentive focus: When having group discussions, our body language can control the level of information that others will contribute. Facing players directly demonstrating eye contact and aligned body positions are good tools to show them that we are listening to what they are saying and care about what they say. If there are any barriers in the way of the conversation, we should adjust the environment to show that we care about what they say. Visually responding to what they are saying can also increase their participation, actions such as nodding our head and smiling when they are making a good point can make them more likely to expand and speak up again in the future. Mirroring the body language of the person is also a powerful way of suggesting agreement and being on the same wavelength. Mirroring is copying the body language of the person we are communicating with. This can quickly become a subconscious habit that regularly helps build rapport with people.

Greetings: The tradition of handshaking to greet people is a powerful tool to support building positive relationships with players. Greeting players allows a short one-to-one interaction, which if given full attention can make players feel like we are incredibly happy to see them, in turn making them feel wanted and important. These are important feelings for players to associate with their coach and with the club they are playing for. Unique greetings further increase the importance and value that players and staff feel within the environment.

Decision-making as Communication

The decisions we make also form a key part of our communication. When making decisions, players and staff in the environment decode the decision which then influences their ideas, thoughts, and feelings. It is important that we understand that as we make decisions, we are consistently influencing the environment. Our decisions should align with the expectations we set and must guide the individuals and the team in the direction of success. For example, if we speak of the importance of our players and staff spending time with their families, then we develop a schedule that allows minimal time off, our decision is conflicting with our values. Players and staff will respond to the decision with confusion and internal conflict, which decreases trust in the environment. They are unsure whether to trust what we say, as it is not reflected in what we decide. With awareness that our decisions are a form of communication, we can put more thought into the impact our decisions have. Another critical method to manage the effect of our decisions is explaining the rationale behind our decisions. For example, when dropping players from the starting line up or squad, or giving certain players less minutes at the weekend, explaining the rationale can prevent players from thinking the reason is something that it is not. A player who has less minutes or is dropped, is likely to think it is personal or it is because we do not think they are good enough and this is not always the case.

Reverse Engineering

Reverse engineering is a term used across the engineering fields to describe the process of deconstructing something to understand the processes and parts that were needed to produce it. It is not frequently a skill that is used in areas outside of engineering, but it is certainly a skill set that can become useful for those in leadership positions, including us. To define reverse engineering simply, it is the method of starting at the end concept and working backwards to discover the parts and processes that are needed to arrive at that end concept, without having a blueprint or set procedure (34). This may seem like a similar process to planning, the difference being that when planning, it is far more common to create steps at random, based on our previous experiences. The key difference with reverse engineering is that the thinking is based on a specific vision, specific set of goals, and a procedure with specific backtracked milestones that need to be met. Reverse engineering helps us increase our success when problem solving and meeting objectives. Rather than acting on instinct or previous experience to meet objectives, it enables us to structure a plan based on the vision, problem, or objective ahead.

Objectify the Vision: The first step of reverse engineering is to turn the vision we have into specific objectives that we want to achieve. For example, if we have the vision of winning the league, we would turn this into a more specific and simpler objective such as achieving eighty points during the league season including twenty-four wins and eight draws.

Backtrack the steps: With clear objectives it is possible to start the process of creating the steps to achieve the objectives by backtracking through the steps. For example, in order to meet the objective of achieving eighty points we would need to have the best team in the league. We then backtrack further to discover what it is that will ensure we have the best team in the league, one of which may be having the best players in the league. We then continue the backtracking process which tells us we must recruit the best players and develop the best players. This backtracking continues until we get to steps which can be started instantly. For smaller objectives this may be a short list of steps. For bigger objectives there may be many steps required across a range of topics. Some topics to consider include having belief and desire, discovering knowledge, developing ability, specific actions and interventions that need to be carried out, environments we need to be in, and reflection and perfection of processes that are required to eventually achieve the objectives, thereby making the vision a reality.

Start from the bottom: Once we have the steps planned out, we start at the bottom and work our way up the steps. At times we may move up and other times we may move back down to do further work before moving up again. The more success we have with each step the more likely we are to make it to the final vision.

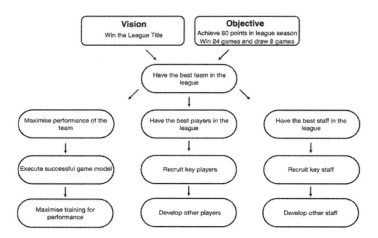

Figure 22: *Reverse Engineering Example*

This is a simple example of how reverse engineering works for achieving team objectives. It can also be used for professional objectives such as the vision of working at a particular level, or even personal objectives such as moving abroad or buying a house. If we can learn to reverse engineer our visions, we can increase the amount of our behaviours that lead us in the right direction, and therefore lead ourselves, players, and staff more efficiently towards success.

Problem Solving

Problem solving must be split into two skill sets. Problem identification, and solution identification. Some of us are quick to identify problems however struggle to identify the best solutions for those problems. We may also be at the other end of the spectrum, great at solving problems but not the best at identifying them. The combination of both skills is what enables us to successfully problem solve.

Problem Identification

In order to improve our ability to identify problems we must be able to identify when there is a difference between what 'should be' and what 'is'. Therefore, we must have a clear idea of what 'should be', and extremely high awareness in our environment to see 'what is'. This vision and awareness must cover all aspects of coaching, from on the pitch during sessions, and throughout the team environment. For example, if we have an expectation of what our build-up should look like in a high level of detail, we can quickly identify where the process is breaking down. If we have only a vague idea, we may not be aware where exactly the problem lies. Similarly, if we have clear expectations of how players should behave at training, we will be very quick to identify when people are not behaving correctly. This process can be broken down into four stages.

1. **Vision of what 'should be':** Visions of what should be happening throughout our environment
2. **Observation of what 'is':** What is actually happening throughout our environment
3. **Acceptance of the problem:** Acceptance of the difference between what should and what is happening
4. **Understanding of the problem:** Delving deeper to understand why there is a difference

Stage three requires humility and acceptance of responsibility. One of the easiest ways to avoid responsibility is to pretend the problem does not exist. As coaches who are responsible for players and teams, we must take the next step of understanding the problem deeper. With experience it becomes easier to decipher the problem, but there will always be times where intentional analysis of a problem is needed to understand it fully. There are many methods we can use to get to the bottom of a problem. A unique model representing the way problems are to be understood (stage four) is called the 'Five Whys'. It is a life changing tool we can use to get to the bottom of problems in our professional and personal environments.

Five Whys

Sakichi Toyoda, one of the fathers of the Japanese industrial revolution, developed the 'Five Whys' technique in the 1930s (42). He was an industrialist, inventor, and founder of Toyota Industries. His method became popular in the 1970s, and Toyota still uses it to solve problems today. The 'Five Whys' theory suggests that when dealing with a recurring problem, asking the question 'why' five times over, will ensure we get to the bottom of what is actually happening. This concept or technique can be used by coaches to find out why performance indicators are not being met, why the team is not getting the desired results, or why people are behaving in a particular way. Here is an example of how it can be used in reference to the previously discussed problem.

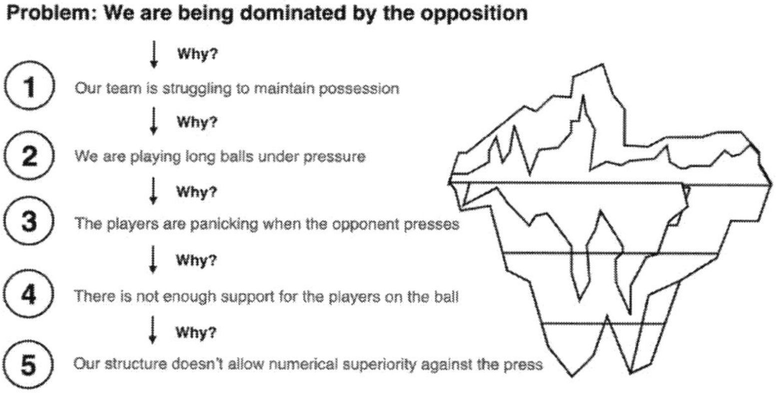

Problem: We are being dominated by the opposition

↓ **Why?**

(1) Our team is struggling to maintain possession

↓ **Why?**

(2) We are playing long balls under pressure

↓ **Why?**

(3) The players are panicking when the opponent presses

↓ **Why?**

(4) There is not enough support for the players on the ball

↓ **Why?**

(5) Our structure doesn't allow numerical superiority against the press

Figure 23: Example of the Five Whys Approach

The more frequently we practice using this process, the quicker the process becomes in our minds. We can get to the point where we get to the bottom of a problem in seconds as opposed to the initial process of needing a pen and paper or sitting and thinking deeply for a while. At the top level, where coaches have decades of experience coaching, they can identify problems before they even arise. The earlier we can identify potential problems, the easier we can solve them and avoid the barriers blocking our objectives. For example, if we have a clear idea for our set piece routines, we can quickly identify when they are not being executed correctly. Identifying this early, enables us to start the process of understanding why. If we can identify why earlier, we can intervene earlier, saving us wasted time practising something incorrectly. The reality is that solving one problem can be the difference between player and team success or struggle. On a results scale it can be the difference between points, leagues, cups, and therefore overall success.

Multi Reasoning

Multi reasoning is an important additional concept to understand. As humans we tend to search for one explanation for why a problem exists. For example, we may believe we have health problems because we do not exercise enough, when in fact, it may be a combination of many factors including stress, diet, exercise, hormonal balance, genetic influences and many others. Once we understand that there may be multiple reasons for problems, it helps us identify a wider range of solutions to deal with a problem. For example, the reason why a team may be conceding too many goals may not just be because of the goalkeeper. It is likely to have many causes, such as defensive structures, number of shots on goal, number of set pieces given away, and individual defensive errors among others.

Solution Identification

Deep problem identification makes the solution identification stage far simpler. Imagine we are struggling to keep possession in the game, and we stop at that level of depth. What solution do we pick to help the team keep better possession? Change of formation? Change of personnel? Change of strategy? If it is a change of strategy, what strategy is the best? What change of personnel is required? Which formation is going to be the solution? In getting to the bottom of the problem, our solution becomes far easier to identify. There are many skills to successfully solving problems:

1. **Identifying Potential Solutions:** What options are we aware of to help fix the problem?
2. **Selecting Solution:** Which solution is most suitable to fix the problem?
3. **Implementing the Solution:** How can we best implement the solution?
4. **Review of Solution:** What impact has the solution had?

Now we have certainly seen coaches try to find solutions from level one, two and three problem solving. 'Look after the ball'. 'Stop playing long balls'. 'Relax on the ball'. The real solution and detail come from level four and level five. The solution may be, 'get more support for players on the ball'. The solution may be changing the structure to increase the numbers in the areas where possession is being lost or maybe it is beating their high press by utilising a different strategy. Of course, this is just an example to demonstrate the principle. There are so many factors to consider when coming up with a solution to the problem, and these depend on the many factors within the game. Due to the vast number of factors involved both on and off the pitch, it is sometimes necessary to identify different potential solutions even when we have a deep understanding of the problem. The solutions we pick when problem solving should always refer to a game model, a culture, or an agreement. One key consideration is that a solution may be 'no intervention'. Preparing for these situations pre-match may make the in-game problem solving even easier. Caesar was recorded as saying "Experience is the best teacher", and problem solving in football is no different. Some key questions to consider when deciding on the intervention:

Timing: When is the best time to implement the solution?
Personnel: Who is the best person to implement the solution? (technical team, captain, management?)
Location: Where is the best place to use the intervention?
Selection: Is an intervention needed at all?

Using these questions will help with the implementation stage. After the implementation, as always, reflection is the critical stage that will enhance the learning experience of dealing with the problem:

Success: Was the solution successful?
Alternatives: Could it have been more successful if executed differently?
Next time: How would we deal with this problem again in the future?
Selection: What would have happened if we did not intervene?

Below are some key skills involved in dealing with problems. Intentionally developing these skills will assist when we are required to solve problems:

Researching: Reading and asking others about problems they have faced and solutions they have used can give us better insight into finding potential solutions and selecting a solution based on our own scenarios.

Emotional Intelligence: Understanding the state of others can help identify the deep level problem and the butterfly effect of each solution. This will help narrow down and select the solution.

Creativity: With the game ever evolving, new problems will be encountered, meaning we must combine previous solutions and ideas to create a solution we may not have used before.

Risk Management: Most solutions will have a level of risk otherwise they would not need to be discussed or evaluated. Being able to weigh up risk and reward in relation to our goals will help select the right solution in a higher probability of situations.

Group Management: In scenarios where we are discussing problems and solutions with others, managing the discussion process will enable us to identify the right problem and the right solution more efficiently.

Coaching Behaviours

While many of the skillset attributes discussed so far have evolved around work off the pitch, the skills we have on the pitch are also vital to achieving success. There is a dedicated chapter in this book that focuses on the principles of training sessions and designing sessions. This this particular section is focused on the skills we can use during our training sessions. These are coaching behaviours that we can improve to enhance happiness, development and performance for individuals and the team. Researchers and educators have created many frameworks to evaluate coaching behaviours during training sessions. These include instruments such as the Domain Five Observation Instrument (DFOI) (35), the Arizona State University Observation Instrument (ASUOI) (36) and the Coaching Behaviour Assessment System (CBAS) (37). The following framework is more focused on the range of skills in a sequential order from the initial stage of setting a session objective, all the way through to behaviours used during the session, and to the evaluation at the end of the session. There are twelve attributes from start to finish that we can work on to better ourselves as coaching practitioners during training sessions.

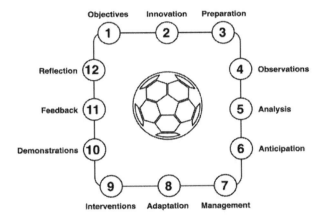

Figure 24: Twelve Coaching Behaviours

1. Objectives: Do we want to be thieves or want to be pickpockets? We may ask what is the difference? However, when Steve Kerr said he is "among the best pickpockets in the game of thieves that involves all NBA coaches" it really gave great insight into how we think as coaches. In a world with the internet, coaching sessions are so easily accessible. From session plans that can be downloaded to session videos that coaches and clubs have recorded. While this can be a huge benefit to coach development, it can also hold us back in our coaching journey. Our objectives should be focused on ensuring maximal happiness, development, and performance for the players and the team in relation to our short and long-term objectives. The best coaches will achieve three things:

A. Set the most relevant objectives in relation to success
B. Design a session which most efficiently meets those objectives
C. Execute the session with methods that ensure the objectives are achieved

When creating objectives for upcoming sessions the key is to reverse engineer from our long-term objectives all the way back to the immediate objective required. For example, if working in an academy system with an under eight team, our objective may be to ensure our players are signed by the club by the time they reach the under nine stage. If we then step back through objectives, we can identify the requirements for players to be signed at the end of the season. We should have objectives based on the period of the season we are in, which should then dictate what is required in that week and on that day. If working with a senior team, it may start off with the season objective of winning the league, then may move backwards all the way to winning the game at the weekend which then asks the question, what does the team need to win the game at the weekend? What needs to be covered today to ensure this is achieved? Clarity in what we want in the future increases the clarity to understand what is required today.

2. Innovation: This is another great skill that we can develop and work on to support the design of the most suitable and effective sessions. Innovation has been defined as "an idea, practice or object that is perceived as new by an individual or other unit of adoption" (38), or "the process of transforming an opportunity into fresh ideas that can be widely used in practice (39). Every coaching session is an opportunity for us to innovate and bring something fresh to the players, the staff we work with and coaching as an industry. Should we wait for others to innovate so that we copy, or should we be the innovators who take coaching to the next level. In 2017 Julian Nagelsmann revolutionised training by setting up a videowall next to the training pitch which enabled the players and staff to watch training clips during the session (40). Whilst this was an expensive innovation, there are many innovative ideas we can bring to training sessions with or without the use of technology. Exposing ourselves to a variety of coaching sessions from a variety of sports, by a variety of coaches, in a variety of environments are some of the methods of broadening the concepts we have in our mind. The broader the concepts, the bigger the urge to innovate, the more likely we are to consistently deliver innovative coaching sessions. In other words, innovation is also said as "an idea, practice, or object that is perceived as new by an individual or other unit of adoption" (Daugherty et al., 2011; Grawe, 2009; Rogers, 1995). Meanwhile, Tidd, Bessant, Pavitt, and Wiley (1998) defined innovation as a process of transforming an opportunity into fresh ideas and being widely used in practice

3. Preparation: In an ideal world we all have an hour to take our time and prepare and set up our sessions. However, it is not always a possibility. Some of us have had to travel between different locations and rush through traffic to make it to the session on time, in some environments there is a session on our pitch which finishes just before ours starts, and in some cases we are rushing from a full-time job to coach in the evenings. What does this mean for us in terms of preparation? It simply means maximising the time and space we have prior to the session, to best prepare ourselves and the players. At times this has meant warming players up off of the pitch so that when the pitch is ready the players can go straight into the session. In other environments it has meant introducing the session via video or tactics board, so the players are aware of what to expect throughout the session. If we think further in advance, we may send videos and pictures to players hours before or the day before the session to start priming the mind for what they are going to be working on. The key for preparation is using our schedule and environment to maximise the state of players and staff for the session ahead. In multidisciplinary environments, using the preparation stage to align the work of all staff, also supports meeting the session objectives. If we are fortunate enough to work in an environment where sessions are planned days or weeks in advance, this preparation time may be used to make adjustments based on any changes to the needs of the players or team, or changes such as player or staff availability.

4. Observations: Once the session starts, what are we looking for? There are so many different factors to observe throughout a session, particularly when working with larger numbers. No matter how much experience we have and how focused we are, we are never going to be able to observe everything. Focuses range from, the success of the session structure and flow, individual actions, unit actions, team actions, on the ball, around the ball or away from the ball, relationships between players, work rate of players, the list goes on. So how do we deal with the never-ending list of observations? It all leads back to our objectives. Our focus should be on whether the session is achieving its objective. Of course, it does not mean we ignore other aspects, it is often beneficial to have a notepad or another member of staff who can note down any other observations. If we are recording the session, we can review in more detail after. In relation to our objectives, we should be able to identify key indicators of what success and failure looks like. For example, if one of the objectives was to improve the high press of the team, it would therefore influence aspects such as the coach position we should use, the detail we are looking for, and the triggers for success and failure. If we are working with another coach, we may be able to delegate observations to them, such as monitoring the team that is building up, or monitoring the realism of the session in relation to match. It is our observations that allow us to analyse the success or failure, the areas to improve, and the areas of strength.

5. Analysis: While we are making observations, it is the skill of us identifying what the information means that is key. For example, if during the high press the opposition keep playing through the press, most people can see this, but being able to correctly identify why it is happening, takes us to the next level. What is going wrong for the team high pressing? Which individual or unit is causing the problem? Or is it related more to the design of the session. As discussed in the problem-solving section, the most efficient way to analyse is to have pictures in the mind that the situations can be compared to. If we have a clear picture of how we want to high press against a variety of situations, we can then compare the pictures we are seeing to the expected pictures and pick out the areas that are different. For example, if we are observing the opposition training team play a number of successful long passes in behind, and our original picture of the high press involved having a free centre back to deal with long balls, we can check to see whether the training picture has a free centre back dealing with those passes or not. This of course may be a subconscious process of observation. What did we expect to see vs what are we seeing? If we are seeing something different to what we expected, why is that? Is the problem with what we expected to see, or is the problem with the execution of what we expected to see? Is the planned structure of the high press the problem, or is it not being executed in the way we need it to be executed?

6. Anticipation: Experience gives us the ability to anticipate what is going to happen next. This can significantly help us identify times where management or interventions are going to be needed. Can we identify when the structure of the session is too small before it becomes a problem? Can we identify when a player is going to struggle before they are struggling? Do we need to wait for the opponent training team to beat our press and score before we identify that there is a problem? A great example of this is when coaching a team, a specific tactical topic, such as preventing crosses into the box. Do we wait for crosses to come into the box to identify a problem, or can we anticipate the problem coming by the triggers such as poor body shape or slow aggression in the press. If we can anticipate these problems it enables us to intervene earlier in the session and show the exact picture we want to coach, without having to rewind and repaint pictures. Experience will support us with this ability; however, we can enhance our ability to anticipate by studying the topic we are coaching in a higher level of detail. This means watching several different teams working with that topic. For example, if delivering a session on counter attacking, we can watch several counter attacking teams play and identify the key principles and pictures that we want to use in our session. We can then identify these in our sessions before seeing problems. Once we understand that our defensive structure significantly impacts counter attacking success, we can then deal with the defensive structure before seeing failure in the counterattack.

7. Management: There are a number of factors that we must manage during training sessions, most importantly, the players. We can do this using different forms of communication. Some players will need praise, some players may need criticism, and some players will require specific body language from us. Managing players during sessions is heavily dependent on the relationship we have with them, the type of person they are, and the status they have in the team. To critique the captain too heavily in front of the group may negatively impact the respect players have for them within the team. It may be better to talk to the captain individually or address the unit they are in. Similarly, for players we do not have good relationships with, it may be smarter to deal with them in a different way to the other players. Of course, we must be honest, but the emotional intelligence we use when managing players on the pitch can have a significant impact on meeting the session objectives. Managing players with discipline, critique and praise can increase focus, work ethic, decision-making and quality throughout a session. Getting the balance right can be extremely valuable.

8. Adaptations: While observing, analysing, anticipating, and managing players, another aspect to develop is our ability to adapt the session when required. What are the chances that our planned session is 100% perfect? There are always changes we can make to support the observations we have made. Maybe the area size is too big and is challenging for a team keeping possession or maybe the numbers on each side mean one team is working much harder than the other? Maybe it would be better if goalkeepers were added. There used to be an idea that adapting our session meant that the session design was wrong, however, it is now more common to hear coach educators encourage us to adapt the session to improve it. A great challenge is to ask ourselves mid exercise, how can we make this exercise better to meet our objectives? Most of the time, there are numerous changes that can be made. Being brave and doing this is a valuable way of developing, as we can observe a direct relationship between the changes we make and the outcomes that are affected. For example, pitch size increases tend to equal easier possession and more difficulty pressing. A narrow-shaped pitch equals more vertical passes and less horizontal possession. Neutral players can increase possession but decrease realism. Many of these principles are discussed in the chapter titled 'Training Session Principles', but our bravery and comfort in adapting our session can be the difference between meeting our objectives or not meeting our objectives.

9. Interventions / Moments: One of the best ways to enhance our interventions is to plan some of the key interventions in advance. When designing the session, can we manipulate and anticipate the events that will occur and plan the intervention accordingly? For example, if coaching counter pressing, we can create a large pitch which is going to challenge the players, and we can therefore anticipate moments where the distances are too big to counter press. We can then plan an intervention to explain the strategy of what to do when we are unable to get pressure to and around the ball quickly. With planned interventions we can anticipate the situation earlier and have increased clarity on the strategy and detail we want to give to improve how the players deal with the situation.

10. Demonstrations: Depending on our playing experience, demonstrations can be our strongest attribute or our weakest attribute. It is key to understand that they can also become our best developed attribute if we spend the time working on them. The importance of demonstrations will heavily depend on our environment and objectives. When working with foundation phase players, ball mastery and individual development exercises may take up far more time than working at senior level. While demonstrating exercises perfectly is not always a requirement for developing players, it certainly helps for several reasons. Firstly, in some environments it can help gain buy-in from the players, and secondly it can increase the tempo of the session. It is far easier to show a player the type of pass that is required than describe it and guide them. At the other extreme, there are players who demonstrate something a player cannot do and then are unable to teach it. Being able to demonstrate to a good level and being able to teach brings a great opportunity to more efficiently develop players. If there are demonstrations we can improve, why not spend the extra time that players do?

11. Feedback: After the session there are several feedback processes that we can use to enhance our development. This involves both receiving and giving feedback to players and staff. We may wish to do this directly after the session, we may prefer to do this later in the day or even the next day. When the feedback process is right, it is a great opportunity for development. If we like to critique ourselves then we may need to reflect on our session before gaining feedback from others. If we want to give players video feedback, it may need to be arranged for a later point. If we prefer to give or receive more generic feedback, we can of course do this directly after the session in a debrief format. The key to any feedback session is to focus on it benefiting development, without becoming detrimental to happiness or performance. If we have a satisfying session which ends with an active spirit, sitting to debrief for thirty minutes may kill the energy that has been created through the session. If the session was poor, a debrief can be used to improve the mood before everyone leaves the environment. Receiving feedback from staff and players is a process that needs to be managed carefully. The purpose of receiving the feedback must be clear and suitable to the environment. There may be some players and staff members less suitable to give feedback than others. Some may be hypercritical, and some may merely say what we want to hear. This means we should think about the different feedback structures such as one to one meetings, small group meetings and organised feedback vs casual feedback. Casual feedback can be a valuable method of receiving feedback, where instead of having meetings with players we casually ask them how they found training. This may be over the lunch period or over a phone call later. There is no right or wrong when it comes to giving or receiving feedback, however the use of feedback can become a key part of our development process if used in relation to the environment, players, and staff we are working with.

12. Reflection: Self-reflection can be a difficult task to maintain. We all have exceptional sessions, and we all have lousy sessions. Watching the poor sessions can be a painful experience. However, through the pain of watching ourselves we can certainly identify our strengths and weaknesses, which will support us putting more emphasis on them in the future. Research has suggested that reflection as an intentional process can begin with some discomfort and end with learning and deeper insights (41) .When watching our session back, we may identify that we adapted the exercise too late, it may then encourage us to be braver in future in adapting the exercise earlier. We can use the coaching behaviours in this section to regularly reflect on the skills we contain to discover the areas we should intentionally focus on developing. Dewey (1991) refers to reflection as to an active and intentional process that can begin with some discomfort with an experience and end with learning and deeper insights.

Key Messages

1. Develop a growth mindset to develop our skills, embrace the challenges we encounter, search for improvements, and persevere through setbacks.

2. Ensure we are working harder than those we are working with, utilising a wide range of content, in an efficient amount of time.

3. Stay aware of our ego and keep control in difficult situations, to utilise the information it gives us in a controlled and calm manner to create the best outcomes possible.

4. Develop further awareness of ourselves, those around us, and the group dynamics in our football environments.

5. Increase our awareness of how our biases influence our beliefs and opinions, to then decrease this impact and utilise more objective opinions.

6. Leadership starts with leading ourselves, so ensure we are living the life that we expect of those around us. Our behaviour must reflect the behaviours we expect of those within our environment.

7. Develop a wider range of communication skills to increase communication abilities in a wide range of situations where different objectives are required.

8. Practice reverse engineering by using thought processes which start with the objective, then work backwards through the actions that are required to meet the objective.

9. Practice going deeper when analysing problems to improve identification of accurate problems and therefore utilise more suitable solutions.

10. Intentionally practice using a wider range of coaching behaviours to increase the impact we can have through training sessions.

References

1. Dweck, C. S. (2006). *Mindset: The new psychology of success.* New York: Random House.

2. Barić, R. and Bucik, V.,2009. Motivational differences in athletes trained by coaches of different motivational and leadership profiles. *Kinesiology, 41*(2).

3. Wright, N. D., Bahrami, B., Johnson, E., Di Malta, G., Rees, G., Frith, C. D., & Dolan, R. J. (2012). Testosterone disrupts human collaboration by increasing egocentric choices. *Proceedings of the Royal Society B: Biological Sciences, 279*(1736), p2275-2280.

4. Conoley, J. C., Conoley, C.W. (2010). Why does collaboration work? Linking positive psychology and collaboration. *Journal of educational and psychological consultation.* 20(1), p75-82

5. Content Catnip. (2018). What is a Pepeha in Maori culture? How can I write one? [Online]. Available at https://contentcatnip.com/2018/05/21/what-is-a-pepeha-in-maori-culture-how-can-i-write-one/(Accessed 22 December 2019).

6. Cherniss, C., Goleman, D., Emmerling, R., Cowan, K. and Adler, M. (1998). Bringing emotional intelligence to the workplace. *New Brunswick, NJ: Consortium for Research on Emotional Intelligence in Organizations, Rutgers University.*

7. Salovey, P., & Mayer, J. D. (1990). Emotional intelligence. *Imagination, cognition, and personality*, 9(3), p185-211.

8. (Dijk, C. F. V., & Freedman, J. (2007). Differentiating emotional intelligence in leadership. *Journal of Leadership Studies, 1*(2), 8-20.

9. Luthans, F. (2002). Positive organisational behaviour: Developing and managing psychological stengths. *Academy of Management Executive*, 16, 57-75

10. Briner, R. B. (2000). Relationships between work environments, psychological environments, and psychological well-being. *Occupational medicine, 50*(5), p299-303.

11. Friedman, H. (2017). Cognitive Biases that Interfere with Critical Thinking and Scientific Reasoning: *A Course Module. SSRN Electronic Journal.*

12. Pronin, E., Kruger, J., Savitsky, K., Ross, L. (2001). You know me, but I know you: the illusion of asymmetric insight. *Journal of Personality and Social Psychology,* 81(4), p639-656.

13. Williams, J. B., Popp, D., Kobak, K, A., Detke, M. J. (2012). The power of expectation bias. *European Psychiatry*, 27(1), p640.

14. Henry, T. (2018). Thierry Henry explaining Pep Guardiola's Coaching [Online]. Available at https://www.youtube.com/watch?v=HFvaZqgr3GQ (Accessed 24 March 2020).

15. Epictetus, A (2013). *Enchiridion & the discourses of Epictetus: Including the fragments.* Hardpress Publishing

16. Sinek, A (2018). *Start with why.* Penguin Books. United Kingdom: London

17. Butler, J.K., Cantrell, R.S. (1984). A behavioural decision theory approach to modelling dyadic trust in superiors and subordinates. *Psychological reports.* 55, p19-28.

18. Norman, S.M., Avolio, B.J. and Luthans, F. (2010). The impact of positivity and transparency on trust in leaders and their perceived effectiveness. *The leadership quarterly*, *21*(3), p350-364.

19. Neal, K. L. (2014). Six key communication skills for records and information managers. Woodhead Publishing Ltd: Oxford

20. Keyton, J. (2011). Communication and organizational culture: A key to understanding work experience. Thousand Oaks, CA: Sage

21. Fordham, J. (2019). Jurgen Klopp reveals his passion for Rocky films and how they got him into an embarrassing situation at Borussia Dortmund [Online]. Available at https://talksport.com/football/605964/jurgen-klopp-rocky-films-borussia-dortmund/ (Accessed 12th March 2020).

22. Bender, W. (2017). *20 strategies for increasing student engagement.* Learning Sciences International: US

23. Taylor, L. & Parsons, J. (2011). Improving Student Engagement. *Current Issues in Education*, 14(1).

24. Mahajan, M., & Singh, M. K. S. (2017). Importance and Benefits of Learning Outcomes. *Journal of Humanities and Social Science, 22*, p65-67.

25. Stiggins, R. J. (2002). Assessment crisis: The absence of assessment for learning. *Phi Delta Kappan*, *83*(10), p758-765.

26. Gale, D., Robbins, B., Tollin, M. (Producers), and Carter, T. (Director). (2005). Coach Carter [Motion Picture]. Paramount Pictures. US.

27. Mourinho, J. (2014). Mourinho tells funny Balotelli story. [Online]. Available at https://www.youtube.com/watch?v=AwXgfBzK_L4 (Accessed 18th March 2020)

28. Losada, M., & Heaphy, E. (2004). The role of positivity and connectivity in the performance of business teams: A nonlinear dynamics model. *American Behavioral Scientist, 47*(6), 740-765.

29. Bennis, T. (2019). *Mental toughness: 30 days to become mentally tough.* Vaclav Vrbensky

30. Passmore, J., Oades, L. G. (2014)
Positive psychology techniques: active constructive responding. *The Coaching Psychologist*, 10 (2). p7173.

31. Oades, L & Passmore, J. (2014). *Positive Psychology Coaching*. In J. Passmore (Ed). Mastery in coaching. Kogan Page: London.

32. Cuddy, A. J., Wilmuth, C. A., & Carney, D. R. (2012). The benefit of power posing before a high-stakes social evaluation. *Harvard Business School working paper, 13-027*.

33. Manusov, V. (2015). Facial Feedback Hypothesis. *The International Encyclopaedia of Interpersonal Communication*, 1-5.

34. Raja, V. (2008). Introduction to reverse engineering. In *Reverse Engineering* (pp. 1-9). Springer, London

35. Shangraw, Rebecca. (2017). The Domain Five Observation Instrument: A Competency-Based Coach Evaluation Tool. Strategies. 30. p37-47

36. Lacy, A. C., Darts, P. W. (1984). Evolution of a systematic observation system: The ASU coaching observation instrument. *Journal of Teaching in Physical Education*, 3(3), p59-66

37. Smith, R.E., Smoll, F.L. and Hunt, E., (1977). A system for the behavioural assessment of athletic coaches. *Research Quarterly. American Alliance for Health, Physical Education and Recreation*, 48(2), p401-407.

38. Rogers, E. M. (1995). Diffusion of Innovation. Free Press. New York: NY

39. Tidd, J., Bessant, J. (2013). Managing innovation: Integrating technological, market and organizational change. John Wiley & Sons: New York.

40. Bundesliga. (2017). Hoffenheim coach Julian Nagelsmann introduces videowall to revolutionise training. [Online]. Available at https://www.bundesliga.com/en/news/Bundesliga/hoffenheim-coach-julian-nagelsmann-introduces-videowall-to-revolutionise-training-454562.jsp. (Accessed 18th March 2020)

41. Dewey, J. (1991). *How we think*. Prometheus Books. Buffalo, NY:

42. Serrat, O. (2017). *Knowledge solutions: Tools, methods, and approaches to drive organizational performance*. Springer Verlag. Singapore

43. Caryl, E. (2011) The investment model of commitment processes. *Handbook of theories of social psychology*, 4(6), p218-231.

44. Goman, C. K. (2009). *The nonverbal advantage: Secrets and science of body language at work*. Berret-Koehler. US: San Francisco

45. McIntosh, C. (2011). *Cambridge essential English dictionary.* Cambridge University Press. United Kingdom: Cambridge

66

TEAM CULTURE

CULTURE PRECEDES POSITIVE RESULTS. IT DOESN'T GET TACKED ON AS AN AFTERTHOUGHT ON YOUR WAY TO THE VICTORY STAND. CHAMPIONS BEHAVE LIKE CHAMPIONS BEFORE THEY'RE CHAMPIONS

Bill Walsh

Introduction

Objective: The objective of this chapter is to demonstrate why culture is so important in achieving success and how we can understand, implement, and maintain a culture to enhance happiness, development, and performance.

If we think of some of the most famous sports teams in the world, from Manchester United and Barcelona, and outside of football, teams like the New Zealand All Blacks rugby team, they have all had a period of success which has been heavily linked to a definable culture. Sir Alex Ferguson's reign as head coach saw Manchester United win 38 trophies across 27 years (1). Barcelona won twenty-nine trophies in a ten-year period between 2009 and 2019, including three Champions League titles. New Zealand's famed All Blacks are the most successful rugby team of all time, holding the number one world ranking for almost a decade, with a win percentage of nearly eighty percent (2). Behind these successful periods there are clear cultures that have been identified by those within the structures. Culture has many different definitions which are typically focused on a group of people having a combination of beliefs, behaviours, and characteristics. Historically, culture was more of a natural phenomenon as it was heavily dependent on geography. One-hundred years ago, the majority of people in most countries were of the same race and religion and were therefore likely to have similar beliefs and similar characteristics. There was less need to focus on building a culture, as a culture already existed that merely needed to be led. Fast forward one-hundred years, and we live in locations where race and religion can be extremely diverse, therefore creating groups of people with different cultures. As a result of this, now more than ever, it is critical we understand culture and can create a culture that builds common beliefs between our players and colleagues. In some cases, clubs have a culture that is set regardless of the coach they hire. Barcelona are an example of this, where they have turned down coaches not because of their potential for results, but because they do not fit into their culture. Other clubs allow coaches to come in and dictate the culture of the club. In both environments our understanding of culture can help unlock the door to our achievement of success.

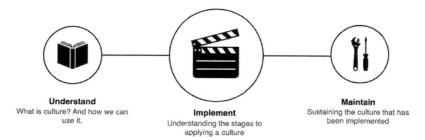

Understand
What is culture? And how we can use it.

Implement
Understanding the stages to applying a culture

Maintain
Sustaining the culture that has been implemented

Figure 25: Three Cultural Management Skills

Understanding Culture

When we walk into a religious building, there are often no signs telling us how to behave. When we walk into a nightclub there is no one telling us what to say or how to dance. What is it that guides us to behave so differently in each environment? We certainly do not behave the same in all environments. When people ask, 'what is a culture', this is a simple method of describing it. 'An unwritten feeling that guides our behaviour.' It is this feeling that aligns desires, beliefs, values, and actions, pulling people in one direction with one way of getting there. Working across different football environments we are likely to encounter a variety of cultures. Sports leadership author Jeff Jansen suggests that there are several different cultures we can find in any team sports environment (8). Some of the characteristics of these cultures are consistent throughout sports environments, particularly across a variety of locations. Below are six common types of cultures we may encounter:

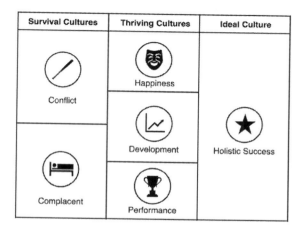

Figure 26: Three Culture Categories

Survival Cultures

1. Conflict: This culture lives in an environment where everyone is focused on themselves and competing for their role, reputation, or image within the team. This focus creates cliques, conflict, negativity, and frustration. These characteristics can be identified on the pitch, off the pitch and more than likely across both. This culture has more of an emphasis on survival and destroying others within the environment, than destroying opponents. In this environment, oxytocin, dopamine and serotonin are likely to be low. This means that players and staff are hunting for ways to boost themselves using methods such as creating cliques, close bonds with one or two people as opposed to the large group, passing responsibility onto other people, and demonstrating individual performance actions to show individual superiority as opposed to team success. Players and staff will also struggle to make it to their individual self-actualisation as they will still feel the void of belonging and a limited internal and external self-esteem.

2. **Complacency:** This culture also lives in an environment where everybody is focused on themselves. However, instead of players competing, they have accepted where they fit within the environment and are focused on staying in the same place. These people have a sense of satisfaction with their role in football and have more of a focus on areas outside of football such as their personal relationships with family friends and spouses, or financial and image related areas such as money, cars, clothes and business. These people are fulfilling their desires outside football and use football as a stable vehicle that allows them to keep focus on these desires. Of course, this is a dangerous mentality within a competitive environment. It will often lead to a peaceful comfortable environment that has average relationships, average performances, and minimal individual development. Neither the conflict nor complacent cultures are likely to produce success.

Thriving Cultures

3. **Happiness:** Cultures that focus on happiness can have huge success in a sporting environment. While they may not produce the best tactical performances, or develop the game of football for the future, they can certainly win titles. Reports and interviews suggest this culture is key for Carlo Ancelotti. The Everton F.C. press release explained how Carlo Ancelotti revealed that establishing strong relationships with his players and staff is central to his philosophy, and cultivating a family environment is a key element of his managerial style as he treats the members of his squad as people, not just players. Football players such as David Beckham have often spoke of Ancelotti's focus on the well-being of the players. Cristiano Ronaldo also stated, "From the first time I met him he made me feel very comfortable. You then see the way he works, the way he is as a person and you begin to understand why everyone speaks so highly of him" (9). This culture is based on the continuous family feeling in the environment to improve performance, which also allows a level of fulfilment within the individuals. One of the challenges with creating this environment is that the quality of performance is often very dependent on the quality of players you have available. It enables you to 'get the best' out of players' current level of ability but may not develop their current level of ability to meet their maximum potential.

4. **Development:** While relationships are a key part of the hierarchy of needs, the top level of self-actualisation involves the opportunity for individuals to become the best version of themselves. For this, individual development is critical. The ability to meet potential is based on working on important strengths, as well as potential weaknesses that may hold players or staff members back. The development culture creates an intense environment where expectations of everyone are huge, and decision-making is always focused on pushing players and staff to be better. This individual focused approach is heavily reliant on the repetition of activities and mindsets that support 'being the best version of yourself'. For success with this, players must become more obsessed with being the best as an individual, than they are with winning with the team. When Pep Guardiola is coaching his players after the final whistle, it gives you an indication of his expectations of individual development. Even after winning a game, in a moment where he could be celebrating the victory, at times he focuses on how individuals must improve further. There are players who have loved the drive of the expectation to become better every-day, and players who have not found happiness in this type of environment. This range of experiences is maybe best summed up by Mario Gotze who stated: "Pep Guardiola was technically one of the best coaches, playing under him was a tremendous enrichment. But I had the feeling that he thinks only about the pitch and leaves out the people and the outside. The empathy was not that big. A world class coach needs empathy, every athlete is also human, and you should combine both" (11). This suggests that in the development culture, players get

better, but they do not always have a fulfilled experience. To get a further understanding of these cultures we can study individual sports and understand how far competitors must be pushed to be better than their competition. Tennis players, sprinters and gymnasts are three examples where athletes are frequently pushed close to breaking point in order to ensure the development process is maximised. Where the line is drawn between pushing athletes and abusing athletes is another topic to consider when understanding this type of culture, as it is very dependent on the characteristics of the groups we are working with.

5. Performance: Cultures that centre around performance are often focused on results, league tables, and trophy cabinets. While all cultures will have an element of focus on these, the degree of the focus is key. In these cultures, coaches often use pressure to boost performance. They do this using methods such as shouting at players and giving punishments and/or short term rewards for success such as performance bonuses. The challenge with these behaviours is that while they can boost testosterone (which can increase performance), they can also increase cortisol (which can decrease performance). Only people who thrive on pressure may be suitable for working under these conditions. It is understandable that performance must be a measure in any sporting environment, however, when performance is the sole element it can certainly limit the potential of the group. The pressures of the financial side of the game and the club or coach reputation is often the reason for this heavy performance emphasis. When behaviours are based on performance, behaviours that jeopardise happiness and development are likely to be acceptable. An example of this type of behaviour may be abusing players or staff with the objective of pushing them to work harder. The abuse may increase work rate, but it may also sacrifice happiness and the likeliness of people developing individually. The desire is not a problem when it is balanced with a focus on development and happiness. However, when performance is the sole focus, we miss an opportunity to bring happiness and individual development to the group. Combining all three creates the *holistic culture*.

Ideal Culture

6. Holistic: A holistic culture focuses on all three of the key objectives, happiness, development, and performance. The key for this culture is identifying when to base decisions on each aspect. When is the right time to use happiness as the basis for a decision as opposed to performance? How can we make decisions that are based on all three where possible? When we can successfully achieve this there are many key positive outcomes. From a hormonal perspective, this environment is likely to cause high levels of oxytocin, serotonin, testosterone, frequent dopamine boosts and low cortisol levels. This hormonal balance is likely to significantly enhance performance. Furthermore, this culture will support the achievement of self-actualisation within Maslow's hierarchy of needs and therefore promoting creativity, problem solving, and fulfilment of purpose. If looking for a footballing example of this culture, the easiest club to find at this moment may be Jurgen Klopp's Liverpool team. Though we can never be one-hundred percent sure, visually it would appear that the players and staff are extremely happy at the club. Virgil Van Djik, Mohammed Salah, and Sadio Mane were all nominated for the FIFA Player of the Year award, last season they won the Champions League, and have won the premier league this season. In a Sports Joe article by Melissa Reddy, there are several quotes from Jurgen Klopp which cover all three objectives. "Everything we do in life is about relationships, family, teamwork, everyone we help, helps us, everyone we meet in our day, it was clear that we had to develop, and a lot of players that are key today were young. For getting more confident you need results on the way there and we had them" (10). It appears he is able to cover all three aspects within his culture. Robert Lewandoski's quotes about Jurgen Klopp also support this idea. "He was one of the main factors behind my development and he opened the door to the big wide world of football for me. He's able to find the right balance between fun and more serious criticism. He made me realise that I had more potential than even I had imagined". To reflect the performance success, Lewandoski won four trophies working under Klopp scoring 103 goals in 187 games. (28).

Once we understand the variety of cultures that can be created, we must understand the variety of factors that create and develop cultures. Some of these factors are more commonly discussed than others, however, they all play a role in the make-up of a culture within a football club environment. These factors include:

Figure 27: 14 Components of Culture

Vision: Having worked for six different clubs across three countries thus far, the most successful moments have been when the club has a clear vision. A vision is a visual objective that can cover a wide range of aspects, which give direction on a short-term and long-term basis. The vision is the start of culture. With a vision you can reverse engineer the process to create a mission statement and a set of clear objectives that need to be achieved in order to get there. The vision, mission statement and objectives drive the process of culture creation. When there is confusion within the culture, or difficulty in identifying a culture, it is likely there is no clear vision throughout the organisation, or the visions of people within the organisation do not align. This is extremely frequent across many clubs in the football industry. With business organisations buying football clubs, we are seeing a higher implementation of these business principles, which should increase the clarity and consistency of club cultures. A successful vision is one that allows staff and players to fulfil their hierarchy of needs and meet individual achievements through fulfilment of their purpose.

Beliefs: What a team believes in is the sum of what most individuals within the group believe. The neural theory behind the law of attraction and the cognitive triangle demonstrate that what we think, will dictate how we feel and therefore how we act. This is powerful as an individual. In a group environment it becomes even more powerful. It turns individual effort into synergy. "Synergy is the interaction of elements that when combined, produce a total effect that is greater than the sum of the individual contributions" (5). In other words, with synergy 1+1=3. As previously discussed, beliefs alone will not win the team a title. What they will do is certainly increase the probability of success, if the beliefs are aligned, positive and followed through with action. There are different categories of beliefs which have a significant impact on culture. What does everyone believe about themselves? What does everyone believe about the team? What does everyone believe about the world? All three should be aligned. If someone believes that they are the best player, and believes the team is the best, but believes that there are huge limitations on what can be achieved in the world, there will probably be a limitation on what they will achieve. Similarly, if they believe in the team and the world, but do not believe in themselves they will again be limited. We must make sure players and staff have positive beliefs about themselves, the team, and the world. Believing something is achievable, is the first step towards achievement.

Desires: While desires are not commonly discussed in relation to culture, it is an important building block in building cultures. People have a wide range of desires as discussed in Maslow's Hierarchy of Needs, ranging from basic needs to actualisation needs such as creativity and problem solving. A successful culture must fill the gaps between basic needs and actualisation needs, to enable players to focus on stage five, which is key for happiness, development, and performance. A culture that leaves gaps in one to four, such as players having a low self-esteem, or a low sense of belonging, will be searching to meet these needs through behaviours outside of the culture. An example of this would be showing off expensive clothes and cars to demonstrate a sense of fulfilment or spending a significant amount of time focusing on social groups outside of football, to find that sense of belonging they are missing. The desires of a player or staff member will significantly influence their beliefs, values, and standards. The key to understanding their desires within the environment is to figure out why they are working in football. Whatever the desires are, it is critical that they align within the group and with the culture. Players motivated by money can often be a problem. While this approach may not be what we are looking for, there have certainly been teams that have had success through motivating players with pay increases and bonuses. The biggest challenges come when players and staff are motivated by different desires and there is no cultural alignment. Every individual must win as a person when the team wins as a club. Meaning all players must meet their desires by the team meeting their objectives.

Psychological Conditioning: Styles of implementing a culture can be divided into two groups. There are cultures implemented which focus on manipulation of people to conform (operant conditioning) and cultures focused on inspiring people to conform (classical conditioning). Cultures making use of punishments and rewards to control behaviour are extremely common in many football environments. Running laps if you are late. Fines if you misbehave, time off for good results. These are manipulation methods. According to reports across multiple platforms such as the Guardian, Chelsea F.C. under Frank Lampard, have a list of fines up to £20,000 for different types of behaviour (3). Alternatively, Nuno Espirito Santo has a different approach at Wolves. "We don't use fines here, it does not make sense," he told the Sunday Times. "Money, for a football player, is not an issue. You have a big star. He comes five minutes late and I say, 'ok, I'm going to fine you £5,000' and he goes, 'Tomorrow I come ten minutes late. The day after I come 15. Are you going to fine me?' Nuno went on to give an example of how inspirational conformity works. "I remember we did it, we didn't start the session until the player came and when the player comes, he feels so bad. He was expecting everybody running already so he says, 'Sorry, gaffer...'. No, no. We just wait. So, everybody was waiting, fucking freezing, waiting, waiting. When the guy comes, nobody claps. 'OK, are you ready? We start now you're here.' It works. No argument, no conflict." (4). No reward for being on time, and no punishment for being late. Just an expectation of behaviour where players associate being on time with being part of the group. A culture with most of the group being on time and having to wait for the player running late, can be enough. Whether we should use rewards and punishments or let the culture inspire behaviour through values, is dependent on many factors such as the type of players we are working with, the length of time we must work with them and the previous culture they have worked under. The key is finding the right balance between manipulating cultural conformity and inspiring cultural conformity.

Values: According to the business dictionary, values are "important and lasting beliefs or ideals shared by the members of a culture about what is good or bad and desirable or undesirable. Values have a massive influence on a person's behaviour and attitude and serve as broad guidelines in all situations" (6). When searching for values, there are hundreds of different ideas we can incorporate into our culture. The key is selecting the right ones that represent the desires, beliefs, objectives, and methods, then following through with demonstrating actions, which consistently fit in with the values. F.C. Barcelona place values as a high priority in their club across community, development and first team structures. They state that "Values must be present in every aspect of our athletes' training programmes. These values are respect, effort, humility, teamwork, and ambition. Here at La Masia we believe that values and attitudes are learned and therefore must be shared by all the agents that are involved in the training process - athletes, coaches, and families, so that these values and attitudes can forge their personalities" (7). Barcelona suggest that values form personality, which is certainly a possibility. They influence decision-making. Values guide us on what we should do within the culture. For example, a value of respect dictates how everyone should communicate and behave in the environment, covering situations like dealing with conflict, listening to each other, and turning up on time. One single value can cover decision-making across a wide variety of situations.

Person or Player: Another key factor to understanding culture is to understand how far the principles extend. Some cultures are limited by the location or the group they are in at the time. These are focused on the role that someone must play within a specific environment. Alternatively, there are cultures that are focused on the person. This meaning that players and staff are expected to represent the culture regardless of the environment they are in. An example of this is a religious leader who would always be expected to demonstrate positive behaviours related to the religion, regardless of where they are and who they are with. A schoolteacher on the other hand, is expected to behave a certain way at school as a leader of their classroom, but after leaving the school they have freedom to behave in ways they would not within the school. In relation to football, both types of culture are present. I have worked with coaches who explicitly say to players, "What you do outside of football is none of our business, however when you are here we expect focus and hard work", and I have also worked with coaches who have put heavy emphasis on the importance of representing the clubs culture 24/7, "the 24/7 professional". The more suitable option will be dependent on the environment and previous culture. If we walk into an environment as a coach where the culture has previously promoted freedom when not working, for example allowing players to party and drink publicly, it may be a challenge to set a culture of being a 24/7 professional. In a club that is used to having disciplined players both on and off the field, allowing them freedom to party and drink may cause chaos. Therefore, analysing the current culture is absolutely critical before implementing your culture.

Expectations: Environments vary significantly regarding the expectations of players and staff. In some environments there may be written rules, and in others, players are expected to understand the expectations through observations of behaviour. There are club cultures where players are expected to spend the whole day at the training ground, and other cultures where players can leave by midday. Bielsa is famously known for keeping players at the training ground for long hours, on many occasions, from 9am until late in the evening (12). There are also elite football environments where players are finished at midday. In any environment, if the players feel the expectations are too extreme or do not align with the mission, they are likely to lack 'buy-in' and end up rebelling against the culture. In some environments, if players feel the expectations are too low, they may take advantage or rebel. According to reports, Bayern Munich players ran secret sessions because players felt like the expectations from them in training were not enough (13). There are a wide range of expectations that can be considered, such as being on time, work ethic, lifestyle management, level of sacrifice and many more.

Norms: Behaviours that are 'normal', frequent, or typical in an environment can be labelled as norms. They are unwritten rules of how to behave in order to fit into the environment. This can range from the way players and staff communicate, the way they greet each other, to the way they bond socially. This is a useful method of creating an identity. Norms build a sense of belonging within a group that allow players to feel more comfortable and to focus on higher needs such as creativity and problem solving. Examples of norms include greeting each other with handshakes and hugs when they first see each other, singing songs in the dressing room or making fun one another. Norms tend to be led by the alpha males within the environment. Once the influencers use these norms, many others feel like they must use them to stay relevant within the group. John Lundstram, an integral part of Sheffield United's successful 2019/20 season, explained how it is normal for players to stay behind after training to socialise, stating how close the group is as they socialise, on what is nearly a daily basis, sharing countless coffees and dinners (16). For this group, socialising and sharing coffees and dinners after training is a norm, as it does not have to be adhered to, yet it is a regular action by those in the group.

Rituals: Most coaches involved in team sport have heard of the initiations. Football has many fantastic examples across clubs such as Liverpool, Bayern Munich, and Arsenal, where new players have sung a variety of songs, from Bob Marley to Whitney Houston. This is one example of a club ritual. A ritual is something that routinely happens based on a specific cue. A team praying together before starting training, a team huddle before going out to start a match, or initiations for new players. Rituals can be used for many reasons and tend to be for controlling the feeling within the environment. Initiations bring a sense of humility as ego needs to be dropped to be able to sing in front of the group (unless they are a great singer). A team huddle may be focused on increasing the team unity. The most famous ritual in sport may be the Haka performed by the All Blacks, which has been used for over one-hundred years to build a sense of pride, strength, and unity (17).

Hierarchy (Organisational vs Cultural): The hierarchy within the club may be one of the most challenging aspects to control. In many clubs there is already a hierarchy in place when joining. In some clubs the players and staff have direct relationships with members of senior management such as the Chairman or CEO, in others there is a chain of authority that must be followed. A hierarchy is a system in which members of an organisation or society are ranked according to relative status or authority (19). It is important we understand there are two hierarchies always running at the same time. There is an organisational hierarchy, which is based on authority, legalities, finances, and control. There is also a cultural hierarchy, which is based on the feeling everyone has within the structure. We should always ensure that the organisational hierarchy keeps our authority, but the cultural hierarchy must encourage happiness, development, and performance. While executing this we must ensure no one starts to feel as though they are above others within the cultural hierarchy. Influencing cultural and organisational hierarchy enables us to manage the day to day feelings of the players and staff we are working with. A key method when identifying or creating a hierarchy is the use of language. The famous half-time team talk by John Sitton, when he was Head Coach at Leyton Orient, provides perfect examples of phrases used that demonstrate the enforcement of a hierarchy, which creates a culture of fear and conformity. "I run this f**king football club until

I'm told otherwise by the fucking circus above. That performance is the f**king straw that broke the camel's back and it will not be tolerated in this dressing room while I am in charge. If I'm gonna take abuse from the bunch of cockroaches behind me, I'm gonna take abuse by doing it my way, and that's f**king conformity, not f**king nonconformity. You, you little c**t, when I tell you to do something, and you, you f**king big c**t, when I tell you to do something, you do it" (29). This may be the clearest example of enforcing an organisational and cultural hierarchy that has the coach far above the players in the team.

Interests: As football continues to become more multi-cultural around the world, teams are less likely to have the same common interests among the players and staff. What is clear from research into building relationships, is that common interests are a key way in which people can relate to one another, but how do we as coaches create these common interests in the team to help build stronger relationships? If you can recall the celebrations after Manchester City won the 2019 Premier League, Noel Gallagher came into the dressing to join the team in singing 'Wonderwall'. This was not the only time the Manchester City players had been recorded singing together as a team. This is an example of how music can be used to build relationships. There are many other examples of songs within football team environments such as the French National Teams use of Vegedream's song, Coupe A La Maison, at the 2018 FIFA World Cup. The players in the squad built a common interest, an interest that builds a bond between players. Music is just one example that can be used. Other examples can range from the films, digital gaming, or practical games such as pool or Teqball (football table tennis). These types of games are often installed into a players' lounge or communal area at clubs to support the interaction between players and to create common interests within the group.

Boundaries: Setting a long list of rules can make people feel as though they are in a prison as opposed to a football club. What we can do instead, is set a reasonable number of boundaries within the environment that will limit destructive behaviours. These should focus on the critical things that matter. In some cases, this may just be one boundary such as 'whatever happens in this environment must stay with us in this environment'. This was a key boundary within the Manchester United environment, under Sir Alex Ferguson (27). Having too many boundaries is likely to backfire; however, one or two boundaries may make players aware of things which will have them excluded from the group. When setting the boundary, the punishment of breaking the boundary must be clear. The boundary must be breakable, but also easy and possible to stay within. If the boundary set is too harsh, we may find we must exclude too many people, which can lead to losing the dressing room very quickly.

Priorities: Once a culture is in place, it is important that there is a conscious or subconscious understanding of the priorities, between the different cultural aspects. There will be times where values or beliefs within the culture may clash. If a player is asked a question in an interview about an event that happened within the club, they may must decide between 'protecting the team' or 'being honest'. Which value is more important? This must be clear in order to avoid conflict between players and staff when someone prioritises the perceived, incorrect value. This can be particularly important from a technical team perspective. Many decisions such as designing a training programme require clear priorities in reference to what is important in the club. Examples of these are, is the individual player development more important than the team? Is data more important than gut feeling? Is athletic development more important than technical development? Priorities such as these will impact many day-to-day decisions such as training session design and coaching styles.

Environment Design: At some levels of coaching, there are limitations on the influence that we can have over the environment design. At senior professional level, there is often a lot more freedom to influence the environment. At all levels we can have some influence. Environment design refers to factors such as the layout of changing rooms, the décor around the training ground, the seating arrangement for meals, the cleanliness of the facility and many other aspects. The environment influences how we feel. The feeling should promote the behaviours we expect. In environments where structure is important, there may be a set table layout for eating meals, whereas in environments where freedom is more important, the layout for eating meals may change frequently, to encourage different types of interactions. Small details such as the number of seats at a table can have a significant influence on the relationships in the environment. Small tables for three or four people may create small cliques of the same people, who sit together every day. Bigger tables encourage communication between bigger groups, and one large table may bring a bigger sense of togetherness. These details also apply to changing room layouts. Which players should be next to each other? Is it better to keep people together based on the strength of their relationship, or can we find ways to encourage players with weaker relationships to build stronger relationships? What does the colour of the environment mean? Author Karen Haller suggests that colour is at the core of our DNA and is an important component when making decisions about environment design (18). Environment design is an opportunity to reinforce the culture we set within our team environments.

Human Importance of Team Culture

Maslow's hierarchy of needs tell us that belonging to a group is a critical component which enables people to demonstrate higher end desires such as creativity and problem solving. Culture gives us this sense of belonging. The only way we know we belong, is by sharing the same ideas, morals, beliefs, and behaviours. Ever been in a social setting and felt extremely awkward because there is no one we can relate to? How would we feel as a football coach, sitting at dinner, with a group of ice hockey coaches, who are all discussing the sport in depth? Awkward? Out of place? That feeling is due to our desire to belong. Our desire to ensure we are not excluded from groups that we want to belong to. How different would we now feel amongst a group of football coaches, who all love sharing knowledge and ideas? Would this bring out the best in us? Would we be more likely to feel a sense of belonging? When we have an increased sense of belonging, we also develop an increased level of trust. We are more likely to trust those within the group we belong to, than those from outside of the group who are different to us.

Behavioural Endocrinology has a huge impact on our desire to belong to a culture. As humans we are hunting for oxytocin. Oxytocin being critical in the team culture process. When we enter social settings and group environments, we instantly start searching for oxytocin by finding people we can trust, to develop a group we can belong to. When in environments by ourselves, such as attending a conference without any friends or colleagues, we often quickly look for people we can relate to. We will search for someone who looks or behaves similar to us, as we trust those similar to us, more than those who are different from us. Therefore, having one common culture increases trust and togetherness in an environment. Once the players feel safe and trusted, all energy and focus can be placed on happiness, development, and performance. Serotonin also increases when we have a recognisable role within an environment, where we can make ourselves and others proud. We only do this when we are happy with the specific role. When we are lacking this feeling, we often try to find it in other areas. A player who is happy within the environment and loves their role, is far more likely to gain a serotonin boost and therefore wants to make everyone proud. When players are unhappy within the environment and they do not place value on their role, they search for serotonin by buying bigger cars, better clothes plus many other behaviours.

In summary, team culture is a critical component when attempting to achieve success. It creates a sense of belonging for those within the team which increases fulfilment and happiness, increases development as they become closer to self-actualisation, and improves performance through trust, problem solving, and creativity.

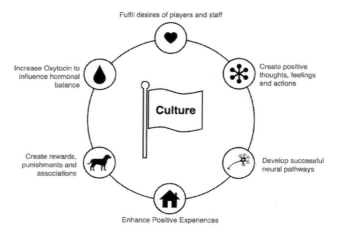

Figure 28: Impact of Culture Summary

Implementing Culture

Designing Culture

A one size fits all method when designing a culture, does not exist. There is no culture that will work at every club in the world. This is one of the factors which relate to why coaches may be successful at one club and unsuccessful at others. A coach cannot simply take the culture they have created, to a new group of players, staff, and management and expect that it is going to be a success. What we can do as coaches, is plan a culture in relation to the type of club we are looking to work at, then adapt it when joining a club. Once we understand the culture we want to create, it indicates to us which clubs would be a good fit for us and which clubs would not. Designing a culture can be executed with four steps:

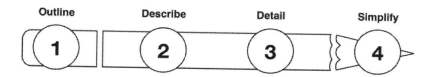

| Outline | Describe | Detail | Simplify |

Figure 29: Culture Design Process

Step 1: Outline: Have an idea of a vision for the next step in our journey. Do we have a vision for what we want our football environment to look like? What achievement is next in our coaching journey? These questions should give some guidance as to the type of culture we want to create.

Step 2 Describe: How do we want people to feel in our environment? Describe the outcomes we want from the culture we want to create? What aspects do we want to focus on the most? What behaviours do we want the staff and players to demonstrate?

Step 3: Detail: How will we achieve the description? What are the details around the characteristics of culture? Beliefs, values, desires, expectations, priorities, boundaries, norms, rituals, environment design, hierarchy, etc.

Step 4: Summarise: Once detailing the culture, it is vital to summarise it into a simplified format that can be easily understood but still explains positive and negative behaviours. This may include use of acronyms. Jurgen Klopp summarised his expectations using:

'T' for terrible (to play against)
'E' for Enthusiastic
'A' for ambitious
'M' for mentally-strong machines (10)

Analyse the Clubs Current Culture

In an ideal world, we would walk into our new coaching role and from day one, stamp our authority with the new culture that we want to set. In some cases, this may work. In other cases, the implementation of the culture may be a gradual process. The answer to which approach we use is based on the analysis of the current culture within the club. Before joining a club, it is critical we understand their culture to identify; one, how we can fit into the club and two, how we can adapt the culture to create the environment that will bring success. The level of understanding we can gain is dependent on the resources and access we have available. Some of us may know players or staff within the club we are joining, meaning we can pick their brains to answer some of the important questions. Some of us may not know anyone, in which case, it may take networking to build relationships and online research of publications and articles relating to the club, the staff and the players. Out of all the cultural characteristics, the following are the most important ones to understand.

1. Vision: What vision does the club have for the upcoming years? When working at Tottenham Hotspur between 2011- 2013, there was a clear message sent from the top which spread throughout the club. The club must become a champions league standard club. The specific message our development department received was that everything we did must be of a Champions League standard, whether it was an international group session or a local development session. If we can identify a vision such as this before arriving at a club, we can then align our vision with the club vision and design our objectives and culture accordingly. We can reverse engineer the question, what is it going to take to ensure everything within my control, makes this club a Champions League standard club?

2. Organisational Hierarchy: What does the club structure look like from top to bottom? Who are the decision makers? Who are the influential people on the decision makers? And where do the key relationships lie within the structure from ground staff all the way up to the owners? At times, the chef is related to the owner or the groundsman is a friend of the Technical Director. Understanding this structure provides us with an overview of the club and an indication of how they operate. In some cases, the top may start with franchise owners. Organisations such as Red Bull and The City Group have multiple clubs that fall under one umbrella. In this instance, it is important to understand how each club fits within the group, as it is likely the clubs are prioritised based on the mission and vision of the organisation.

3. Desires: What are the players and staff looking for from football? Are there common desires between the group? Are they hungry for success or hungry to move on to a bigger club? Are there staff members who want to change their role? Answering these questions will be significant when attempting to motivate players and staff through culture. Implementing a culture focused on winning trophies in three years, is not going to motivate players who want to move to bigger club at the end of the season. There are certain triggers that will dictate these answers such as the age range of the players and staff, and the standing of the club in the football world.

4. Expectations: What current expectations are placed on the players? If our expectations of players are quite different to the expectations currently placed on the players, we may need a transition process to apply our expectations. Coming in with a complete change of expectations at either end of the strict or relaxed spectrum, is likely to have a negative impact. Therefore it is critical to understand what has previously been expected of them, before putting in place our own expectations. Indications of expectations can be found by understanding what a day in the life of the staff and players look like? How many hours a week do they train for? How many hours a week do they spend at the training ground? How much freedom do they have outside of work? These questions will support the design and implementation of our culture.

Adapting Culture

Once we have designed our culture and understood the culture within the environment we are going into, we can now adapt the culture to ensure successful implementation. How can we adapt our vision to fit the vision of the club? How does this then impact our objectives? What factors are critical to implement straight away? Which factors can be introduced gradually? Which factors should not be implemented at all? How can we use aspects of our culture to get the best out of the environment we are entering? All these questions need to be considered with ego aside, and happiness, development and performance of the staff and players at the centre. If the analysis of the club environment is far away from the culture we would like to implement, it informs us that we need to make significant adjustments, or maybe the club is not the right fit for us, at the time. When we move to clubs that have a culture that is similar to the culture we have designed, we are likely to find the implementation process far easier.

Initiation of Culture

Every time we work at a new club, there will be an initial moment where people are waiting to get a feeling for how things are going to change. At times this may involve a big, detailed, presentation, in other situations it may be a brief introduction, before getting straight to work. This moment can be key to setting the tone regarding the culture moving forward. This initiation phase must be applied across all members of the club who are going to have an influence on the happiness, development and performance of the players and staff in the team. This may mean having initial meetings to present the culture to members of senior management, staff, and players. There are many ways to do this, and the key for success, is finding the right type of information and the right balance between too little information and too much information. In one environment, a long presentation which goes into a great amount of detail may be suitable, in other environments a short five-minute speech may be enough to obtain the buy-in required from the players. If entering an environment where there have been minimal rules and expectations, explaining a long list of rules may be the start of a difficult period of cultural implementation. At the end of the initiation, ideally everyone will be in agreement of the culture moving forward, walking away believing that the changes are going to benefit them as an individual, and benefit the team in achieving the set objectives. We must use cultural analysis, and emotional intelligence to tell us how we most effectively initiate the culture, with the new group we are working with.

Diffusion of Culture

Once we have initiated the culture, the diffusion process must take place. To understand how to diffuse a culture, we must first understand the different groups of people within a football environment that will dictate the success of our implementation. Some of the following concepts and principles have been adapted from the business theory of 'Diffusions of Innovations' (21). This business theory is based on the concept that different groups of people within a social system react differently to change, and these reactions will dictate the way the change spreads throughout the environment. It suggests that for an innovation to self-sustain, it needs to become widely adopted by those within the environment, and specific types of people need to play a role in the spread of the innovation. Use of the word diffusion carries deeper connotations than the word implements. To implement is to put a decision, plan, or agreement into effect. To diffuse is to 'spread something over a wide area or between many people'. To build a successful long-term culture we need both to occur. We can picture implementation as the initial phase of introducing the culture, and diffusion as the continuous phase where the culture must continue to spread and develop. Within a football environment the main method of spread will be through the staff and players themselves. There are many moments when we may not be present with the players and other staff, meaning we are relying on others to enforce and spread the culture. When the players are receiving treatment, it is the physios who are spending the most time with them, when they are at the gym, it is the conditioning staff spending the most time with them, when we are away for a matchday and the players not in the squad stay behind, it is another staff member that will be working with them, and most importantly, when players are in the changing room, it is often the players managing each other. In all these situations it is critical for the culture to be present and directing behaviour. Therefore, it is important to obtain the buy-in from individuals within the team. Here are some key groups of people within a social system that must be considered when attempting to implement and diffuse a culture. The end goal that we are looking for is cultural cohesion, where the high majority within the environment, support the culture and the direction it is heading. Below are the key groups with significant influence over the success of cultural diffusion.

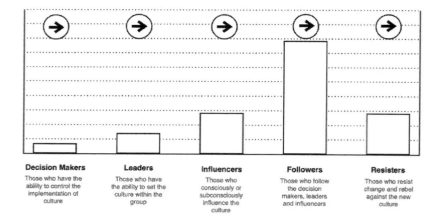

Decision Makers	Leaders	Influencers	Followers	Resisters
Those who have the ability to control the implementation of culture	Those who have the ability to set the culture within the group	Those who consciously or subconsciously influence the culture	Those who follow the decision makers, leaders and influencers	Those who resist change and rebel against the new culture

Figure 30: 5 Key Groups for Cultural Diffusion

Decision Makers: Having the decision makers on board with the culture must be the starting point. There must be complete cohesion and clarity between ourselves and the people that make the final decisions. It is critical to have support in making decisions that affect culture. This can be from factors such as recruitment, scheduling days off, or funding of training camps. In creating a culture based on players arriving on time for training, we have a player consistently arrive late, we may need the decision makers to fine the player, in order to support the culture. If it continues, we may need further action to be taken by the club. If the decision makers do not understand and support the implementation of this culture, they may refuse to take action and leave us to manage the situation. This is just one example of the many situations that require the support of the decision makers. How many times have we seen clubs recruit players who do not fit into the culture of the team, which results in problems for the coach? This is another classic example of the importance of cohesion with the decision makers. To have success in this process, we sometimes must be flexible. Even if we have already adapted the culture for the club, we may find ourselves in a meeting where other aspects need to be adapted. Certain clubs may have procedures in place such as win bonuses, rules and rituals that may not align with our culture. Being flexible but staying strong on the principles that are critical to success, could be the answer to ending these discussions productively. The objectives of these meeting are:

1. **Cultural cohesion:** Everyone is on board with the culture
2. **Cultural confidence:** Certainty that we can have success with the agreed culture

Leaders: Once there is cultural cohesion with the decision makers, it becomes important to start the diffusion process amongst the players and staff. The people at the top of the hierarchy should have the right experiences to implement a culture that benefits all in the environment. As coaches this should be us. What we can take from TED speaker Arthur Carmazzi, is that we can change our perspective of how we look at culture, from a top to bottom approach, to an approach where those below us have an opportunity to provide feedback and feel a part of the culture implementation (22). This is where leaders become involved. There will be several players and staff in our environments who take pride in leading within the group. These people are critical in supporting us and in diffusing and managing the culture. With their role being so significant, it is imperative that we bring them into the discussion around the culture, in order to obtain feedback from them. This may mean having a meeting with the staff and players who are comfortable enforcing a culture. This is likely to include the captain and vice-captain as well as any staff who directly work with the players in larger groups. At the end of this meeting or meetings, it is critical that these people buy-in to the culture and are prepared to enforce it where possible. On a side note, this is also a great time to identify conflicts within the group and start to address the key conflicts which may affect the diffusion of culture. For example, in creating a family culture, who are the players who do not get along in the group, and how can we work on these while diffusing the culture?

Influencers: The third group of people that need to be on board are the influencers. In the theory of diffusion of innovation, these people are the ones who other people follow, who do not wish to be leaders but aid in enforcing behaviour. In business, influencers have become a critical part of setting trends. When Adidas release a new trainer, their influencers will wear them first and publicise its release, and as a result, Adidas know others will purchase these trainers. We need the same thing to happen when diffusing the culture. We need to have the influencers demonstrate the behaviour so that the followers within the group (who make up the majority) follow those behaviours. Within any club with staff and players there are likely to be a few of these key influential people who do not want the responsibility of leading. Cristiano Ronaldo could be an example of a player like this. Significantly influential in terms of setting standards of behaviour, however, does not necessarily focus on leading the team through enforcing punishments and managing people's behaviour. A method for having players like this on board may be using individual meetings to illustrate the importance of their role in the team. Take the time to understand what they desire, and if possible, give them that in return for having the right influence on the squad. Once these players fit into the culture and demonstrate the right behaviours, the followers will follow.

Followers: The fourth group of people are the followers. The followers within the group tend to listen to the leaders and follow the influencers. They are very unlikely to rebel against the group culture, so often need less attention in reference to their behaviour. If they do not follow the influencers, they are likely to listen to the leaders. While it is not so important to spend time discussing culture with them, it is still important that we spend time managing them as people. Sometimes the followers will feel like they are not being seen or heard as people or as players. If this becomes the case, they can turn into resisters.

Resisters: These are the people who did not and do not want to see change occur. They are often the leaders or influencers who are not in a position of leadership or influence. For example, the young upcoming player in the group, or the players who are used to leading and influencing but are now no longer in the starting line-up. This is the group that can cause conflict within the culture and can start demonstrating behaviours that do not align with what we want to achieve. Sir Alex Ferguson famously sold and let go of players before they could become a part of this group. "Ravel Morrison might be the saddest case, he possessed as much natural talent as any youngster we ever signed, but he kept getting into trouble, it was painful to sell him to West Ham in January 2012, because he could have been a fantastic player" (23). In an interview with Gary Neville, he speaks of how Sir Alex Ferguson advised him to let go of Valencia players who were not heading in the same direction as the team (24). We may come across similar situations with staff members who want to be in a different role or want to lead or influence. Not to suggest that letting go of players and staff is always the answer but resolving the situations must be a priority. Conflict resolution and management of people follows in the chapter titled *Concepts for Managing Players and Staff*. How can we turn our resisters into followers, influencers, and leaders?

Stages of Cultural Diffusion

During the process of implementing and diffusing a culture, we are likely to experience various stages that need to be overcome to reach high performance. With football coaching being an industry heavily dependent on results, performance must be achieved as swiftly as possible. To reach this point of high performance, there are phases of cultural diffusion we must go through. In 1965 Tuckman first presented the 'four stages of group development', which in later years was adapted to five stages (25). Forming, Storming, Norming, Performing, Adjourning. This model is more frequently used in business; however, its principles can certainly be related to culture implementation in football. From experience and anecdotes, there is a critical stage after performing, which I label 'developing'. Maintaining high levels of performance can be one of the most challenging tasks when working with football teams over long periods of time. How often do we see teams that start well under a new coach before performances start to drop? How many teams maintain their level of performance throughout an entire season? One of the biggest ways to keep focus on performance is by a having new levels to strive for, on a constant basis. Higher expectations within the culture, new interests to develop the group bond, and environment design development to enhance the dynamics within the group. Striving for perfection. The best way to maintain levels of group culture is to consistently develop the group culture. Throughout a season, players' behaviours may slip outside of the culture if we do not keep pushing the characteristics of culture such as beliefs and expectations. Enhancing the culture to make it stronger will be key for maintaining high performance.

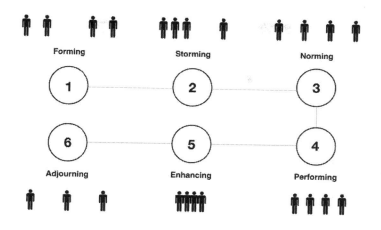

Figure 31: Stages of Cultural Diffusion

Forming: In football, the forming stage can be challenging. As coaches we can enter roles and have a high-pressure fixture in a matter of days or enter groups where the relationships between players and staff are broken. Factors such as these make the first stage extremely important. The forming stage is the introduction stage where new members join a group or new groups form. In most footballing environments it will be us as the coach joining a team which is already formed. As a result of this, the previous regime has a heavy influence on the state of the group, as we arrive. Hence the analysis of the current culture is so important. During this phase we can expect to see players with a variety of emotions, from sad and disengaged to excited and extremely engaged. Some players may be disappointed in a new coach arriving as they are aware that things are going to change, and some are going to be relieved there is a change of coach, hoping that the environment will improve. In this phase the key boundaries and expectations must be laid to create the foundation. Meetings with the leaders, influencers and resisters should be had during this time, and you would hope meetings with the decision makers would have been had prior to starting work. In this stage, all players and staff are also on high alert, watching and listening to everything that is being said. It is a critical time to obtain the buy-in through both our actions and words. However, it is just as critical that these words and actions are realistic and sustainable over the long term. We should therefore not promise what we cannot sustain.

Storming: During the storming phase, high alert continues as everybody is focused on the impression they are making, and roles tend to become available as coaches must evaluate the abilities of the players and staff. Having been in this stage on multiple occasions, it can feel like being in a lion's den with everybody trying to gain an advantage. Everyone is looking out for enemies and allies, people they can trust and people they cannot trust. As players and staff take over each other's roles and responsibilities, tension amongst the group increases. Rash decisions create heavy emotions, and those with similar emotions can latch together to create cliques in order survive the environment without being isolated by themselves. Where possible, it is important to keep the group together and heading in the same direction. In some cases, this will not be possible, and we must be prepared to let people go if they are not heading in the same direction. Conflict is likely and at times it may not be visible to everyone. Identifying these situations and dealing with them is also crucial. As coaches when this occurs, we must be on high alert, observing body language and changes in relationships within the groups. Too many changes in roles and responsibilities are likely to shake up the environment. The more changes the more you can expect followers, influencers, or leaders to turn into resisters. The key to this stage is to change enough to start moving in the right direction, but not so much that people are lost in the change of direction, as well as aligning purposes for everyone to work towards their professional goals which supports the achievement of the team's goal.

Norming: The third stage of group development is where the group has started to stabilise. During the norming phase, most players and staff have accepted their roles and have started performing them to support the group. In some cases, there may be a few situations which should still be dealt with. However, overall, the group are functioning together. This may now be the time to start dealing with the few resisters that should create complete harmony within the group. During this phase it is still possible to return to storming if the staff, and players are not managing the culture to ensure that behaviour is aligned. Often in this phase, coaches take their foot off the gas and sit back and relax without monitoring what is going on, which is then the end of 'the manager effect'. When this happens, the team tends to return to their original culture and performance level before there was a change in coach.

Performing: Once the decision makers, leaders and influencers sustain the culture within the group, the team can enter the performing stage. Not all teams enter this stage, but this stage produces the highest level of performance. There is enough structure and trust in the environment where people know where they fit into the group and can effectively fulfil their roles and responsibilities. In this stage oxytocin, serotonin and testosterone are likely to be at their highest. Dopamine opportunities are present for all involved. There are no cliques that people latch on to out of desperation, cliques occur only out of similar interests such as language or relationships outside of football. In this moment, the key is managing individuals to keep them performing. There will be moments that create opportunities to ruin the group dynamic, such as poor results and new players or staff joining or leaving, these situations must be managed. One of the best ways to keep going through the performing stage is to consistently enhance the environment.

Enhancing: As a coach we should be enhancing performance week in and week out, but do we also focus on enhancing the culture? In any culture there are weaknesses or areas that can be improved. Maybe some players are starting to attend training later, or the work ethic in training has decreased. We must keep on top of these things and find new areas where the culture can be improved to ensure performance continues. Often coaches wait until they have fallen back into the storming phase before they attempt to enhance the culture. For example, only using team building activities when there are problems within the team. By this time, it is too late and influencing group dynamics for a second time is always harder than the first time. As leaders it is our duty to protect the happiness development and performance of the group. As soon as we have let it go once, we have demonstrated our vulnerability as leaders. Development must never stop to ensure performance is kept to its maximum.

Adjourning: After the performing and enhancing stages comes the adjourning stage. In football this is the end of the season. At this point players and staff may leave and new players and staff may arrive. It is critical to reflect across the season and acknowledge the efforts of those who deserve it and prepare for the forming of a new group. If many in the group stay together, it is more likely that we can move through the stages much quicker. Too many changes equal a return to forming, fewer changes equal quick movement back to norming and performing. Sir Alex Ferguson ensured that any new players that came in were aware that they would need to adapt to fit into the current culture within the Manchester United team (24). This enabled the team to keep one culture and move through the development stages quickly, as opposed to adjusting every time new players and staff join the group. When preparing for off season, while it is important to allow players a physical and mental break, it would be positive to encourage interaction between the group to keep the dynamics positive and stable for the new forming phase.

Maintaining Culture

"The art to truly maintaining anything is to develop it". Once we have implemented a culture which is achieving success, how do we maintain it? Having one successful season can be an amazing achievement, but how do the best coaches in the world sustain a long-term successful culture? There are five key methods we should use to sustain a successful culture.

1. Enhance ourselves: Sustaining a culture of hard work and discipline is of course beneficial for gaining success, however the challenge is that we must also sustain that culture within ourselves. After a successful period working with a group of staff and players, it is then an easy option to change our behaviour believing that success will continue. The issue is that when staff and players observe the changes in behaviour, they are often likely to follow. If we start spending less time at the training ground, players are likely to also spend less time there. It is certainly difficult to have expectations of others when we do not demonstrate them ourselves, especially when it was practised previously. As discussed, after achieving success we must increase the standards and expectations to simply sustain the levels of success. As such, we must also increase our standards and expectations of ourselves to set the example to the group we are working with. We must enhance ourselves, to push those around us to enhance themselves.

2. Psychological Conditioning: Once we can sustain and enhance the culture within ourselves, it then gives us more leverage to condition the behaviour of others within the environment. By us sustaining quality and intensity in our coaching behaviours during sessions, we can push players to maintain their quality and intensity. Once we identify behaviour in players or staff that do not align with the culture, it is critical we deal with it immediately. It is only normal that once implementing a successful culture, there will be players and staff member who may push the boundaries at times. A staff member who does not complete their report with the same detail, or a player who stops completing their injury prevention work. Allowing this to happen is accepting that it is allowed as part of the culture. Dealing with this early sets the standard and lets everyone know that the culture is still to be followed by everyone within the environment. To identify these moments, we may need to sit and audit the culture, by assessing the day to day behaviours that are occurring.

3. Cultural Auditing: With analysis becoming prevalent in sports environments, we are consistently auditing the development and performance of the players and team. However, who is responsible for auditing the culture? Who is responsible for monitoring what time players are arriving? Which activities players are participating in both inside and outside of football? Without this type of information, how can we be aware when the culture is slipping away or changing. One of the methods to deal with this is to have cultural auditing meetings, where key staff members responsible for the players and staff meet to discuss observations of the current team culture, and areas to enhance the team culture. In these meetings we can start to identify any players or staff members who are behaving outside of the culture so that these situations can then be dealt with. Maybe one of the analysts has experienced a player who is no longer coming to review their clips, or the fitness coach has observed a player who is not focusing during their sessions. Auditing the culture to identify these areas allows us to deal with the issues before they affect team performance.

4. Managing adversity: In every successful environment there is bound to be adversity. When adversity arises, how we deal with it may enhance the culture or cripple the culture. Examples of adversity may be losing a critical match, dealing with a player who wants to leave, or even negative media coverage of the team or a player. During adversity, the mindset must be focused on how we can use the situation positively to benefit the players and the staff, while protecting the team from any negative influences. It is our mindset that will determine the outcome of the adversity. Can being knocked out of a cup competition be used as leverage to improve the league performance? Can a key player leaving be used as fuel to set the standard that no player is bigger than the team? The perspective and spin we put on the adversity will dictate the culture moving forward. Staying calm during adversity and using it to our advantage not only helps maintain the culture, but can also enhance the culture to take happiness, development, and performance to the next level.

5. Managing transitions: As well as adverse moments of difficulty, we may also experience moments of transition within the club structure. When these changes are above us, we may have limited control over the culture which follows. When it involves players and staff, we should hopefully have an influence over those moments. The 2019 Rugby World Cup winning coach, Rassie Erasmus, shared his presentation to the National Team explaining how getting the 'right people' is more important than getting the 'best people' in a team sport (26). If we have an opportunity to control transition moments such as letting people go or bringing new people into the environment, we must make sure we bring in the 'right people' as opposed to just the 'best people'. The 'right people' refer to those who will be able to fit into the culture that has been set, without expecting the culture to adjust to them. If we are unable to control who comes in and who leaves, it is then critical to manage the situations to ensure cultural maintenance. This may mean a culture induction for new players and staff to explain the culture and informing them that the culture is bigger than the people in it. When players or staff members leave, it often means there is a gap within the culture. For example, the staff member who makes jokes and entertains everybody in the team has a social role beyond their contractual role. How does that role now become filled? Maybe there is a player who is a leader within the group, how do we now assign a new leader and who should that person be? Decisions in these moments can take the culture and the group back to storming stages or can enhance the team to take them to the next level of performance.

Summary

1. **Culture builds the foundations for success:** Before even addressing tactics, strategies and formations, culture should be the first factor that is addressed in any high performance environment.

2. **Understanding culture:** There are many different factors which contribute to the culture in any environment. Understanding and planning for these allows us to have the greatest influence.

3. **Analyse before applying:** Before applying any culture, it is critical to understand the current culture in the environment, and adapting the new culture where necessary.

4. **Simplify the culture:** The most important aspect when designing and implementing a culture is simplifying it so that it can be understood by everyone.

4. **Live the culture:** We must live the culture ourselves in order for the diffusion process to start and continue throughout those in our environments.

5. **Diffuse instead of impose:** The best way to implement a culture over a period of time is to diffuse through the decision-makers, leaders, and influencers.

6. **Move the resisters:** Identify which resisters can be brought over to become followers, influencers, or leaders. Create a strategy for executing this movement to bring about positive outcomes where possible.

8. **Manage the process:** Observe and manage the shifts across the stages of cultural diffusion. Identifying which stage the group is in can help identify methods that can be used to move towards the next stage.

9. **Audit the culture:** Once a culture is implemented, it is not always going to sustain itself. Regularly auditing the culture with analysis, meetings and discussions with others is a great way of keeping on top of any cultural changes.

10. **Develop to Maintain:** If we want to maintain a culture, the best method is to keep developing it, creating higher expectations of everyone within the environment.

References

1. O'connel, H. (2013). Here are the 38 trophies that Sir Alex Ferguson won at Manchester United [Online]. Available at https://www.the42.ie/alex-ferguson-trophies-900075-May2013/ (Accessed 27 March 2020).

2. Tarabay, J. (2019). What makes the All Blacks so Indomitable? It is in their DNA [Online]. Available at https://www.nytimes.com/2019/09/17/sports/rugby/new-zealand-all-blacks-rugby-world-cup.html (Accessed 27 March 2020).

3. Dawnay, O. (2019). Chelsea players are fined £20,000 if they arrive late for training and £500 for every minute, they miss of Frank Lampard's team meetings. Available at https://talksport.com/football/629050/frank-lampard-chelsea-fine-list/ (Accessed 27 March 2020)

4. Austin, S. (2020). Nuno Espirito Santo: Why Wolves don't fine players. Available at https://trainingground.guru/articles/nuno-espirito-santo-why-wolves-dont-fine-players (Accessed 2 April 2020)

5. Tutar, H., Altinoz, M., & Cakiroglu, D. (2014). A study on cultural difference management strategies at multinational organizations. *Procedia-Social and Behavioral Sciences*, *150*, p345-353.

6. Clyne, M., & Clyne, M. G. (1996). *Inter-cultural communication at work: Cultural values in discourse*. Cambridge University Press.

7. F.C. Barcelona. FC Barcelona Identity: Knowledge of the Club, its history, and its values. Available at https://www.fcbarcelona.com/en/card/759581/fc-barcelona-identity (Accessed 2 April 2020)

8. Janssen, J (2015). *How to Build and Sustain a Championship Culture.* Winning the Mental Game.

9. Lennox, P. (2020). Ancelotti outlines managerial philosophy. Available at https://www.evertonfc.com/news/1609731/ancelotti-outlines-marial-philosophy (Accessed 3 April 2020)

10. Reddy, M. (2019). Jurgen Klopp: Living and breathing Liverpool. Available at https://www.sportsjoe.ie/football/jurgen-klopp-interview-180798 (Accessed 3 April 2020)

11. Lacey, A (2018). Mario Gotze points to huge difference between Pep and Klopp. Available at https://extra.ie/2018/06/09/sport/soccernews/mario-gotze-points-to-huge-difference-between-pep-and-klopp (Accessed 3 April 2020)

12. Hytner, D. (2018). Perfectionist Marcelo Bielsa brings radical approach to Leeds United. Available at https://www.theguardian.com/football/2018/aug/04/leeds-united-marcelo-bielsa (Accessed 3 April 2020)

13. Sports Staff. (2017). Bayern Munich players' ran secret training sessions' behind Carlo Ancelotti's back. Available at https://www.independent.co.uk/sport/football/premier-

league/bayern-munich-secret-training-sessions-carlo-ancelotti-arjen-robben-franck-ribery-a7980666.html (Accessed April 4, 2020)

14. Wilson, S. (2017). Rio Ferdinand reveals how Sir Alex Ferguson reacted when Paul Scholes got sent off. Available at https://www.givemesport.com/1197043-rio-ferdinand-reveals-how-sir-alex-ferguson-reacted-when-paul-scholes-got-sent-off (Accessed 5 April 2020)

15. Unwin, W. (2020). Nuno Espirito Santo: What makes Wolves boss one of Europe's leading managers? Available at https://www.bbc.com/sport/football/51962924 (Accessed 5 April 2020)

16. Taylor, L. (2019). Sheffield United's Chris Wilder: the old school manager with new ideas. Available at https://www.theguardian.com/football/2019/nov/23/sheffield-united-chris-wilder-manager-non-league (Accessed 5 April 2020)

17. 100% Pure New Zealand. Prepare yourself for the energy and awe of the haka. Available at https://www.newzealand.com/us/feature/haka/ (Accessed 5 April 2020)

18. Haller, K. (2019). *The Little Book of Colour: How to use the Psychology of Colour to Transform your Life.* Penguin Books. UK: London

19. Diefenbach, Thomas & Sillince, John. (2011). Formal and Informal Hierarchy in Different Types of Organization. Organization Studies. 32. p1515-1537.

20. Sitton, J. (2010). John Sitton- Angry Football Half-Time Team Talk- Leyton Orient F.C. Available at https://www.youtube.com/watch?v=nYDIMWpcKql (Accessed 10 April 2020)

21. Rogers, E. M. (2003) *Diffusion of innovations.* Simon & Schuster. US: New York

22. Carmazzi, A. (2019). Creating Sustainable Organizational Culture Change in 80 Days. Available at https://www.youtube.com/watch?v=r2XE87EoI7M&t=1056s (Accessed 10 April 2020)

23. Mannion, D. (2019). Ravel Morrison: Why Sir Alex Ferguson and Manchester United had no choice but to get rid of the hugely talented player. Available at https://talksport.com/football/435276/sir-alex-ferguson-manchester-united-ravel-morrison/ (Accessed 11 April 2020)

24. Neville, G. (2020). Gary Neville opens up on his time at Valencia & explains why he'll never coach again. Available at https://www.youtube.com/watch?v=_qk04dh4Rxg (Accessed 28 April 2020)

25. Egolf, D. B. (2001). *Forming Storming Norming Performing: Successful Communications in Groups and Teams.* Writers Press Club. US: Bloomington

26. Erasmus, R. (2019). Talent vs Mindset: Again, same clever friend taught me this many years ago. Available at https://twitter.com/RassieRugby (Accessed 28 April 2020)

27. James, D (2013). Silence speaks volumes on how Sir Alex Ferguson ran Manchester United Available at https://www.theguardian.com/football/blog/2013/may/11/alex-ferguson-manchester-united-manager (Accessed 28 April 2020)

28. Zakarian, A (2019). Bayern Munich star reveals how Klopp helped make him World Class. Available at https://www.vbetnews.com/bayern-munich-star-reveals-jurgen-klopp-helped-make-world-class/ (Accessed 25 April 2020)

29. Sitton, J. (1995). John Sitton- Angry Football Half-Time Team Talk- Leyton Orient F.C. Available at https://www.youtube.com/watch?v=nYDIMWpcKqI. Accessed 21 June 2020

"

MANAGING STAFF & PLAYERS

I'D SAY HANDLING PEOPLE IS THE MOST IMPORTANT THING YOU CAN DO AS A COACH. I'VE FOUND EVERY TIME I'VE GOTTEN INTO TROUBLE WITH A PLAYER IT'S BECAUSE I WASN'T TALKING TO HIM ENOUGH

Lou Holtz

Introduction

Objective: The objective of this chapter is to discuss a variety of methods used to manage both staff and players from an individual perspective, with the aim of increasing the happiness, development, and performance.

While creating a culture helps influence the behaviour of the group, management of individuals will help keep players and staff striving to develop and perform within the culture. After a challenging experience as the Chelsea F.C. manager, Andre Villas Boas discussed the importance of managing individuals as opposed to only managing the team. "At Tottenham I learnt to be completely different. The day to day is everything with every single individual. Each person requires a different type of response and different type of person from you. You cannot be the same person to every single player, you must be a different person to each individual." (13). The idea behind managing people is to influence their individual behaviours which can positively influence the group's performance. Poor management of individuals equals decreased success. Great management of individuals equals increased success. Happier players, better players, with better performances. Neuroscientists say that 95% of our behaviour is controlled by our subconscious, and our subconscious is motivated by emotion and not by reason (2). This means that managing individuals 'emotions is key to influencing behaviour both on and off the pitch. Decisions made on the pitch are certainly more likely to be influenced by the subconscious, as emotions are even more dominant under the pressure of time and expectations. This makes managing individual's emotions and thoughts one of the key components of successful coaching. As well as referring to players, this also refers to colleagues and management across the club hierarchy.

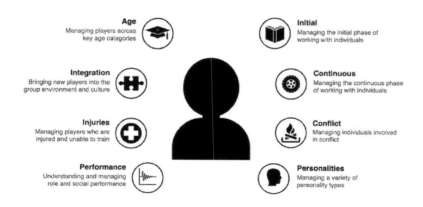

Figure 32: Individual Management Priorities

There are several situations we may come across in a coaching environment where individual management will play an integral part in achieving success. From the first day of meeting anyone at the club, the management of these situations can dictate the success we are going to have. How can we keep everybody in an optimal emotional state which then influences their decision-making towards the objectives that have been set?

Initial Management

When discussing a coaching role, our expertise must kick in before even stepping onto the training pitch. The initial discussions with senior staff and management are the first vital steps to ensuring a smooth and successful experience. Clear objectives must be identified, along with clear methods of meeting these objectives. Objectives can vary between league standings, cup competition success, player development or sales, or in modern cases, can be based on statistical data that predicts long term success. The methods may include style of play, recruitment of players, or behaviour during matches and press conferences. This will depend on what is most important to the club. In some cases, coaching roles have minimal pressure to meet both the objectives and the methods, for example, a team desperate to stay in the league may have a strict objective to avoid relegation without any focus on the methods used. However, more and more clubs now have expectations of both objectives and methods, with the most common method being focused on style of play. With 'Club Philosophy' being the common trend in football, there is often an expectation of a coach to implement a certain model of play which fits in with the identity of the club. This needs to be clear in the initial phase of taking a coaching role. Is there a model already in place to follow? Are there expectations regarding the image of the model that should be put in place? When discussing these points, the agreements should align with our genuine beliefs about what is possible, and what we believe in. Agreeing to unrealistic objectives, or methods that we cannot sustain over a period, is likely to cause problems in the future. It is better to modify the initial objectives and methods and agree on them, than to agree on meeting objectives and methods that we are unable to fulfil. Once coming to an understanding regarding objectives and methods, the next consideration is to whether these align with the players and colleagues' individual desires. If they do, fantastic, if not, then there will either need to be meetings with the players and colleagues to try to align their desires with the set objectives and methods, or possible changes in the staff and playing department. It can be of critical importance, that all players and staff are pushing in the same direction to achieve one goal using the same set of methods.

To align players and staff objectives with the clubs, it is vital that we first understand each person's aspirations, which can best be discovered with individual meetings. Once we understand what the players and colleagues want, we can identify which players and staff members align perfectly with the club goals, and which players and staff members may need to find alignment or move club. Here are a few examples where these may not align:

1. Players who want to win trophies when the club wants to survive relegation
2. Staff who want to win matches when the club prioritises developing players
3. Players and staff who have no aspirations, when the club has huge objectives
4. Youth players who want opportunities to play, when the club wants to use experienced players.

The initial phase with the technical team can be a huge challenge when joining a club with staff members already in place. It means that they have their own objectives and methods which need to be aligned before starting work. The methods can be a challenge as they have often experienced working under several previous coaches, who have had their own methods of working. The staff must buy into new methods, as the influence they can have daily, is sometimes far greater than we are aware of. This influence may be through their body language, their technical, tactical, and physical instructions when working with the players, or even more likely, the conversations they have in the canteen or on WhatsApp. It is becoming more and more of a common trend for coaches to bring their own technical team with them into a job, so that they do not go through these processes and can be efficient from the first day of training.

For many of us, this is not a common reality, therefore we must use the initial phase to align everyone working at the club with the same objectives and methods.

Continuous Management

After the initial phase is complete and all parties are aligned, the continuous phase now starts, where day to day management of all parties is critical to success. Our culture and leadership may be enough to manage most people in the environment, however, there are several specific players and situations which may need different management techniques. One factor to consider when managing people, is each person's interest and influence, which has been utilised as a key business principle for managing stakeholders (6). The table below summarises how different focuses are required based on these factors:

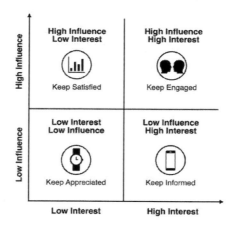

Figure 33: Management of Influence vs Interest

Across club management, staff and players, everyone has a different level of interest and a different level of influence. How to treat each individual must be unique to their interest and influence. Making a mistake of managing people incorrectly can create many difficulties. The first challenge is identifying any outliers who may need a management style that is outside of our leadership style. For example, if we lead with trust, honesty, and openness, a player who cannot be trusted, may need a different management style to the rest of the group, to ensure that his behaviour aligns with the group. A more common scenario is a coach who leads by strict authority but has a Chairman that cannot be treated with harsh words, so the management style for the chairman must be adapted. How many times have we seen a clear fall out between coaches and senior management? How many times could this have been avoided with a management style suited to their influence and interest? The levels of focus include the following:

Low interest | Low Influence: Keep them feeling appreciated. For people who have minimal interest and minimal influence, minimal attention can be given to ensure we have enough time to manage those with higher interests and higher influence. This does not mean ignoring them, as everyone in the environment has a contribution. The practical contribution may be minimal.

A cleaner's practical contribution may not influence performance but the energy they bring into the environment and the example they set with their work ethic and perfection can often have a subconscious effect. A frequent short discussion can go a long way to ensuring they are okay, whilst also making them feel appreciated in the environment. Their feeling of being appreciated can go a long way in ensuring they bring the right energy to work every day, and it often only takes a small amount of time and effort.

Low Interest | High Influence: Keep them feeling satisfied. For those who have a limited interest but have a high influence, it is critical that they are kept satisfied with the aspects they are interested in. These are often at management or board level and may have a close relationship with the key decision makers, meaning they are the people who can have an influence without us even seeing it. A typical example may be a board member who only really has an interest in the youth programme at the club and has minimal interest in the senior team. To keep them satisfied, it may only take one trip to the academy to watch the young players train. Minimal effort to ensure satisfaction.

High Interest | Low Influence: Keep them feeling informed. In every club environment, there are bound to be people with a heavy interest and low influence. This could be kit managers, administrators, or groundsmen who are fans of the club, but have no links to the decision makers. People in this situation generally appreciate being informed of what is going on, as everybody who is passionate about a club loves to feel a part of the club. Engaging them in conversations around their work is key to making them feel valued. Updating the administrator on a change of plans or informing the kit manager of a delay in training time can be critical to keeping them on side. Once again, even when their practical contribution to performance is minimal, the energy they bring can either support the journey to success or make it that little bit more challenging.

High Interest | High Influence: Keep them feeling engaged. Among the key decision makers, it is highly likely there will be at least one person who has a key interest alongside their influence. People who have both influence and interest are likely to be the ones to support or fire us when difficult situations arise. It is vital that these people feel like they are part responsible for the day to day events that happen, as if challenges arise they will support us, as they are indirectly supporting themselves. To manage these people, they may need regular meetings and conversations to update them on what is happening, but also, we may need to listen and seek advice to gain further understanding of some of the situations they may be dealing with. Of course, there is a line that must be addressed to create an understanding of the level of influence they are to have on coaching decisions. It is critical that this is set in the initial phase as previously discussed. Some influential and interested people may want to tell us how to play and which players to play, others may want to share their observations with us. Whatever we decide to set must be stuck to, never make the mistake of changing the objectives or breaking the methods, without agreement from the influential and interested people.

Conflict Management

At some point in a football season, there is bound to be conflict between people within our environment. As coaches it is our duty to be aware of, and manage these conflicts, particularly if they are between players or staff. At times, conflicts resolve themselves, in which case the best way to manage it can be to observe it, and let it play out. There are however conflicts which may not resolve by themselves, some of which we can identify early. For example, a physical fight is likely to require intervention, whereas an argument over a poor pass may not need any intervention. The key trigger that will let us know whether an intervention is needed, is whether there is acceptance of responsibility on at least one side of the conflict. Conflict normally continues when there is no acceptance of responsibility on either side. For example, if two players lunge into a dangerous challenge on the training pitch, and one player apologises after, the conflict will likely resolve itself. If there is no apology or acceptance of responsibility, it is likely to continue into a progressive conflict. For full conflict resolution, it is key that all parties understand their responsibility for the conflict. This is critical in sports teams as results can be heavily dependent on genuine player relationships (7). There are three key mechanisms that people use to deal with conflict before resolving it. While these strategies can make it appear that the conflict is resolved, the conflict is often just hidden or postponed. These mechanisms are often used when the discomfort of the confrontation is high, but the discomfort in resolving the conflict is even higher.

Avoiding: Avoidance can be a strategy people use to minimise or hide the conflict. In a team environment, avoidance can cause further problems, as while they are avoiding each other, there will be a clear decrease in team cohesion which can be observed and absorbed by others within the group. Avoidance can also split the dressing room. Players are likely to feel like they must only talk to the party(s) on one side of the conflict. If those involved in the conflict have used avoidance as the mechanism to deal with it, when they are forced to be in contact, the conflict can explode. A typical example would be two players who have had an argument over a comment made about their personal life. After the argument, the two players may decide to stay out of each-others way to manage the conflict, which works for a few weeks. In the meantime, players subconsciously take sides, until there is a moment in training between the two players where there is a 50/50 challenge they are both expected to go for. What happens? A return to conflict via a viscous challenge, which is not about winning the ball, but is likely about the previous unresolved conflict.

Competing: Competition is a key requirement of a successful dressing room, even between teammates, to battle for a place in the starting line-up. The challenge comes when the players compete to make the other person suffer, as opposed to competing to make themselves better. Conflict can create competition that is about bringing other players down, which has two negative effects. One is that the other players performance can decrease, and the player trying to bring other players down also has a performance decrease, as his focus on being better has also decreased. Within a team environment it is critical that competition must be focused on becoming better, not making others worse.

Accommodating: When one party feels too much discomfort in the conflict, and the other party(s) do not appear to take responsibility for the conflict, they may decide that accommodating the other party is the easiest option. This meaning they allow the behaviour to preserve their comfort, even though the conflict may still be there internally. The internal conflict is forcing behaviour that does not align with the feeling they have inside. While it does preserve harmony, it can again leave a conflict that can explode at a later point when they feel tired of accommodating the other parties' behaviour. This typically happens with captain-player relationships and coach-player relationships. While the player may not agree with the captain or coach, the discomfort in having conflict with the coach or captain may leave the player feeling that it is better they accept the behaviour, even though they do not agree with it. This also happens with the head coach/manager and other members of the technical team, as again, the conflict discomfort is often too high. Eventually, the internal conflict will cause unhappiness, as well as a decrease in development and performance.

Ideally, before any of the 3 mechanisms are utilised, we should use a conflict resolution strategy to deal with the situation. A conflict resolution strategy often requires a mediator; however, this mediator does not always have to be us. Sometimes this responsibility can be given to someone we trust will execute the steps in the correct order and in the correct manner. Examples of people we can use for this includes, the captain, a member of senior management, or another member of the technical team. It is key that they are neutral and will not carry a bias towards one side. The captain would not be a good mediator for a conflict situation between his teammates when he is also personal friends with one of them. Below are four steps that can be carried out for full conflict resolution:

1. Understand the Incident: The first stage to resolving conflict, is understanding the incident that has taken place. In most cases there is an incident that has taken place that can be identified as 'conflict'. Understanding exactly what has happened in this incident and how it started is critical to understanding why there is a conflict. At times, the incident explains the reason for the conflict, however, often the events prior to the incident better explain why there is a conflict. It is important that both parties can explain what they believe happened and how the incident made them feel before looking beyond the incident.

2. Look beyond the Incident: Once the incident has been fully understood, with all parties contributing, it is then the time to understand if there were any issues prior to the incident that may have been the underlying cause. Perhaps a previous conflict that was not addressed, a continuous personality clash, or continuous difference in opinion. Dealing with these is the key to repairing any damage caused by the conflict, and preventing further incidents happening. Can both parties understand where the incident started, and see the other parties' perspectives around the incident(s)? Often it is a lack of understanding of the other parties' feelings that cause the clash in conflict. One area to be sensitive around is the potential differences in the two parties. Examples of these can be race, culture or their role within the team. The ideal outcome from this step, is finding a mutual agreement of miscommunication.

3. Request and Identify Solutions: Once both parties have shared their viewpoint, it is important to then support them in identifying how they can both improve the situation to deal with the conflict and prevent the conflict from reoccurring. The question to ask is, how can we make this situation better? The key outcome from identifying solutions is to align beliefs and perspectives, and if needed create interventions that all parties can cooperate with, where they all feel like they are putting in equal effort to make the intervention work. If one or some parties feel they should put in more effort than the other, it is possible there will be a feeling of favouritism, which is a concern during conflict resolution. The mediator must always appear to be equally on both sides, even if there is an internal bias. If all parties do not appear to be enthusiastic about sticking to the solutions, it is an optional idea to turn the agreements into a written agreement for extreme circumstances. The ideal solution from here is to simply realign the thoughts and beliefs in relation to the culture within the environment, which should limit long term conflict if aligned correctly.

4. Observation and Intervention: After interventions have been created and agreed on, it does not mean the conflict is completely over. After all parties walk away from the conflict resolution, continuous observation is needed to monitor the situation. If we are not going to be too close to the players, we may need to identify someone else within the group, who can also monitor the situation, and report back on the progress. If there are any moments where one of the parties are breaking the culture or intervention, further intervention may be needed to remind them of the situation, and ensure they continue with the work they are doing to prevent further conflict.

Preventing Conflict

The best way to deal with conflict, is to avoid it in the first place. Emotional intelligence, reading of body language, and speaking with players on a regular basis can be key to identifying potential conflicts. Utilising the captain or senior players is also a great way to understand what problems are happening within the group. Based on the three conflict behaviours previously discussed (avoiding, competing, accommodating), here are some key indicators to look out for:

1. People that isolate themselves
2. People that avoid each other
3. People that regularly compete with one another
4. People that are regularly mocked
5. People behaving outside of the expected culture
6. People that form sub-groups

Conflict Revolution

We have all heard the phrase 'losing the dressing room', but what does it really mean and how does it happen? Conflict revolution (losing the dressing room) is the process by which one major conflict, or many conflicts cause a revolution to overthrow the leaders within the group. There are many cases where players, or the whole team have intentionally underperformed to ensure the coach is fired. Of course, players will not openly admit to this but when you see news of the coach under pressure, followed by a heavy defeat with minimal effort to prevent it, it does paint a specific picture. It is exceedingly rare that this happens due to one conflict, it generally precedes a lack of effort in dealing with continuous conflicts, whether it is between players themselves, or players and coaching staff. Therefore, it is critical that conflicts are dealt with early on. When we feel like a full revolution is coming, it may not be too late, however a huge personality shift is needed to express our desire to understand whatever conflicts are present, whether they are visible or not. Remember, as discussed, some conflicts do not have an incident to observe and therefore emotional intelligence and reading body language can be the key to identifying a potential revolution. A squad of players is always going to have more power than a coach, so we must think very carefully before trying to fight against a revolution from the staff and players we are working with.

Managing Personalities

Managing players over a period of time can be exhausting, but can become far easier and far more rewarding once we understand how players differ. Of course, every player is unique, with many different personalities, however if we can identify traits of each player, we can start to identify strategies for managing them. From experience and research, below are five key personality traits, with most players showing one of these to be their dominant trait. Most players will have a level of all the traits but identifying their dominant trait will allow us to understand how to manage them slightly differently.

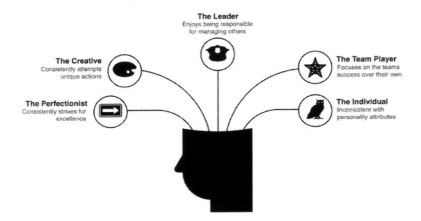

Figure 34: Key Personality Types

The Perfectionist: Once we have a perfectionist within our group it can have huge benefits for the team when harnessed correctly. The perfectionist loves training, but also has high expectations of training quality and improving in every session. We can use this desire, as a standard for other players if we want to create a group environment where everybody focuses on their development every day. When they are striving for perfection, they also expect perfection from others, including the coach. Managing the perfectionist can mean putting on extra small group or individual sessions to help the player improve and giving them regular objectives to achieve and focus on. It also means understanding that when they are not playing very well, they are likely to be overly critical of their performance, and sometimes they can even be over critical when they are playing well. Managing their perspective and giving them regular positive feedback is especially important, as they will often only give themselves negative feedback internally. Their thoughts are often based around the idea that 'they are not good enough'. Positive appraisal is the key to turn this into 'they are good enough', while allowing them to still improve each day.

Tips:

1. Use their focus on being the best as a standard
2. Encourage them to push other players to strive for perfection
3. Use positive praise to balance their self-talk

4. Observe and manage their workload to ensure they avoid burnout or injury

The Creative: Ever heard the phrase 'they are just a bad trainer'? This is often the creative. We are running a finishing session, and instead of scoring the easiest way, they want to lob the goalkeeper or put it through their legs. They like doing things that others cannot do and hate restriction during training. When we find most of the group completing exactly what is asked, we can identify the creatives as they are normally doing something else. They are the least common player type, as it takes a brave person to choose their creativity over conformity. The reason why they get away with non-conformity in training and matches is often because they produce unbelievable quality in comparison to the rest of the group and can execute actions that others simply cannot. One of the hardest parts of managing a creative, is ensuring they conform without limiting their creativity. Session design and tactical flexibility is critical in managing these players. Mundane repetitive exercises become boring for them and tactical limitations with a lot of instructions also become boring. They will often rebel against them if they feel too restricted. Which coach wants regular conflict with one of their most creative players?

Tips:

1. Use their creativity within our tactical structures
2. Create sessions in which they can demonstrate their creativity
3. Always give difficult challenges to ensure they are pushing forward
4. Push them physically, as they can easily slack off and depend on creativity to perform

The Leader: Hopefully as a coach it is easy to identify the leader, as they should have similar personality traits to us. They should never be afraid of confrontation and should be very aware of their environment. Sometimes the best way to discover a leader is to observe how others behave around them. The leader may be quiet but well respected by teammates and peers. It is our job to use the respect they have, to build their leadership skills. If we try to build a leader who is not respected by the group, we are preparing the team for conflict situations. Leaders must be respected before they are followed. One of the keys to managing the leader, is giving them enough power to influence but not too much where they can compete for power. We must always stay in control while allowing the leader to have influence. They are most likely our captain, however, if we have numerous leaders, we can create a leadership group that discuss issues and report them to us on a 'need to know' basis. A strong leader may often be key to pushing a team to success. Roy Keane, Carles Puyol, Sergio Ramos. Three recent captains who have led their teams to continuous success, including winning the Champions League. When assessing the players traits on the pitch, and stories from off the pitch, it is easy to identify their clear leadership traits such as strength of character, communication, and motivation.

Tips:

1. Use their leadership to manage the dressing room
2. Manage their power, and ensure all players know we are still in control
3. Never put down the leader(s) publicly unless it is constructive
4. Regularly give responsibilities to ensure they feel like a leader

The Team Player: When identifying player traits, the team players are often the ones who do not stand out with any extremities and have a continuous work ethic and mentality. These players are the core of most team sport environments, as they decide to fit in when their traits are less extreme than others. For example, if putting together a team of creatives, the most extreme ones will stay as the creatives, and the majority will become team players and conform within the group. While team players may be easier to manage, it is still important to invest time in them so that they do not feel like they should show extreme behaviour to get attention from the coach. Ignoring team players is a quick way to develop more extreme behaviours within the group. Any sign of negativity or complacency should be dealt with immediately to keep their team player attributes. Whilst they may not be the top goal scorer, or the captain, they still make up a critical core of the group.

Tips:

1. Remember to praise and speak with them regularly to keep the feeling of equality
2. Deal with any negative or complacent behaviour immediately
3. Encourage individual qualities to promote their unique attributes

The Individual: The most challenging player type is the individual. The players who have fluctuating moods and fluctuating performances often fit into this category. These players may demonstrate behaviour which is difficult to understand due to their emotional inconsistencies, which can vary on a day to day basis. This means that one day they can show incredible ability, and the next day they can look like they do not enjoy the sport. The key with this type of player is understanding that the emotion needs to be managed more carefully than the technical and tactical aspects of the sport. Most of the time, the emotions for them have nothing to do with the sport, and everything to do with their personal life and their personal challenges. These players are most at risk of faking injuries, alcohol or drug abuse, and regular conflicts with players and staff. To get the best out of them, we must focus on getting the best out of the person, before discussing the player. This may require daily conversations, objectives, motivation, and praise. Their sensitivity means that they can become insecure or disinterested in minutes but can also become motivated and focused within minutes if the right buttons are pressed.

Tips:

1. Spend time understanding the person behind the player
2. Read body language early to intervene with necessary intervention
3. Invest in the person daily to get the best player, as frequently as possible
4. Set agreements and interventions to help them manage when they are struggling emotionally

Utilising Personality Traits

Within any environment there are hundreds of traits that will have an influence over success. These may vary between each person. Many of the negative personality traits come from a positive place and can be a treasure if utilised correctly. For example, while aggression may be a negative trait in many moments, it can be beneficial when we need someone to motivate players before a game or intimidate opposition in a big game. Of course, we must manage the aggression so that they do not end up in fights or end up being sent off. If we can allow them to release some of their personality in the right moments, there may be less of the emotion held inside for critical occasions where they must control it. Similarly, a moody personality can be difficult to manage as they may appear up one day and down the other. This can often be because they are extremely sensitive, and their emotions fluctuate to extremely high and extremely low levels. If we can manage their emotions and keep them high, we can reap the extreme benefits of their high mood which is often happiness, laughter, and enthusiasm. Easier said than done, but possible when we take the time to understand and manage them correctly. We have three tasks in managing the traits:

Understand: Where the traits come from
Identify: Which traits can be positively utilised
Manage: Influence the traits towards being utilised in a positive way

Managing Age Factors

When coaching, the age of the group we are working with is one of the most important factors that contributes to all the decisions we make. Age is important when working with first team players, academy players, or players in recreational teams. To take the understanding of age to the next level, we must understand the different measurements of someone's age, and understand how age affects the expectations of the players we are working with.

Chronological Age | Psychological Age | Athletic Age

There is one key principle that applies to working with players, whether at the senior professional level, or the amateur youth level. The chronological age of the player does not necessarily represent the emotional or athletic age of the player. We often have this idea of how a player should look and act based on their chronological age, but this is not the reality. Understanding this principle allows us to better manage the players to ensure their development is as efficient as possible.

Chronological Age
The age based on number of years since birth

Psychological Age
The psychological, emotional, social maturity

Athletic Age
The maturity of the human bodies capacity

Figure 35: Measurements of Age

At age fifteen, a young player called Wayne Rooney was playing up numerous age groups playing with the under-nineteens (8). A year later, he was training and playing with the Everton senior team before making his debut appearance in the Premier League. While his chronological age was far younger than the rest of the Everton squad, he was an early athletic developer, meaning his athletic profile could be compared to players aged many years older than him. This enabled him to handle the workload and physical competition of professional players in the Premier League. Other professional players can testify that this is not the situation for all young players. At age sixteen, Jesse Lingard was playing a year down with the under-fifteens age group due to his late athletic development. He did not start playing regular first team football at Manchester United until he was in his mid-twenties after going through numerous loan spells at different clubs to try and prepare him for life at the highest level of football. Two players, at sixteen-years-old who were athletically completely different. As well as the physical differences which are easily noticeable, the psychological, emotional, and social age of players also differs from their chronological age. There are players age sixteen who find it easy to socialise with players in their thirties, who can handle some of the dressing room competition, and manage the pressure of playing in front of millions of people on TV. There are also players age twenty-one who struggle to socialise with other adults, who struggle to be strong in a competitive environment, and cannot manage the pressure of the expectations of so many people. Identifying these differences is important to managing players' growth and development within the team. They may need extra support during challenging times and may need a senior player to help integrate them into the team and mentor them through the journey.

From an athletic perspective, players who are late developers and are behind the rest of the group may need an altered program or may need to train and/or play with a different age group at times to manage their development. An eighteen-year-old, late physical developer, who has a professional contract with the first team may still need to play matches at times with a youth team where they can express their technical and tactical qualities. A player with excellent dribbling and footwork, may find it hard to execute their one-vs-one dominance against players who are physically far stronger and quicker. By playing with a group closer in physical development, they can dominate and be reminded of their abilities, while being mentored through the process. Similarly, with Jesse Lingard, a critical aspect to the journey is everyone (most importantly the player) understanding that patience is key, and eventually they will athletically peak. If there is a player who is training with an age group where their athletic development is behind the rest of the group, program modifications are necessary. A typical example is when a player signs their first-year professional contract and trains full time with the first team on an elite training program. During the first season, particularly pre-season, their training load must be managed, with a balance between the progression of fitness and freshness. Furthermore, they may need to go on to an individualised physical program to support the players development into senior football. This integration should be gradual, until eventually they are prepared to fulfil the full first team program without an increased risk of injury in comparison to the rest of the group.

Youth and Instant Gratification: In some cases, we will experience a youth player who expects everything now and is extremely eager to play. While the belief they are ready to play and should be starting is an essential confidence tool, it can become detrimental to themselves and the club if they are not playing. These players do not want to sit on the bench. Our coaching eye and experience are critical in deciding whether they are ready to play, or if they are better off on loan, or sold, or even kept in a lower age group. Jadon Sancho decided to leave Manchester City, one of the richest clubs in the world, competing for the Premier League and Champions League titles, to go to Borussia Dortmund where he would start first team football instantly, instead of having to wait (9). Initially, many frowned upon the decision, but it is now clear to see that he was ready to play Champions League football and compete in a top European League where they are competing for the title. This is not to say that if he stayed at Manchester City he would have been better than the players currently in the starting eleven but it does mean that his time would not have been best utilised playing in an under-twenty-three league, when he could be competing for Champions League and Domestic League titles each season. His excellent assist and goal stats, plus England National Team caps also support this argument. While instant gratification is still labelled as a negative trait, it is a trait that is ever increasing in the world of sport, which is a representation of current society. The key to dealing with it, is accepting it, and managing it, not ignoring it, fighting against it, and hoping it will go away.

Whether it is an Academy contract for a player who expects to play up an age group, or a professional who expects to be starting for the first team, the players contract and their value will generally dictate the club's decision. A player's impatience is justified when they deserve what they are asking for. The challenge currently is that many children have been brought up gaining awards and praise when they have not necessarily worked hard enough for them. Similarly, in youth programs, players are promised equal game time regardless of their work ethic in training and matches, and regardless of their attitude to development and growth. If a fifth-place athlete gets a medal, and the player who has been lazy all week is guaranteed equal minutes at the weekend, the desire to work hard to be the best, may be reduced for all. Later in life it can often mean that they feel like they deserve an award when they have not demonstrated excellence in what they have achieved. The reality of the results driven world, particularly in the football world, is that the best players play, and no one will play due to sympathy or equality. This means that players must be better than most of their peers in order to get the outcomes that they desire.

Tips:

1. Identify if the player is ready, if they will be ready, how far away they are from being ready to play
2. Advise the player on the likely pathway we believe they should take
3. Listen to the players desires after we have advised them
4. Advise the club on recommended action based on what has been identified, and what we have heard

Senior Players: At some point in most players' careers, they will become a 'senior' player where they have passed their athletic peak but have a lot of experience to offer. As their athletic abilities decline, there will be a point where they do not meet the requirements of the starting eleven, and eventually the requirements of the squad. Identifying this point at the right time is particularly important for managing the dressing room, as the senior players are often the most influential. When we identify the time too early, we can cause upset by dropping, selling, or releasing the player. If we identify the time too late, results may suffer as they do not perform to the required level. Rather than dropping a senior player completely, adapting their role may be the best way to manage the process without causing conflict.

Tips:

1. Can they play in a different position where the athletic requirements are lower?
2. Can they make substitute appearances in key games?
3. Are there games where they can play without sacrificing the result?
4. Are there games where their experience may be vital for the team?
5. Can mentorship roles be given to them to keep them involved in the teams' performance?
6. Can they start education programs to prepare them for life after football?

Managing Performance and Motivation

Assessing and influencing player and staff performance is a key part of our role. Often, we assess the quality of people's performance based on their work output. For players this is the quality they demonstrate on the pitch, for staff it may be the quality of their reports or work they execute with the players. How often do we consider their performance in and around the training ground and work environments? To differentiate between these areas, I have divided performance into two areas, namely, social performance and role performance.

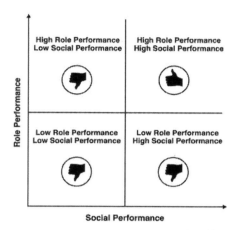

Figure 36: Role and Social `Performance

Role Performance: Is everyone consistently contributing to the performance of the team, to the level that is expected? Each person in the tribe is responsible for performing their role to the best of their ability within the workload they have been set and within the hours they are expected to work. The art of maximising people's performance is not to maximise the number of hours they work, but to maximise their efficiency when they are expected to be working. What performance contribution are they giving to the tribe?

Social Performance: Is everyone consistently contributing to the culture of the team to the level that is expected? In a recent interview Jurgen Klopp said "it is not for me to create an atmosphere in a room, each person is responsible for that" (12). Each person is responsible for their contribution to the mood and the togetherness of the team. They must bring the right energy daily and promote the agreed ideas of the culture we have set. All behaviours must promote the group being closer, together as one.

To really maximise role and social performance within our environment, it is extremely helpful to understand the people we are working with. This can apply for both staff and players. Knowing what motivates each member in our environment as a person, will gives us a significant advantage in increasing their social and role performance. We can then use this understanding of motivation as a tool to reward performance in relation to their desires and use their desires as targets and objectives. There are many models of testing which can be used to identify our dominant human desire. Most people desire multiple feelings, however from experience there will normally be one lead desire which dictates most of their behaviours. Here are eight dominant desires that motivate human behaviour (PIPAUSSS):

1. **Power:** People who have felt powerless in situations where they wish they had power, are likely searching for power so they can have control in future difficult situations. Dealing with people searching for power can be incredibly challenging, as they may threaten our role. However, if we can give enough power to keep them fulfilled while limiting their power enough to keep us in control, we may be able to increase their performance.

2. **Influence:** People who have previously tried to have influence but have been ignored often search for positions where people will listen. We must always try to listen to the opinions of these people, even if we do not want to use their information, listening may make them feel far more empowered.

3. **Perfection:** People who have been heavily criticised for small mistakes and errors who now crave perfection to demonstrate they do not make mistakes and errors. Rewarding their high-quality work and pushing them to increase their quality will motivate them to increase their performance. Criticising them without recognising their quality can cause major disappointment.

4. **Achievement:** People who feel as though their achievements were not recognised, now crave achieving on a level where people will notice their achievements. Recognising their achievements will ensure they feel appreciated and perform better at work. Setting achievable aligned targets will keep this person motivated to improve and work harder.

5. **Usefulness:** People who have previously been made to feel that they are not good enough to help people, now want to help others in order to show that they are useful. These people can be extremely beneficial in our environment, especially if they have quality. They like to be given tasks to do to help, so use them and their expertise frequently.

6. **Security:** People who have felt significantly unsafe or at risk at some point in life, now crave consistency in terms of lifestyle and relationships. Ensuring their job and status within the team is safe, will allow these people to perform. Too much of a threat that puts their role at risk may make them panic, therefore reducing their performance quality.

7. **Self-Expression:** People who have felt restricted in terms of displaying their thoughts, beliefs and emotions go on to crave the opportunity to express them. Allowing these players and staff to share their ideas and creativity will increase their motivation to perform. Making their life at work rigid will limit their role and social performance.

8. **Significance:** People who have previously felt insignificant when they felt they have far more to offer than those who have been treated as significant, will crave being viewed as significant. Making them feel important to the success of the team is likely to increase their work ethic, capacity, and efficiency.

While there is no test to find these specific desires, we must utilise our emotional intelligence and communication to identify which desires the players and staff have. Being able to identify these traits in people within our environment will help us not only understand their behaviour, but it will help us best utilise their skillset to motivate them and maximise their role performance and social performance. Where possible, we can encourage all these feelings to be present within our environments.

Managing Individual Situations

New Player Integration

Joining a new club can be an overwhelming experience, especially when it's one of the player's first transfers. Often, they must go from a comfort zone, to a completely unfamiliar environment. There can be numerous considerations when a player moves club:

1. Must the player learn a new language?
2. Is the player moving to a new house?
3. Is the player moving with or without family?
4. Does the player have friends within the club they are likely to bond with?

Understanding these details can help us support the players social transition into the new club. Some clubs will have a dedicated staff member who is responsible for arranging language lessons, housing, and visas, and it is critical that this person keeps us updated. If there are players who may struggle socially, it is important that responsibility is given to some of the squad to support the integration process both on and off the pitch. Regarding technical and tactical integration, there are two different options, which are heavily depend on the rigidity of the club game model, and the expectations of how soon they must be involved in a starting line-up.

1. **Player First:** When signing a player, one approach is to give them minimal technical and tactical information and let them express themselves to show us where their strengths and weaknesses lie. Often analysis is completed before signing a player, however, that analysis is sometimes based on the role they played in the previous club, as opposed to their actual ability. For example, a player with expert dribbling may have been playing for a club where the coach wants his wingers to cross early instead of dribbling. Therefore, when signing him, there is a hidden ability that has not been visible from the analysis. Giving them freedom and informing them of their freedom to express themselves, can be a good starting point to having a full understanding of the players ability.

Game Model First: The opposite approach is to educate the player on the game model from the start, giving them clear roles and responsibilities in the position we want them to play. The benefit of this is that the player may gel quicker with the squad and be better prepared to play early on. However, we may miss an opportunity to further investigate their strengths and weaknesses and adjust their roles and responsibilities to get the best from the player. When taking this approach, are we open enough to identify a player such as Gareth Bale, who was purchased to play as a left back, but eventually showed his ability as one of the best players in the world as a winger and attacking midfielder?

Regular and Irregular Players

In the 2018/19 Premier League season, Manchester City had a squad of thirty-two players, however they used a clear starting eleven for most of their games, with a few players who rotated in, such as Gabriel Jesus and Ilkay Gundogan (10). The key for managing the dressing room was based on the age of the players within the group. All players who made under ten appearances during the season were all under the age of twenty-three. Meaning all the players over 23 made at least ten appearances, and in most cases far more than ten (excluding players with long term injuries). If only all coaches were this fortunate to have a squad with this kind of balance. Ideally when working closer to professional football, a squad should be made up of two demographics:

Regulars: players who play most of the match minutes throughout the season
Irregulars: players who play minimal or no minutes throughout the season

Having both types of players is key to ensuring the dressing room is kept happy, and every individual has a day to day focus. The challenge comes when players who we deem as irregulars have the expectation of being regulars. If we have players expecting to play regularly who are not even on the bench, we will have a big challenge in managing them to ensure they bring positivity to the environment. For the players who are not expecting to play regularly, we can still motivate them to become better and closer to the regular players, to ensure competition is kept within the squad. The idea that a squad can be full of players who expect to play regularly may very quickly create chaos within the group. In some environments, on arrival at the club, we may find an incorrect balance between those who expect to be regulars and those who do not. This meaning we are forced to have players expecting to be in the squad who are left out of the squad on a regular basis. In this situation, managing individuals is the key to a successful environment:

Tips:

1. Keep regular communication and give regular praise to maintain close relationships with them
2. Give them target fixtures for when they should be ready to be in the squad
3. Ensure they are getting friendly-match minutes, and give feedback on their performances
4. Give them leadership responsibilities in supporting the younger players that are playing
5. Be strict with any negative behaviour as soon as it starts, before it spreads within the group

Managing Injured Players

Dealing with injured players is a guaranteed part of coaching, and how we manage the player can have a significant influence on their rehab and their mentality when they return to play. When a player has a medium to long term injury, the challenges are far bigger than just the physical aspect of the injury. From a social and psychological perspective, the player will go through a lifestyle change and must make a mindset adjustment that will affect their day to day life. Waking up every day with a set focus, a regular amount of physical activity, and the feeling of being part of a team of friends, in comparison to having no training or match to focus on, no or limited physical activity, and limited contact with teammates. The change in lifestyle is drastic, with research demonstrating the importance of physical activity, goal setting, and socialising for happiness and well-being (11). We often look at the mind and body as two separate aspects of the player, however they are heavily interlinked. The state of the mind will always impact the body, and the state of the body will always have an impact on the mind. When we cannot fully control the state of the body (during injury), we must ensure we support the management of the mind. Here are some methods we can use as a coach to support injured players:

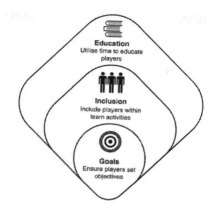

Figure 37: Methods to Support Injured Players

1. Promote Goal Setting: By the time, a player has progressed to elite youth or senior football, they should be used to setting goals, or at least understand the benefits. There are two stages to successful goal setting, one which is commonly known as SMART goals, and one I refer to as Flow Goals. SMART goals are fantastic for setting targets for the future. For example: "I want to be injury free and back in the starting eleven one-week earlier than the expected eight weeks, which is December 1st"

Specific: The goal is to be injury free

Measurable: Being back in the starting eleven is the measure of success or not

Attainable: It is attainable as the injury can be healed

Realistic: Returning one week earlier than expected is a realistic recovery time from an 'eight-week injury'

Timely: There is a specific date to aim for

While this is a great method of setting goals, the goal can often feel so far away that there is a feeling of patience required. In the modern society as discussed, instant gratification is a common desire. I utilise a second stage to goal setting which is described as Flow Goals. Flow goals focus on converting goals into a daily controllable focus. Here would be the flow goal in relation to the previous example. "Every day I am going to eat the best food for recovery, complete the most focused rehabilitation, and watch training and matches to ensure I am in the best place possible to compete when I do return". The wording of the flow goal now makes it very clear in reference to what the player must start doing. This means they start the journey and take responsibility for meeting the target they have set from day one, with a focus on the present moment as opposed to something that is so far away.

2. Increase Social Inclusion: When a player is injury free, they socialise with a full squad of players and a technical team on training days, however when they are injured, they may only socialise with the medical department, which may consist of only a few staff members. The transition of now only socialising with a few people, from socialising with twenty, thirty, or forty plus people can be a difficult one, especially when the player has close relationships with other players. Therefore, it is key to include the injured players in as many social aspects as possible. For example, they can still be a part of team meetings, can still be involved in community events, and even non-physical team building events. If there are key players with medium-long term injuries, it may even be a beneficial idea to create a team building or social event during that period in which they can attend to feel part of the squad. It is also beneficial to try to have the players complete as much of their rehab on or around the pitch when the team are training, as possible. This may mean, where possible, bringing equipment outside for them to use. The positive outcome from this is being able to observe the training, and socialise with players in breaks of the session, while keeping up with the social cues, such as humour and group dynamics.

3. Continuous Education: When dealing with injuries where physical development is limited, it is key to keep the mind stimulated and challenged. If mental focus on the injury is advised, the medical team can take responsibility to update the player on progress and educate them on ways to increase their recovery potential, such as diet, visualisation, and extra rehab exercises they can use. The level of education should be a challenge to stimulate their growth mindset of learning every day. If they have a long-term injury, there is always an option to encourage them to complete a short online course on an area of their interest to complement their rehabilitation programme. For a player who can only complete one to two hours of rehab in a day, they have so much time available, sitting watching television or scrolling through their social media is not going to be the most beneficial use of the period. Giving them learning experiences may also adjust their perception of the injury, as it can become an opportunity for growth in new areas. Who knows, maybe the course during their injury may give them an interest in an area they may follow up on after they retire, or maybe they will use the information on diet and rehab to support other players with similar injuries. If there are players who have previously had the same injury, it can also be a great idea to use them as an 'injury mentor', as they can advise them and have discussions on how to best manage the injury process and stay focused on rehab.

Key Messages

1. Managing individuals for success: A key primary role as coaches is to manage players to maximise their happiness, development, and performance within the environment, where possible.

2. Fair but unique: All individuals are unique, and therefore require unique approaches to dealing with them. However, we must be consistent and fair in regards to the happiness, development, and performance improvements we attempt to make with all players.

3. Initial management: When starting a new coaching role, there is a huge opportunity to agree to objectives and methods which will align everybody's focus and roles.

4. Influence and interest: Understanding that each individual will have a different level of interest and influence, enables us to identify how we can manage each individual.

5. Expect and manage conflict: In any high performance environment there is likely to be conflict. Expecting it enables us to identify it early, and deal with it at the right time to keep the competitiveness, but minimise the negative behaviours.

6. Understanding age is critical: In all football environments there are age factors that we must consider. In development this may be the differences between chronological, psychological, and athletic age. In other environments this may be related to working with senior or youth players.

7. Role vs Social Performance: When analysing the performance of players and staff in our environment, we should consider people's performance socially, as well as their performance in relation to their contractual or agreed expectations. Social performance can be just as important than role performance.

8. The psychology of injury: When players are injured and away from the team, while there is a physical component to manage in relation to the specific injury and required rehabilitation, there are also psychological elements to stay aware of and manage, to ensure the happiness and development of players.

References

1. Dweck, C. S. (2006). Mindset: The new psychology of success (1st ed.). New York: Random House

2. Zaltman, G. (2003). How Consumers Think: Essential Insights into the Mind of the Market.

3. De Menezes, J (2019). Chris Hughton sacked: Brighton sack manager one day after end of the Premier League season. Available at https://www.independent.co.uk/sport/football/premier-league/chris-hughton-sacked-by-brighton-manager-sack-end-of-premier-league-season-a8911126.html (Accessed 1 May 2020)

4. Bailey, S (2019). Shocked. Harsh. A ridiculous decision. No surprise: The football world reacts to Chris Hughton's sacking Available at https://www.brightonandhoveindependent.co.uk/sport/football/brighton-and-hove-albion/shocked-harsh-ridiculous-decision-no-surprise-football-world-reacts-chris-hughtons-sacking-975146 (Accessed 1 May 2020)

5. Hunter, A (2016). Roberto Martínez sacked by Everton after disappointing season. Available at https://www.theguardian.com/football/2016/may/12/roberto-martinez-sacked-everton (Accessed 1 May 2020)

6. Mendelow, A. L. (1981). Environmental Scanning-The Impact of the Stakeholder Concept. International Conference on Information Systems. p. 20

7. Tranæus, U., Ivarsson, A., & Johnson, U. (2018). Stress and injuries in elite sport. In Handbuch of Stress regulation und Sport p.451-466.

8. Adams, T. (2017). August 17, 2002: Wayne Rooney makes Everton debut in draw vs. Tottenham. Available at https://www.espn.com/soccer/club/everton/368/blog/post/3181929/august-17-2002-wayne-rooney-makes-his-everton-debut-in-draw-vs-tottenham. (Accessed 5 May 2020)

9. Ducker, J. (2017). Pep Guardiola left puzzled by Jadon Sancho's decision to leave Manchester City for Borussia Dortmund. Available at https://www.telegraph.co.uk/football/2017/09/08/pep-guardiola-left-puzzled-jadon-sanchos-decision-leave-manchester/ (Accessed 5 May 2020)

10. The Premier League. (2019). Manchester City Squad. Available at https://www.premierleague.com/clubs/11/Manchester-City/squad?se=210 (Accessed 5 May 2020)

11. Hamson-Utley, J. J., & Vazquez, L. (2008). The comeback: rehabilitating the psychological injury. International Journal of Athletic Therapy and Training, 13(5), p35-38.

12. Doyle, I. Jurgen Klopp identifies the surprise inspiration behind Liverpool's Champions League quest. Available at https://www.liverpoolecho.co.uk/sport/football/football-news/jurgen-klopp-identifies-surprise-inspiration-16324615 (Accessed May 8, 2020)

13. Villas Boas, A. (2016). Stars Chat: Andre Villas Boas - Aspire4sport/Global Summit, Amsterdam 2016. Available at https://www.youtube.com/watch?v=ADmE3PlNtK8 (Accessed 1 May 2020)

"

PLAYER PERFORMANCE

COACHING IS UNLOCKING PEOPLE'S POTENTIAL TO MAXIMIZE THEIR OWN PERFORMANCE.

John Whitmore

Introduction

Objective: The objective of this chapter is to simplify performance and explain the key factors that we should identify and develop to increase the probability of high performance.

The Performance Formula is a framework which explains the factors that determine a player's development and performance. The overriding factor that dictate a player's performance is the summary of the decisions they make (mind) and their ability to perform their role on the pitch (body). The relationship between these two factors can be complex. The variety of decisions a player can make is dependent on the ability of the player, and the ability of the player is dependent on the decision-making options and selection from the player. For example, picture a striker being one-vs-one with the goalkeeper. There are only two factors they can control that will dictate whether he will score or not. The decision they make regarding how to score, and their ability to execute that decision. If they only have one technique for finishing such as a placed finish to either side of the goalkeeper, this limits their decision-making process in a situation where a lob or shot through the legs may be a better option. If they have a variety of techniques but are only aware of one which will be successful in the situation, the outcome is again limited. While this relationship is complex, having an initial formula gives us a starting point for understanding the factors we need to develop and identify in players, to increase their long-term performance level. What we are doing here is reverse engineering elite football performance to understand the components that will help us develop individual performance consistently. When we look at the development process, we should be focusing on developing 'elite performers', as well as elite players. Using the term 'elite performers' challenges us to think past football, and start addressing a wider range of components:

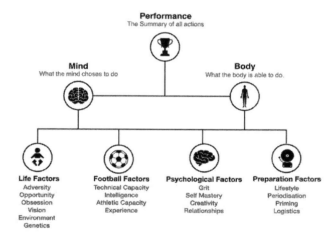

Figure 38: The Performance Formula

If we are looking for elite performers and we get to the first step of understanding decision-making and ability, we will probably find as coaches that we have a deeper understanding of developing what the body is able to do, and less of an understanding developing what the mind chooses to do. To really maximise performance and development, we must understand both what the mind chooses (decision-making), and what the body is able to do (ability).

Mind (Decision-Making)

Johan Cruyff once said, "Football is a brain game, where to run, when to run, when to cover, when to press, when to move, how to move. It is decisions like these that come from the brain that determines whether you're a good player or not" (1). How many times have we seen players with bundles of ability who do not quite make it to the next level because they frequently make decisions that do not meet our expectations? It is easy for us as coaches to brush this off and put the responsibility on the player. "They just do what they want". "They just make the wrong decisions". "They just do not see the picture". What influence have we had over this player's decision-making development? Decision-making is certainly one of the more complex factors to understand. It is not as simple as 'let them play' and they will learn, and it is certainly not maximised by controlling players like robots. Instead, it is developed through a range of life, football, psychological, and preparation factors. While we cannot control all factors, we can influence many of them to best support the players decision-making development process. In order to do this effectively, we must understand the systems, components, and factors affecting decision-making.

Decision-making Systems

According to Nobel Prize winner Daniel Kahneman we have two different thinking systems, labelled systems one and two, more recently defined as autopilot and intentional systems (2). The system that is used is dependent on the factors that have just been discussed. For example, when we are aware of danger, in a state of panic our 'autopilot' system will kick in and decide based on feeling. However, if in danger, but a state of calmness, we can use the intentional system to take a more logical approach. It is the culmination of the factors that will influence which system is used. There are many theories into the systems controlling our decision-making, including a recent concept titled 'The Chimp Paradox' (3). Generally, the theories focus on us having an emotional system and a logical system.

Emotional System: The process used to make quick decisions based on emotion and feeling.

Logical System: The process used to make thought out decisions based on logic and future outcomes.

Emotional System: This system mainly functions within the amygdala and corresponds to our emotions and habits. This system is there to help us make quick decisions when under pressure or in danger. It was developed earlier in the evolution process and can be compared to the system animals use to meet the requirements of their environment. In moments when we must make a quick decision, it is the emotional system that takes over. For example, if we were to walk into our house and find a lion, it would be our emotional system which takes over and gets us out of the house as quickly as possible. In a football match, an example would be a goalkeeper receiving the ball under pressure when they did not expect it, and having to deal with an opponent striker quickly applying pressure, with the risk of them winning the ball. The goalkeeper would likely panic and clear the ball to deal with the danger unless they have strategies for dealing with the situations. While this system is extremely beneficial for animals and is still beneficial for human survival, there has been an expectation of us as humans to make logical decisions as opposed to emotional decisions.

Logical System: The use of the logical system forms intelligent rational thinking which can be used as emotional management in times of difficulty. Choosing to take the time to create a logical decision as opposed to an emotional or habitual decision is integral to making better long-term decisions. The intentional system which mainly functions around the prefrontal cortex, corresponds to our rational and logical thinking. It is believed that this system has been developed in more recent years to help humans deal with the complex demands of modern-day society. This system takes far more conscious effort and energy to function, making it the system which we use to make less decisions than the emotional system. Below is a summary of the characteristics of each system:

Logical System	Emotional System
Bases decisions on rationality and logic	Works on autopilot when it is not controlled
Led by the outcomes we plan	Led by how we feel
Requires a lot of energy	Requires little energy
Slow when under pressure or in danger	Quick when under pressure or in danger
Less prone to errors	Prone to errors
Effectiveness is dependent on intelligence	Effectiveness is dependent on previous experiences

Figure 39: Logical vs Emotional System

With factors such as pressure, time, space, and fatigue, and the understanding that avoiding errors is a fundamental aspect of performance, developing a player's logical and emotional systems is critical to improving their performance. To do this we must ensure players train in situations that involve high pressure decision-making as well as lower pressure decision-making. A centre back with time on the ball playing against a deep block, needs to be able to logically identify how the opposition can be exploited, but under pressure needs to be able to make quick decisions with minimal error.

Objective – Action Relationship

Whether subconsciously or consciously deciding, there are two things the brain must decide on. An objective we want to achieve and an action to best meet that objective. For example, if we walk into the house and see a lion we must decide on an objective in the moment and the action to meet that objective. The exact picture we see will dictate the objective and action. If there is time to open the door and run out, then the objective would be to get out of the house, with the action to open the door and run. While this is a subconscious action, there is still an objective and action. In a football setting, when taking a free kick, there is a selection of the objective which may be to shoot and beat the goalkeeper in the top right corner, and the selection of the action to achieve that. The relationship between the objective and action I call the Objective-Action relationship. The stronger the relationship, the less conscious effort is needed to think of the objective and perform the action. For example, the first time a player learns to defend crosses in the box, they must consciously think about objectives such as when to clear the ball, when to bring the ball under control, when to pass directly off the cross. They should also start using a variety of actions to meet those different objectives. Eventually, a player can decide on the right objective, and link this objective with the right action. In relation to the example, if the objective is to clear the ball, the correct action would likely involve contact that gets height and distance on the ball. An elite defender is likely to choose the right objectives and the right actions, therefore having an elite Objective-Action relationship for those situations. To improve decision-making, we must do three things:

1. Improve the objectives selected
2. Improve the actions selected
3. Improve the Objective-Action relationship.

Influencing Factors

There are six key factors that influence objective selection, action selection, and the Objective-Action relationship. Understanding these factors will give us the best chance of improving and influencing our players' decision-making.

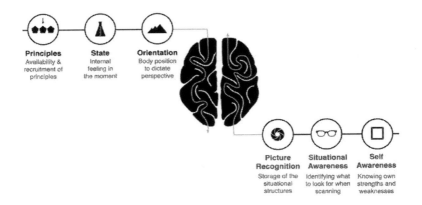

Figure 40: Factors Influencing the Objective-Action Relationship

1. Principles: Having principles to apply in a situation plays a huge role in dictating the decision we make. In many situations the principle is the main factor that will dictate our objective. Where a player is unsure of the principle to apply, they will then lean heavier onto the other factors. For example, if being safe and secure is the key guiding principle during build-up, this can be key in ensuring players do not make decisions that will risk possession. If a player does not understand any principles during build-up, they may turn to previous experience to execute their actions, even though the current picture they are dealing with is different to the experience they are recalling. Principles tend to be more flexible and can be applied across all pictures, meaning the use of principles is more likely to end up in success than the use of pictures which change all the time. Both are useful and have a place in the game.

Tip: Set a clearer list of basic principles that can be applied dependent on the phase of the game. E.g. keep safe possession during build-up.

2. State: The state of the player also has a significant influence over decision-making. State refers to their current feeling, which links to hormonal balance, fatigue, pain, happiness etc. As we know, these factors heavily affect the actions that follow. Why does a player who is consistently shouted at eventually end up making worse decisions? They often end up in a state of stress and panic which then influences the process of which objective and action to select. Another example of how state affects decision-making, would be when a player kicks another player during a high-pressure game Their state causes a different action to the norm which results in a red card. At the opposite end of spectrum, the theory regarding state of flow would suggest that the positive state of being 'in the zone' enhances the selection of objectives and outcomes.

Tip: Educate the player on how their feelings are influencing their decisions and utilise controllable factors to support the player in moving towards a state of flow during performance.

3. Orientation and Perspective: As well as experiences, a player's orientation will dictate their perspective, and perspective is a critical component of decision-making. Are our players orientated in ways that give them the best perspective of what we need to see? Poor body orientation limits the triggers players can see which then impacts what we think, feel, and eventually execute. Players' orientation should be controlled by principles as it should correlate to the next action we select. For example, a player's orientation to be safe and secure may be different to one with an expectation to play forward under pressure. The best orientation gives us the best perspective of the situation we are in, and the better the perspective the more clarity we can have in understanding our available options, and therefore the objectives and actions we can select.

Tip: Explain the variety of possible orientations based on the principle that needs to be applied. E.g. demonstrate different orientations when making a run in behind the opposition defensive line which ensures the player can see the ball and the location where they want to meet the ball.

4. Picture Recognition: The more familiar with a situation we become, the quicker and better the decision will be" (4). This is because as we have more experience we start to observe and recognise pictures. The more pictures we see the more we can narrow down our objectives and actions. This meaning we can start to gauge which objectives and actions are best for each type of picture. For example, when receiving in central midfield, there are a wide variety of pictures to experience, e.g. receiving under pressure, receiving with options to pass back, receiving with space to turn. There are also several, variable factors within each picture. The more variety and repetition a player can get in receiving in centre midfield, will enhance the number of patterns they recognise within that situation. The more patterns they can identify, the better the feeling of which objectives and actions to select.

Tip: Give players variable repetition, which means creating training scenarios with a lot of repetition with a wide variety of situations that they will encounter within match situations, ensuring both success and failure.

5. Situational Awareness: To best utilise their experiences, players must improve their searching, similarly known as scanning. This does not mean just ensuring that players are turning their heads when receiving. Situational awareness is a constant understanding of what is occurring throughout the game. This does require a high frequency of searching. However, it also involves asking the question, what our players are looking for? There are so many options of what can be searched for on the pitch. Often, we refer to space, time, teammates, and opponents. While these are certainly categories of things that can be looked for, our job is to narrow the focus down to what players must look for. If a player had to analyse so much detail every time, they made a decision, the game would be played at a minimal speed. The best players look for the fewest factors but know which factors are critical based on the principle they are applying. These factors may make up the components of their picture recognition. For example, if receiving in between the lines there may be specific movements that attackers make to exploit space in behind which should be identified. This may be a key trigger to look for which identifies a specific picture. Two players can receive the ball in that same situation but may see different pictures.

Tip: As well as ensuring players are searching, try to discuss and identify what triggers and pictures players are looking for when they are searching, then offer insight into which triggers, and pictures can best support them in the situation.

6. Self-Awareness: A player's awareness of their own capabilities will also have a significant impact on the decision they make. What is happening when we observe players making decisions to do things they are not capable of? This can be a positive trait when development is the priority, as the first time a player tries anything the probability is that they are not capable of executing it under pressure. In fact, this is what gives players and us as coaches an indication of which attributes a player must work on. Players must however be aware that they are not strong in that area and place intentional focus on executing it to develop it. When players get closer to a high-performance level, it is critical that they are aware of what they can and cannot execute, so when they need to make the right decisions, they do not select decisions that they are unlikely to have success with, but select actions that have a high probability of success. For a player to be aware of their abilities, they need to have the continuous freedom to execute many actions under match realistic situations within the training environment.

Tip: Frequently ask players to reflect on their ability, by identifying their strengths and areas where they can improve.

These factors enable us to identify potential reasons why players are making poor decisions. At least one of the six is likely to be a problem. Through analysis of the mistakes and discussions with the player, we can identify which aspects are responsible for the decision-making, and then intervene to improve that area.

Conditioning Decision-making

One method that can make a big impact on decision-making is the conditioning of actions. As coaches as we condition behaviours and we alter their feedback process in their cognitive triangle. When players execute the actions that align with what we are looking for, praising their decision increases the likeliness that they will execute a similar decision in the future. This is particularly powerful when trying to develop players who frequently make bad decisions. For example, the winger who always dribbles and never looks up should be praised when they do look up and use another option. The goalkeeper who always plays direct passes in a team where short build-up is important, should be praised for playing short. To take this to the next level, we should be able to explain why the decision was right based on the triggers that were present.

Critical Phases

The use of different systems is an explanation for the critical phases often discussed in football. In a 2014 study focusing on the timing of goals scored across numerous leagues and tournaments around the world, they found that the last 15 minutes of the game had the highest number of goals scored in comparison to the rest of the game (5). The reason behind this could be linked to decision-making. Under fatigue and high emotion, our state plays a bigger influence over our objective-action relationship, meaning a decreased emphasis on principles, pictures, situations, and our own strengths and weaknesses . There has been a similar concept presented by many coaches and pundits who suggest that there is also a critical phase just before half-time. However, there is research that has suggested that there is no correlation between scoring just before half-time and winning the game (6).

Body (Ability)

Role ability is far simpler to understand than decision-making. It is simply the ability to carry out a specific function within football, or more, specifically within the team. The role that a player must execute is dependent on our model of play and framework we have created. The more clarity we have in the roles and responsibilities of players on the pitch, the easier it will be to identify and develop players towards success. In some cases, we may adapt the framework to fit a specific type of player based on their strengths and weaknesses. Either way, we need to have a clear framework that we can then judge players against which works across all phases of the game. The actions within this framework can be broken down into two categories. The variety of abilities, and the quality of the abilities.

Variety of Abilities: How much variety do they have in relation to the required abilities? For example, if we are looking at full backs, how many abilities do they have? Can they head the ball, defend one vs one, jump to compete, sprint to press, deliver crosses etc. The more abilities they have, the more likely they are to perform across a variety of situations.

Quality of Abilities: With the variety of abilities the player has, how much quality do they have when executing them? For example, how much accuracy does a winger have when delivering crosses into the box? How much quality can they execute when they are in high pressure situations against the best players they will be against?

In an ideal world we will have players who can execute all desired abilities with perfect quality. We know this is not possible. However, we can develop a framework which prioritises certain abilities over others, which informs us which abilities need higher quality, and which abilities can be utilised with lower quality. We can do this by categorising abilities into four groups.

Example: Striker

■ Category	🚶 Abilities
Essentials	Finishing | Heading | Agility | Movement
Desirables	Passing | Dribbling | Acceleration | Strength
Non-Essentials	Screening | Crossing | Marking | Tackling
Trademarks	Free Kicks | Penalties | Tricks and Skills

Figure 41: Ability Categories Example

Dividing abilities in these four groups enables us to identify where players must place more focus to ensure the quality of those attributes are high. A striker is more likely to require high quality finishing than high quality crossing. Many of these factors will be dependent on the framework and game models we are working within. A striker who has high quality essentials is likely to have better performances than a striker who has high quality desirables. Trademarks are unique attributes that may enable elite performance but are not necessary for the specific position. For example, a striker does not have to master free kicks, however a striker who has an elite ability when taking free kicks may be able to significantly increase their performance. Understanding the different levels of importance on different attributes guides us in relation to working on strengths and weaknesses. When discussing the topic of developing strengths or weaknesses, the answer often depends on whether the strengths and weaknesses are essential, desirable, or non-essential. For example, if a centre back has a weakness heading the ball, it would be essential, so it is critical to work on the weakness. If they have a weakness finishing, it would not be a topic that must necessarily be focused on. A similar approach can be taken with trademarks, asking the question regarding the impact the trademark will have on player performance. For example, a rabona cross may be a trademark skill, but it may not have as much of an impact on performance as mastering free kick delivery. This question of performance impact can guide whether we give time to developing a player's trademark attributes.

Life Factors

As coaches we control many factors that influence a player's development and performance. There are even more factors outside of the football environment that impact a player's development and performance. Life factors is the first of the four categories that impact performance and development via the mind and the body. In order to understand which life factors are important, I studied the lives of all the Ballon d'Or winners since 2001 to look for common events and trends. If we can identify specific events and trends, we can start to reverse engineer the development process. This means that the hundreds of decisions that are heavily discussed around performance and development, can have some anecdotal concepts to support or critique arguments. From the research, these are the following key trends discovered across most of their life stories:

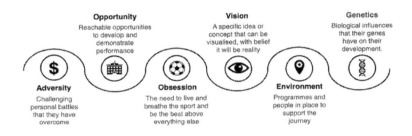

Figure 42: Common Life Factors Across Ballon d'Or winners

Adversity: In every journey to becoming part of the world's elite, adversity is a likely component that people will end up having to deal with. One of the common trends among the majority of the last ten Ballon d'Or winners is major adversity. In 2018, just after Luka Modric won the Ballon d'Or, the Sun newspaper headlined him as "the refugee whose Grandad was shot dead when he was six, who became a world superstar". The article then went on to explain how Modric lived without electricity, running water, and with the sound of grenades, bullets, and landmines daily. Modric stated, "when the war started, we became refugees and it was a really tough time. It was a very hard time for me and my family. The war made me stronger" (7). While this is one of the more extreme stories, it is certainly not the only one. Ronaldo's family upbringing and heart surgery were two serious stages of adversity he had to deal with. Lionel Messi was diagnosed with a growth hormone disorder during his adolescent life leaving him physically behind his teammates. When you analyse some of the winners prior to the decade of Messi and Cristiano Ronaldo, there is 'Brazilian Ronaldo' who dropped out of school at eleven-years-old after his parents financially struggled and separated. Ronaldinho whose father hit his head and died in their family home when he was just eight years old. Kaka who had a career threatening spinal fracture and possible spinal paralysis after a swimming pool accident at eighteen years old. And Shevchenko who had to abandon his home and relocate aged ten-years-old due to the Chernobyl nuclear disaster. While we do not wish these kinds of events on any of our players, it does suggest there may be a clear trend between world class development and adversity. After dealing with such challenges in early life, does it make dealing with injury, high pressure, criticism, and difficult opposition easier tasks to overcome? Or does it increase the desire and motivation to be successful. Maybe it is both.

Opportunity: One of the key debates in England around player development, has been why English players are not the best players in the Premier League. While the argument has several different factors, from academy structures and youth coaching. The key challenge English players have faced since the growth of the Premier League is opportunity. With the Premier League attracting the best talent from across the world, the competition to play in the league is higher than anywhere else. It is just like having a company in Paris that is hiring the best lawyers from around the world. A lawyer who has graduated in Paris and wants to work for that company, would find it extremely difficult without getting experience somewhere else, to become one of the best in the world. While there can always be improvements in the structures that are supporting the development of players, we must better support the players in finding opportunities to perform at the next level, and players must be willing to take them. Jadon Sancho made a brave choice at seventeen years old, to leave Manchester City where they could not guarantee him first team football, to move to Dortmund where he would go on to play fifty-six times with the first team, scoring seventeen goals and gaining eleven England Senior Team caps at nineteen. If he had stayed at Manchester City, would he have fifty-six first team appearances and eleven National Team caps? Phil Foden, also nineteen-years-old at Manchester City, had under half the amount of first team appearances (twenty-two) and is yet to represent his country. How many players are there with the ability to perform, but limited opportunity? As coaches we cannot change the leagues, but we can certainly source the best opportunities throughout a player's development, for them to progress to the next level. Many of the Ballon d'Or winners played for clubs in their teenage years that believed in developing youth players for the first team, meaning they were able to get the opportunity to perform at the professional level from a young age.

Obsession: "It is impossible to follow Cristiano Ronaldo in training. When we arrive, he is already training when we leave, he is still training. I have never seen a player like that!" (8). Fabio Cannavaro, another Ballon d'Or winner was labelled 'Scugnizzo', a smiling cunning street kid, who spent his days playing football in the street, between cars, everywhere". When his parents said, "it is better you go to school, it is especially important for your future", Cannavaro said to himself "I think the good way is to follow the football" (9). Michael Owen won the Ballon d'Or in 2001, but only after finishing his career, did he explain in his book 'Reboot', that his "sheer obsession with trying to be the best was the biggest help in the world. What makes you one of the best as opposed to just a standard player? It is pure obsession" (10). Obsession can be defined as 'an idea or thought that continually preoccupies or intrudes a person's mind. Being the best footballer must be the obsession. Football must continually preoccupy the mind of a player who wants to make it to the top. During development years there are many distractions and opportunities for players to focus on having a more balanced life. One perspective is that a balanced lifestyle is important for teenagers growing up today. However, if a player has an internal desire to play football at the top level, it will take a certain level of obsession with the game to ensure they make it there. Therefore, one of our jobs as football coaches must be to make the game so enjoyable that they would rather focus on football than many of the distractions they will come across. When working with players between sixteen and twenty-three, one of the biggest challenges has been keeping players focused on being the best player, while managing the distractions of relationships, social media, nightclubs, cars, and clothes. If we use the ten-thousand hour rule as an example, while the study into hours of intentional practice may be controversial, one of the findings that is difficult to argue with, is that the more we practice with the right focus and right conditions, the better we are going to be. Therefore, if a player's week starts to be divided between football and too many other distractions, the chance of them maximising their potential is likely to decrease. There is no set answer on how to get the exact balance right between obsession with football, and balancing other life activities, however an obsession with football certainly appears to be a common trait of successful players.

One-Percents: When experiencing the journey of players from youth academies into first team environments, we can start to see what it takes for players to make it over the line. By eighteen, most players can pass, receive, make 'good decisions', win duels and meet the demands of the position they play. What is it that often separates players from the group? The one-percents. According to the butterfly effect, the smallest differences can have a significant difference in outcomes. It is an often-misunderstood phenomenon whereby a small change in starting conditions can lead to vastly different outcomes. Understanding the butterfly effect can give us a new lens through which to view player development and performance. The name 'butterfly effect' stems from the concept that the flap of a butterfly's wings in Brazil can cause a tornado in Texas (11). In relation to football, how does a player know how many free kicks they need to practice ensuring they score the free kick opportunities they have in a match? There is a great video of David Beckham practicing free kicks the day before a critical England fixture against Greece. In the game he takes many free kicks which go wide, hit the wall or are easy for the goalkeeper to save. Eventually he takes a free kick which goes into the top corner and takes England through to the World Cup (12). Now imagine England won the World Cup, it may all have stemmed back from one extra free kick David Beckham took in training the day before the game. No one knows the number of practices required to execute an action in the game but again, what we do know is that more practice means a higher probability of success. Players with a one-percent mindset are more likely to surpass future performance expectations due to the extra work they put in to have marginal gains over their competition.

Vision: During the 2014 World Cup, after scoring two goals and receiving the Man of the Match award, Neymar was quoted as saying "There is no pressure. I've always said that there is no pressure when you are making a dream come true, something that you sought since you were a kid. Today I am playing in matches I always dreamed about" (13). It is not hard to find famous quotes from successful players regarding dreams. Whilst we cannot go back in time and verify their dreams, when the best players in the world speak of having dreams to be the best, it would be crazy to ignore them. Dreams do not necessarily mean the thoughts we have when sleeping, but it certainly refers to the things we visualise for the future when we are awake. It is an extreme version of goal setting, with a specific picture in our mind that creates a feeling we are searching for. Success, achievement, influence, recognition, significance. What does it look like for our players? Each of our players that have an ambition to make it to the top should have a visual image of what they want to achieve. Whether we believe in the law of attraction, or to what extent we believe in the principle of the world aligning with our thoughts, it would be difficult to argue that we are more likely to achieve success without visualising it than with visualising it. How can we encourage our players to create dreams and visualisations of what they want to achieve in the sport?

Environment: Nobody makes it by themselves. While we can look at success being a product of the player the themselves. We cannot ignore the environmental factors that had an impact. Environmental factors may come in the form of club and academy structures, coaches, and family members, or even the geographical environment which have an influence. When considering environmental factors, one of the key frameworks is 'The Goldmine Effect' from Rasmus Ankersen. Ankersen travelled around the world and studied how some countries and cities develop a disproportionate amount of top talent. He discovered that there are certain parts of the world that have produced a huge number of successful athletes, including sprinters from Kingston, Jamaica, distance runners from Ngong, Kenya, and even football players from Rio de Janeiro, Brazil. He called these locations goldmines and searched to find common trends among the locations (14). Some of the trends fit with the findings when analysing the lives of the Ballon d'Or winners. Firstly, environmental constraints. When analysing the careers of the Ballon d'Or winners, there are regular environmental constraints which enforce hard work. The first constraint is the working-class backgrounds. The financial constraint within the family environment meant that hard work was always going to be a requirement to be successful. The challenging concept from working class backgrounds is that we must sacrifice time and energy in exchange for money and success. Whereas middle class families can often exchange less time and energy and use money to earn more money and success. For example, investing and starting businesses rather than working in a factory. This message of hard work and sacrifice correlating with success, is a mentality that is required in football. Money is not going to make someone a world class football player without time and effort. Another common constraint is facilities. The second effect of coming from a working-class background is having limited access to a variety of expense-based activities. Playing football in the street is almost a cost-free activity, until someone is forced to buy a new ball after it has been run over or stolen. Children with a larger financial support system may have the option to also participate in a variety of activities such as martial arts, golf, or hockey that require a level of expense. Children without the financial support are more likely to play football than financially dependent sports. The second common environmental factor is support within the sport. Through the journey of world class athletes, there is frequently a coach within the sport that supported them at a critical stage in their journey. Across the goldmines, Ankersen supported this finding with the observation of critical coaches in the environments who were responsible for controlling the development environment. In three of the biggest goldmines he found that the coach was not previously involved in the sport as an athlete. The key coaches he identified had never participated in the sports they were coaching at a competitive level before. One of the key attributes of the supporting person, is that they must have a desire for the individual player to succeed. Sometimes we intentionally or unintentionally hold players back as their success can make us feel inferior, especially when working with young players. To genuinely want players we are working with to become world class, we must leave our egos at home. The third environment factor is support outside the sport. As well as support from within the sport, there is often support of some kind from outside the sport. This is frequently a parent, a sibling, or a friend who gives them a sense of purpose. Michael Owen often spoke of his father who took him to all his games and was a continuous figure throughout his journey. Cristiano Ronaldo speaks similarly of his mother as a key supportive figure, although he had to move away in his teenage years to join Sporting Lisbon. Lionel Messi's father has been his agent since Messi was fourteen. This person is often the one who keeps the player on track through difficult times, and in the end becomes one of the players biggest motivations. The fourth environmental factor is talent identification and development programmes. The geographic location of the environment will dictate the level of talent identification and development programmes available. For players brought up in remote locations, without any sporting links, it is of course more difficult to break into a system that will help guide them through the development process. Each case is different, however, at some point all players will require an identification and development programme. It is extremely unlikely that a player will break through to top level football without any experience in a development structure. All players studied, that have won the Ballon d'Or, entered a development programme within their teenage years and made professional debuts before their nineteenth birthday.

Genetics: Whether we sit more on the nature or the nurture side, there is no doubt that genetics have an influence on the development of football players. Factors such as height, physique and exercise capacities are significantly impacted by genetics. There are two perspectives we can have around working with players with different genetic make ups. Either, a player is limited by their genetic make-up, or every genetic limitation brings a potential advantage. Lionel Messi had a genetic limitation which brought a huge advantage to football performance. How many times have we watched a player with the first mindset? Thinking about the weaknesses they have because of their physique. They are too slow, they are not able to press, they cannot beat a defender one vs one. While these are common challenges we may find when working with players, there are many players who have won league titles and cups with physiques that we might not see as ideal. Zlatan Ibrahimovic (another example of a player who went through adversity) is somewhere in the region of 195cm tall. Certainly not ideal for one vs one dribbling, running in behind opponents, or pressing the opposition. However, he has won trophies across five European leagues and been nominated for the Ballon d'Or eleven times. If coaches had focused on his weaknesses in not fitting the typical criteria of a striker, maybe we would have released him or made him a centre back? Would we be bold enough to look at his strengths and work with those to support him in becoming the best version of himself? In some clubs there is a set criterion for what each position requires. The key is identifying if we think a player who does not fit those roles, could be good enough to adapt our framework to fit them in? This is particularly challenging during development years, where the athletic differences between players can be huge. Alex Oxlade-Chamberlain who now plays for Liverpool was a great example of how genetics can make performance in the development stages difficult. His former coach James Bunce stated, "he was clearly lacking in maturity. His voice hadn't broken. He wasn't as big and muscly as the others. After being moved down a year to give him a chance to develop his technical skills he thrived, he got challenged, he was coached, he was mentored. Three years later he was in the team as a sixteen-year-old" (15). These are examples of how genetics play a significant role in development and performance.

Football Factors

Technical Capacity

Technical capacity is a term I use to explain the variety and accuracy of motor skills used for actions with the ball. "A motor skill is a learned ability to cause a predetermined movement outcome with maximum certainty. Motor learning is the relatively permanent change in the ability to perform a skill, as a result of practice or experience. The goal of motor skills is to optimise the ability to perform the skill at the rate of success, precision, and to reduce the energy consumption required for performance" (16). Continuous practice of a specific motor skill will result in a greatly improved performance when executing that skill. This motor skill learning generally refers to neural changes that allow an organism to accomplish a motor task better, faster, or more accurately than before" (17). So how does this work? Any active movement requires the nervous system to fire impulses through the body to the right muscles, right force, right order and at the right time. When a player first starts learning an action such as passing, it takes a lot of conscious effort to focus on using the right muscles at the right time, at the right speed, with the right force and in the right order. The more this action is repeated the quicker and more efficiently the brain can recruit the muscles to perform the action with specific force, order, timing, and speed. There are three stages of motor skill development that we should understand:

1. Cognitive Stage: During this first stage, individuals focus on how to complete a motor skill, learning step by step. This is normally unopposed without pressure. This stage varies depending on the motor skills they have which are transferable to the action. For example, a player with good foot and eye coordination is more likely to strike the ball more accurately the first time they attempt to kick it.

2. Autonomous Stage: This is where the motor skill can be executed without thinking within the same conditions the skill had been learnt. Normally, this stage is still unopposed without pressure. For example, being able to play accurate passes during unopposed passing drills.

3. Transferable Stage: This is where the learnt motor skill can be executed in the required challenging situations and environments, for example after learning a skill in training unopposed, the skill can now be executed under pressure during a match.

After working with toddlers, the picture does not become any clearer. The first time a toddler attempts to shoot or pass, there is a clear lack of accuracy, timing, speed, order, and force. As the toddler repeats the action, they are eventually able to strike the ball in a manner that resembles a shot. As a player starts to master these skills as well as more complex skills, the brain develops a vast catalogue of movement solutions (18). Throughout this process of repetition, myelination is occurring around the neurons used to execute the action. As myelination occurs, the neural wiring becomes more insulated meaning less energy and focus is required to execute the action. Therefore, we can drive without consciously thinking about changing gears and using the pedals. When we first started driving, we had to consciously focus on everything. But what happens when we change car, or drive a car with the seat on the opposite side? Suddenly, we must go back to our conscious brain to focus. This is an example of how situation affects action even though the action is perceived as the same._Technical capacity can be divided into two categories:

Technical Selection: The last aspect of the decision-making process, deciding which motor skill to use to meet the desired outcome. Technique selection is limited to the variety of motor skills available and is controlled by the previous experience in the outcomes using the variety of executions. For example, the number of finishing techniques a player has, and their previous experiences in scoring, using those finishing techniques in that situation.

Technical Variety: The number of technique options a player has that can be executed well in a specific scenario. For example, if under pressure from opponent where turning on the ball is required, how many different turns do they have available to choose from that they can perform under pressure? If they only have an inside chop available then the situation (current ball position, body shape, space, and opponent) must be perfect for the inside chop. If they have other options available, they can select the one that feels the most suitable for the specific situation.

Technical Quality: Technique quality is directly correlated to the amount of detailed experience using the motor skill in the situation. For example, how many times has the goalkeeper practiced diagonal passes to the right back with the right feedback process of improving the detail on the execution.

Technical Consistency: The consistency of successful execution of a motor skill. Technical consistency is particularly important at the elite end of football, where most players can execute complex skills, but the consistency of their execution makes a significant difference. As a professional there is an expectation of consistent success with actions. For example, goal scoring would be heavily affected by motor skill consistency of finishing actions.

Technique Considerations

Football actions: When thinking of motor skills there are a few actions which typically come to mind. Passing, dribbling, shooting, receiving etc. There are also other motor skill actions that players can learn, to support their development process. These include factors such as off the ball movements and adaptations within current motor skills. Off the ball movements such as runs where a player checks onside from an offside position in time to check back and run in behind, would be an example of something that may need to be taught as a motor skill, to then have it as a selectable option. Similarly, adaptations during a motor skill can be key when competing. An example would be when in the motion of executing a shot, being able to adapt the action to cut onto the other foot and shoot with the other foot to prevent the opponent from blocking the shot. There are many motor skills within a football match that can support development. The key to identifying these, is to watch football with a detailed eye focusing on the most elite and creative players.

Perception Action Coupling: Actions that require analysis of a situation are likely to be enhanced by a player's perceptual-cognitive skills (19). Perception action coupling is an ability to link information we can sense (see, hear, feel, smell, taste) to an appropriate action which can be selected and executed. For example, a striker who can identify a goalkeeper's position and select and execute a shot that has a high probability of going in. The key to this process is heavily based on a player's perception skills, which is discussed further under the topic of 'intelligence'.

Diagnosing Mistakes: Once we understand the process, we can start to identify the specific reasons for mistakes that players make. Does the player have limited variety? Limited quality in the chosen action? Limited consistency in performing the action successfully or did they select the wrong action for the situation? The diagnosis will always determine the treatment. If a player selects the right action and the execution is poor, then we should be working on the quality and detail in the execution. If the player makes bad decision selections, then they probably need a lot of repetition at selecting different actions in similar situations to identify which ones work best. This can be supported by analysis sessions and discussions. Correct diagnosis improves our chance of correct interventions to best develop the player and improve their performance.

Practice State: As with everything we do, the state we are in has a significant impact on the results we achieve. When developing motor skills, our hormone balance, psychological focus, and attention to detail will significantly increase the progress of myelination, which in turn should increase the performance of the task in the future. Performing in a state of flow is the optimal state to develop motor skills. In this state, a player may fail, struggle, correct themselves, and try again until they see significant improvement and can execute the skill subconsciously.

Rest: In sport we will practice a motor skill for a continuous period, then attempt it again the next day and find we are better at it. There is much research into the role of rest, recovery, and sleep on motor skill learning (20). It has been found that motor skill learning can significantly improve after a period of rest, recovery, or sleep. In these periods it is suggested that neural formations occur to support the processes of the prior actions that have been attempted. The implication for this is the importance of patience with players developing motor skills and identifying when a player has practiced enough and is better off continuing the work another day.

Ecological Dynamics: This concept suggests that we are neurobiological systems in which inherent self-organisation tendencies support the emergence of adaptive behaviours under a range of interacting task and environment constraints (21). More simply put, it is our relationship between our systems and our environment that dictates our behaviour. A key concept to understand is that it is this relationship that gives us affordances (action possibilities) that we can select upon (22). A player with clarity in affordances across numerous situations is more likely to improve the outcome of their action.

Intelligence

Game intelligence is an extremely vague term that is used to explain when players make what is deemed as 'intelligent decisions". But what does game intelligence really mean? There are many definitions such as 'the ability of players to anticipate the actions of others and to select appropriate decisions under time pressure' (23). 'Game intelligence in team sports is usually regarded as something very incomprehensible, and excellent players are often praised for how well they read the game' (24). In order to define game intelligence, we should really start with understanding what intelligence is. The simplest definition of intelligence is 'the ability to acquire and apply knowledge and skills' (25). This meaning the most intelligent players are the ones who at the peak of their performance have acquired and applied the most useful knowledge and skills. Therefore, with reference to 'game intelligence' specifically, players must acquire and apply the most useful knowledge to support game performance. For us to support the development of game intelligent players, what knowledge and skills are we responsible for teaching them?

Rules: One of the key aspect's coaches are responsible for is teaching players the rules of the game. Often this is an expectation of coaches working with young youth players, however there are moments where even for senior players, rule changes require further education. For examples this season, changes to goal kick rules and handball rules, and at the top-level VAR rules. It is key that players understand how the rules will affect what they can expect to be implemented within the game. Match officials are often brought into clubs to support the education process and bring clarity to any additional rules or rule adjustments.

Pictures: When we are educating players about formations, patterns of play, and phases of the game we are giving them pictures that they can form in their mind in relation to what they can expect within a match or training session. These pictures enable players to anticipate situations where they can be a step ahead of other players. At the top level, the detail may be teaching a winger how to beat a full back who prefers to use his front foot to challenge in preparation for the weekend fixture. The power of pictures is helping players anticipate and identify what they have been taught. The downside to pictures is that no two pictures are ever one-hundred-percent identical, so within a picture it is important to look for the principle that can be applied.

Principles: There are several principles of football which will never change. The fact that they never change makes them a critical part of our player education process to increase game intelligence. There is a long list of principles. Some examples include space, time, tempo, and momentum. Once a player understands these principles, it can support the identification of these factors within training and match situations, and therefore make better use of them when required.

Roles: Another aspect of intelligence is an understanding of exactly what is required within their role within the team. When players are asked what they appreciated about their former managers, on numerous occasions they have said they appreciated that they knew exactly what was expected from them on the pitch. Do we define a role framework that explains what a player must do in different moments of the game? Within that framework players should have the freedom to make decisions based on the pictures and principles that they see. Eddie Jones speaks in his book 'My Life and Rugby' about the importance of giving players a framework and then giving them the responsibility to lead the framework and make the decisions they feel are right (26).

Cognitive Intelligence

Knowledge of rules, pictures, principles, and pictures does not become intelligence unless we can apply it as a skill. Our ability to turn this knowledge into skill is dependent on the following cognitive intelligence cycle. Understanding this cycle enables us to identify areas of weakness and develop more cognitive strengths. Players should consciously or subconsciously use all the below attributes to enhance the decision-making process.

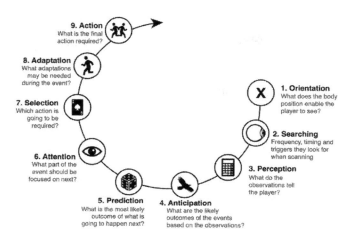

Figure 43: *The Cognitive Intelligence Cycle*

Orientation: What does a player's body position enable them to see? Are players orientating themselves correctly? Body orientation dictates what a player can see throughout the game and should be based on the current situation and anticipation of the next situation that is going to happen or the situation a player wants to make happen. For example, a centre back opening to receive from the goalkeeper, should be orientated to receive and execute the next action, whether it is a pass, dribble etc.

Searching: What does a player see? When consistently orientating correctly it gives players the advantage of what can be seen, however searching (more commonly known as scanning) is the critical part that enables a player to utilise good orientation. Two players can have the same body orientation, however increased searching can increase the useful information a player has, and decreased searching can limit the useful information a player has. There are several research studies that have correlated searching and successful actions such as pass completion, suggesting the importance of the searching aspect of intelligence (27). The most important aspect of the searching or scanning process, is looking for the right triggers and cues in relation to the game situation and the game model.

Perception: What has searching told them? Scanning is great, but if players are not collecting information what is the purpose? What has the player identified that gives important information. Two players can scan in the same situation but identify different pictures and principles. When searching, a player's peripheral vision and awareness will also contribute to a player's perception. For example, a player with poor vertical peripheral vision may focus more on the ball when it is at their feet, than a player with a better vertical peripheral vision.

Anticipation: What is going to happen next? The ability of players to anticipate the actions of others and to select appropriate decisions under time pressure, is essential to expert performance in soccer (28). If a player is defending one-vs-one, once they have orientated to deal with the situation, searched to see what options the opponent has, and identified those options, it is then important a player is able to anticipate which options are the most likely outcome. Anticipating the most likely outcomes enables players to then prepare for the next action that is likely to occur.

Prediction: What will the outcome be? After anticipating what is going to happen next, players must have the ability to predict the outcome of this. A typical footballing example would be after anticipating the opponent is going to take a shot, what is the outcome of the shot going to be? This prediction can then form our next action to ensure players are proactive rather than reactive. If the prediction is that the shot is going to be on target it would indicate that as a defender, they would need to prepare for potential rebounds. If preparing for the rebound before the rebound occurs, it gives an advantage in getting to the ball first. This is the importance of prediction, enabling players to be ahead of the action where possible.

Attention: What do they focus on? There has been much research suggesting that where and what athletes pay attention to, significantly impacts the outcome of the action. There is a key concept named 'quiet eye', which describes the final fixation or tracking of a task-relevant location, prior to the final phase of movement (29). In football, this may refer to a fixation on the exact part of the goal a player is aiming for, or the exact desired location for the pass to be received. Research has found that there is a correlation between the use of the gaze and the performance outcome (30). What we can take from the concept of quiet eye is what we focus on, has an impact on a motor skill outcome. In relation to the example of the opponent taking a shot, the defender's attention may then be on the goalkeeper's hands to identify where they may parry the ball to.

Selection: What do they need to do next? After taking in all this information, players can then select the action to be carried out. As discussed within the motor skills section, the selection is based on affordances. This referring to the available options based on what players are aware of, able to execute, and the situation they are in.

Adaptation: How may they need to adapt? Another key aspect that is often discussed in relation to game intelligence is the ability to adapt and deal with a change in situation. Most football actions such as passing, and shooting, are long enough that they have moments where adaptations can take place. Imagine a striker about to take a shot, then they identify a defender about to slide in front of them to take a shot, they may then adapt by turning and shooting with the opposite foot. There are many critical moments where adaptations such as these, give players an advantage over their opponents. The speed and timing that players can adapt, the more likely we can dominate opposed situations.

Action: The selected action is taken including any adaptations that a player selected either before the action or during the action. As coaches we should educate players on these cognitive intelligence skills and create demands within our environment which require players to utilise them. As players develop these skills there should be significant development and performance benefits which not only benefit themselves, but also benefit the team.

Athletic Capacity

The athletic capacity of players is a detailed topic where a high level of knowledge is required to maximise a players' athletic development and performance. We often work with sports scientists and conditioning coaches who specialise in this area but there are certain principles that can support our understanding and help us work alongside specialist staff members and modify our own sessions to offer the benefits the players need. Athletic capacity has an influence on both the decision-making processes and the body's ability. For example, a player with quick acceleration and speed will have more options in one-vs-one situations when trying to beat an opponent. An increased athletic capacity increases the number of affordances available for players when performing. A player who is quick, strong, mobile, with a high jump height can physically compete using a wider range of actions than a player who is slow, weak, immobile with a low jump height.

Environment vs Genetics: The nature, nurture argument has previously been discussed in the chapter titled, 'Understanding Behaviour', and being aware of that argument is critical when focusing on developing the athletic capacity of players. The genetic base will have a significant influence on a player's development, but the environments we create will also play a significant role. The combination of the environments a player develops in and their genetic base, will dictate their athletic outcomes. As coaches we can only control the environmental demands that we place on players that will have a guaranteed influence. Within our training sessions, how can we incorporate exercises and games which meet the athletic demands that players require for development and performance? This may involve considering factors such as warm up activities, pitch size, number of players in each exercise, frequency, and duration of exercises, and homework we expect players to complete in their own environments. Encouraging individualised homework programmes can be a beneficial method to supplement the work completed at training. This way athletic work is being carried out across several of the players environments. The external environments outside of football are covered under the lifestyle section, inclusive of key elements which affect athletic development such as sleep and nutrition.

Limitation vs Utilisation: Our perspective of a player's athletic ability is likely to have a significant influence on the development and performance of the players we are working with. If we are looking at the weaknesses that a player's athletic capacity brings, we will miss the opportunity to utilise that attribute as a strength. For example, it is common as coaches, to see a small player's height as a weakness because they are unable to compete physically with the average players in the group. If we flip our perspective, we can identify the strengths of a smaller player that can enhance their development and performance. For example, a smaller player may have closer ball control, or may be able to turn in smaller spaces. How can we utilise these strengths to develop beneficial skillsets? Can we encourage our small midfield player to receive in midfield under pressure and move the ball quickly to beat pressure from opponents? It is often athletic constraints which force other strengths to be developed. If playing in midfield against stronger and quicker players, attributes such as body orientation, decision-making speed, and first touch, may be of paramount importance to have success.

Physical Work ECE (Ethic, Capacity, and Efficiency): When we look at some of the best physical athletes in the world, there is an exceptional level of dedication to athletic development that is often undertaken. This work extends far beyond the team training schedule, and includes many other attributes such as extra training, nutrition, recovery, and flexibility sessions. The level of commitment to maximising the bodies potential, is a full-time job containing many of the lifestyle factors to be discussed, within the preparation factors.

Reverse Engineering Requirements: Where do we start when designing sessions to build players athletic ability? Often, we start with what other coaches have done or what we have seen online. If we use the skill of reverse engineering, we can start with the two most important factors. What does the game require from the player for maximal performance? What does the player require to maximise their potential? The culmination of these two factors should dictate the planning of developing players athletic capacity.

The Athletic Journey: The physical development journey of players can be an absolute rollercoaster. One year a player may be the tallest in the group, the next year they may be average. One year the player may be the quickest in the group, the next year they may be one of the slowest. There are periods of the development journey where players must deal with growth-related injuries and decreases or plateaus in performance. We must be aware that each journey is unique, meaning a one-size-fits-all method should not be applicable. A lack of understanding regarding the challenges of players' journeys, is a certain way of decreasing happiness, development, and performances of players within our environments. The extremely tall centre back at thirteen, needs different attention than the nineteen-year-old who is unable to physically compete with players in the age group below. Even when players sign professional contracts, there are often years ahead of key athletic development where players must take their athletic capabilities to the next level, while potentially having to perform on the weekend. Look at some of the world's best players, aged eighteen in comparison to aged twenty-five. Their physiques are often far apart. We must keep happiness, development, and performance in mind throughout the process of this athletic journey.

Fitness vs Freshness: Understanding the balance between fitness and freshness is one of the keys to maximising development without jeopardising performance. Each individual has different fitness and freshness balances. Often this balance is dependent on other lifestyle factors. For example, in an ideal football environment all players could complete double sessions every day and still perform at the weekend. This is not likely to be possible, however some players will be able to complete more double sessions than others. Within youth environments, some players will be able to handle training five times a week while still performing at the weekend, whereas others may not manage this balance. The key is understanding that each individual is different. We often devise a training programme for all players and think that it is perfect for everyone. The challenge with this is that there will certainly be some players who can do more and some players who should not. Those who should do more are risking injury by pushing their balance further towards fitness, and those who are not being pushed far enough towards fitness are missing out on the opportunity for further development. Using individualised programmes on top of the team programmes is the best solution to ensure all players find their ideal balance between building fitness and managing freshness in time for performance.

Football Experiences

The experiences a player has throughout their football journey is one of the most critical factors in influencing happiness, development, and performance of senior players. To ensure the journey is successfully utilised, we should ensure that all players have a high quantity, high quality, and wide variety of relevant experiences that will support the three objectives. One concept we must understand, is that while we are often promoting a specific style of play in line with a club philosophy, how many of the players are going to end up playing first team football for the club? If ten-percent of players manage to get promoted and consistently play within the first team at the same club they grew up in, the academy has done exceptionally well. But even in this case, what about the other ninety-percent of players? How can we utilise the football experiences we give players, to ensure they can be successful within the club, as well as at another club? The loan system for players age eighteen to twenty-three, where clubs send their players to lower league clubs has been one of the key methods used to make up for the lack of variety and competitiveness in development environments. Below are some of the experiences we should consider in relation to supporting the football journey of our players.

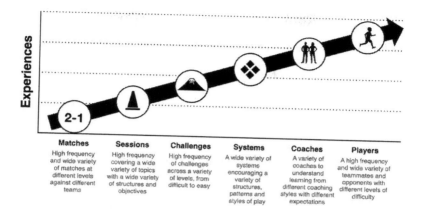

Matches	Sessions	Challenges	Systems	Coaches	Players
High frequency and wide variety of matches at different levels against different teams	High frequency covering a wide variety of topics with a wide variety of structures and objectives	High frequency of challenges across a variety of levels, from difficult to easy	A wide variety of systems encouraging a variety of structures, patterns and styles of play	A variety of coaches to understand learning from different coaching styles with different expectations	A high frequency and wide variety of teammates and opponents with different levels of difficulty

Figure 44: *Key Experience Factors*

Matches: We should ensure players experience playing a high quantity of matches, with a high quality of football, with a variety of match situations and match environments. For example, can we increase the number of matches players play per year without causing burnout? At youth level, some clubs ensure their players compete in over sixty matches per season, at other clubs players play less than thirty. Over a season it is a significant difference, but over ten years the difference can add up to three hundred matches. Obviously, the more matches players play each season, the more expertise is needed to manage the physical maturation of players. At senior level, there are clubs that only play competitive fixtures, and there are others who regularly play against other teams in midweek friendlies. Being aware of the impact of quantity helps us identify when match frequency can be increased. Quality of matches is also an important factor to consider. Can we find the quality of opponents that will push players to develop and be better? This may mean playing against older age groups at times to ensure competition. Most importantly players will require a variety of experiences. When reverse engineering the experiences of senior players, we can identify that they compete in a wide variety of matches. There are matches where players experience beating a high press, playing against a deep block, dealing with direct passes, playing against large crowds, and playing on bad pitches with poor weather conditions. How do we ensure that senior players never encounter something brand new which they have not previously experienced? By ensuring as much variety as possible.

Sessions: Once we have identified the variety of experiences a player must have throughout the football journey, it then indicates what we need to include in our sessions. There are often debates between topics such as unopposed-vs-opposed sessions, which are only beneficial if understanding the benefits of the different session principles. What we can be clear about when discussing session experiences, is that players need a high quantity, a high quality, and a wide variety of session types. There are often limitations for increasing the number of sessions players have per week, however if we put thought into the programme, we can often find ways to increase session frequency. For example, fitting in sessions after matches for the players whose load has not been too high, or giving online or homework sessions for players that we do not have access to enough. Players should not reach first team level without experiencing dealing with long balls, and at first team level, players should not experience beating the block in a game before they have worked on it in training.

Challenges: With adversity being such a heavy influence on the development of players, knowing we cannot control factors outside of football that cause adversity, we should control the level of challenge players experience in sessions and matches to ensure the development of grit and determination. By manipulating games and sessions we can ensure players are experiencing the challenges that will prepare them for their next steps in their journey. At senior level this may mean giving players the right challenges that will prepare them for the next fixture. At development level it may mean challenging them in line with becoming the best player at the club, or the best player in the world. To achieve this, we must pay attention to the variety and quantity of challenges that players require. Does our quick winger need to experience playing against a quicker and stronger full back so that they develop their skill as well as their athletic ability? Does our strong midfielder need to play against older stronger players to challenge them to develop their technical capacity? Do our weaker players need to play against younger players to feel success and build confidence? Being aware that each player needs to be individually challenged, should guide us towards offering a variety and high quantity of challenges throughout their journey.

Systems: Often we have our preferred systems, some of us prefer to use a four-three-three, some prefer a three-five-two. What do the players need? When coaching at the senior end of football, there are many teams with players who are uncomfortable in a different formation, the typical example being centre backs who are only comfortable playing in a back four. How can we offer variety through players' football experiences, to ensure they are prepared for potential expectations when arriving in new environments? Even within systems, there may be game models that vary across cultures. A player can go through a whole academy system, then on arrival to the first team discover there is a change of coach who wants to adapt or change the system of the first team. After ten plus years of one system, they now need to adapt and change, whereas in those ten years we could have provided a bigger variety to ensure when any changes arise, players are prepared.

Coaches: A key discussion between those in charge of youth clubs and structures, is how to manage players transitioning through the age groups. One point of discussion is often how long players should spend with a coach. There are examples of coaches staying with an age group for many seasons, but also examples of players changing coach every age group. The similar discussion is often had in schools with regards to how long pupils should have the same teacher. There are benefits to consistency, however variety is critical to long term growth. Players working with a variety of coaches better prepares players for what they may deal with as a senior player. Senior players may work under many coaches throughout their career, sometimes this can be three different head coaches in one season, alongside any assistant or specialist coaches. Players experiencing a wide variety of coaches may enable them to have success when working under a wide range of coaching styles and personalities.

Players: The last key factor affecting football experience is the players they share the journey with. The variety and quality of players is of particular importance through a player's journey. Through training sessions and games, we should attempt to mix a wide variety of players, with a variety of qualities. The easiest way to do this is to mix age groups within the club. If the age groups are frequently mixed, players may now get the opportunity to compete with and against a far higher number of players than they would if they only train within their own group. Within this higher quantity of players, we will likely find a variety of personalities, a variety of leadership styles, and a variety of qualities that can be experienced.

Importance of Football Experiences

1. Increased brain efficiency: Advanced research has found that an increase in quantity and variety of relative experiences decrease the demand placed on the brain for analysing situations, making decisions, and acting based on those decisions. Decreased brain demand enables focus to be placed on other factors to enhance development and performance (31).

2. Increased ability: If we can acknowledge that the body adapts to the environment, it makes it clear that the experiences we create in the environment will influence the development of the body. If our environment creates a lot of long-distance running opportunities, we will be more likely to develop players that have a better endurance base than those in an environment without those opportunities. We should utilise the experiences to enhance a player's bodily functions towards their future requirements.

3. Improved pattern recognition: Experience brings about a better quality prediction of what is going to happen on an individual or unit level during the game. For example, a player with a higher quantity, quality and variety of experiences is more likely to identify the outcomes of what central defenders may do when under pressure, meaning they can better anticipate the next situation and regain the ball accordingly.

4. Improved solution identification: It is our experiences that help us identify problems and test solutions so that we can pair the right solutions with the right problems. "Are we making the right mistakes this week to be successful at the weekend?" (26). Are players making the right mistakes this week, to be a better player next week and be the best player in the world, in the future? The more mistakes a player makes the more problems they will experience, and the more solutions they will experiment with, allowing them to eventually find the best solutions.

Psychological Factors

Grit

Without a doubt, grit is the most important attribute in predicting success in meeting significantly difficult objectives. The football journey from youth football to senior football is full of hurdles. In England, academy players must go through the sign, retain, and release process up to five times. At the end of the under-eight season, there are seven and eight-year-olds who are told whether they are going to be offered the chance to sign for an academy or must look elsewhere. Then on at least three occasions between under nine and under eighteen youth players must go through retain and release meetings where the club decides if they want to keep them or not. At under-eighteen, there is again the retain or release process where players are either offered a professional contract or told they will be released. Even once a player signs a professional contract, they must compete to get into the matchday squad, and then compete to get into the starting eleven. Once they are in the starting eleven the challenge is then to keep their place, and move to a bigger club, and in some cases break into the National Team. Within the National Team setup, players then have the challenge of breaking into the starting eleven, keeping their place, and for a select few, they then compete to win a Ballon d'Or and be named the world's best football player. For most players, the journey from playing football in their early childhood years all the way to their retirement, is a twenty-five to thirty-year football journey. Along this journey there are often several setbacks, from injuries, to being released, to dealing with being on the bench and not playing and many more challenges both inside and outside of football. What is it that gets players through these hurdles to the top, and what is it that holds other players back? There are many reasons. It certainly is not solely down to skill level. Being skilful does not keep a player focused when injured, or make a player complete extra hours of training, and certainly does not keep a player hungry to succeed after being released. Research from football and other areas demonstrates that the main reason is grit. Grit is the desire to achieve long-term goals even in the presence of failure or setbacks (32). A rare research study found that grittier players are more likely to invest greater amounts of time in soccer-specific activities and work toward their sporting goals in comparison with less gritty players. The study also suggested that gritty players perform better on sport-specific-perceptual-cognitive assessments than less gritty players (33). In a study lead by 'grit expert' Angela Duckworth, they found that grit could predict someone's success more accurately than IQ. In summary of the study, they stated that the achievement of difficult goals entails not only talent, but a sustained and focused application of talent over time (34). These findings align with the identification of life factors of Ballon d'Or winners, which found that overcoming adversity was a common trend between many of the players. Cristiano Ronaldo, Lionel Messi, Kaka, Luka Modric, Andriy Shevchenko, Ronaldinho, Brazilian Ronaldo all overcame adversities to achieve success as a football player.

Identifying Grit

When we are assessing players, whether that be our own players or potential recruits, if grit is a key attribute to long term success then it should be something we try to identify in players. But what are the indicators of a player who has high levels of grit? Below are some indicative behaviours to help us identify them:

1. Regularly completing extra work both at home and before or after sessions when no one is watching

2. Continuing through physical thresholds and difficult conditions

3. Disappointment if not selected in the line-up or squad but channels the feeling towards working harder

4. Eager to return to play when injured with heavy focus on rehab as if it's a football session.

5. Striving to complete set challenges and compete with opponents even when they are stronger.

6. Willing to listen but stubborn in their beliefs

7. Lead through setting an example of their work ethic and application without waiting to follow others.

8. Focus on long term vision and goals

Developing Grit

While grit is a key factor to success it is one of the most challenging qualities to instil in a player. Grit is heavily dependent on events that occur away from football in the personal lives of players. A difficult factor to accept is that the old school 'shout at them and punish them' mentality in coaching, is likely to develop grit in players. Coaches with these methods creates adversity within the football environment by making it difficult to survive mentally. More modern methods of coaching are player-centred and often create more of a sense of comfort for players. What methods can we use to develop grit within players if we want to keep our environment player-centred?

1. Encourage players to set and invest time into long term goals

2. Educate players on channelling energy into achieving their goals after failure

3. Create individual moments of failure through coaching sessions and training matches.

4. Allow players to be frustrated when they are struggling, but push them to 5. keep persevering

6. Be an example of grit by displaying strength to continue through difficult situations

7. Praise effort and work rate over achievements

8. Help players find their 'why' for having grit

Self-Mastery

There are many key areas that players should understand and develop to become masters of themselves. Once a player can master themselves, they are far more likely to achieve success. The following six concepts of self-mastery should be identified and promoted in our coaching environments.

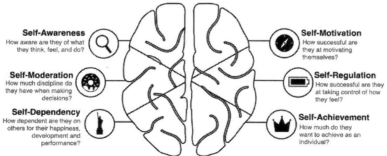

Self-Awareness
How aware are they of what they think, feel, and do?

Self-Moderation
How much discipline do they have when making decisions?

Self-Dependency
How dependent are they on others for their happiness, development and performance?

Self-Motivation
How successful are they at motivating themselves?

Self-Regulation
How successful are they at taking control of how they feel?

Self-Achievement
How much do they want to achieve as an individual?

Figure 45: Key Self-Mastery Concepts

Self-Awareness: As coaches we have a responsibility to tell players what they are doing well, what they are not doing well, when their attitude is not correct, when their body language is poor, along with many other observations. While being aware of these aspects makes us better coaches, players being aware of these things makes them better players. Our job as coaches should be to improve players' self-awareness so they can identify these things in themselves before anyone tells them. If a player can identify when they have poor body language, they can then correct it for themselves. If we must be the ones to identify poor body language, players will wait for us to identify many other things and even worse, what will they do when we are not there to identify these things for them? A player with high self-awareness will be able to identify their own feelings, thought patterns and behaviours, and change them to support their happiness, development, and performance. Where possible this should also extend beyond football. How self-aware are players in life? Do they have their own beliefs and values or are their views based on what other people tell them?

Self-Motivation: if we are consistently shouting at players and pushing them to do more, what does this tell us about the motivation of the player? In most cases it is not high enough. A player's motivation to be successful should be higher than our motivation for them to be successful. Why is this often not the case? Maybe because for years, players have been waiting on the coach to shout at them before they step up and push harder. This creates many challenges. What will they do when we are not there to motivate them and how will they ever know how much they can achieve if their levels of effort are dependent on someone else's expectations? A lack of self-motivation is one of the reasons why players drop out or decrease their participation in the game. When they get to an age where they have control over their life, parents stop taking them to training, school football finishes, relationships and money start becoming motivation, how can we ensure a player's motivation to develop as a player and person is still high on the priority list? The best players are often motivated towards being the best version of themselves.

Self-Moderation: As a player makes it through their football journey, the temptation to become involved in activities that can have a negative impact on their lives increases. Eating unhealthy food, drinking alcohol, getting into many relationships, and enjoying late nights out are just some of the examples that may be encountered. There are three approaches to dealing with players who go through moments of wanting to experience these things. One extreme is we discipline, where we try and tell players never to participate in them. The opposite extreme is allowing players to do whatever they want. The middle ground is educating and supporting players in finding the right moderation for them to achieve the happiness, development, and success they are looking for. For some players this may mean drinking a glass of wine with dinner, and for some players it means not having alcohol at all. Some players can go to a nightclub on a Saturday night to celebrate a win where others find it better when they do not attend the club at all. Once a player can understand that they must find the right moderation, they can start taking responsibility for their own decisions. There are premier league winners who have had success while hiding their detrimental lifestyle habits, so what makes us think we can control all the players we are working with? Education and support are the keys, especially in key development years, where their understanding of life is still forming.

Self-Regulation: Who is responsible for the way we feel? We are so quick to blame others for how we are feeling, which makes us a consistent victim of the world. To conquer this feeling of being a victim, we ourselves must be able to regulate how we feel and teach our players to regulate how they feel. Some days players will turn up after having a long day at school, or at senior level they may have had a fight with their partner at home. In these cases, while we must be supportive, we must teach players how to get themselves into the right space psychologically before training and playing. This teaching should then also be carried into life, so that even in the hardest situations, players can still focus on the task at hand. There are some extreme situations where regulation may not be the answer, such as death of a family member or a mental illness. These situations may need counselling or specialist treatment. However, on a day to day basis, dealing with everyday issues, players must learn to regulate their emotions and return to their optimum state to perform. Regulation factors may include psychological aspects such as regulating thought processes and mindset, as well as physical regulation such as nutrition, stretching and exercises.

A key component of self-regulation is the ability to "predict how we will feel in the future. As it turns out, we are terrible at it. We are not good judges of what will make us happy and we have trouble seeing through the filter of the now. Our feelings in the present blind us to how we will make decisions in the future when we might be feeling very differently" (35). One of the most challenging decisions, is whether to make decisions based on how we feel in the moment (instant gratification), vs how we will feel after (delayed gratification). Should we eat the chocolate now because we are craving it, or not eat the chocolate because we will regret it after? When working in a team sport environment, it is important that players want to feel team and individual success. As coaches we influence the feelings they get from both situations, and if players are educated on affective forecasting, they can better predict how they will feel after making certain decisions. There are many decisions in the game of football that are affected by our affective forecasting. For example, shooting from 40 yards without much practice due to the feeling of excitement at the possibility of scoring, vs retaining possession for the team and sticking to the philosophy, which is likely to bring long term success. The instant gratification option is going for individual glory, whereas the delayed gratification option is the retention of possession. The key for players making the right decision is basing their decisions on the objectives they have set. This may be individual based, or team based. If we are in agreement with those objectives, it is then our job to ensure we praise decisions that align with those objectives, particularly decisions where their initial feelings have been put aside There are four aspects of affective forecasting that players can consider when making decisions:

1. **Valence:** Will the feeling following the action be a positive or negative one?
2. **Emotions:** Which emotions will be felt after the action?
3. **Intensity:** How strong will the feeling be?
4. **Duration:** How long will the feeling last for?

Self-Dependency: Who is responsible for a player's development? As coaches we believe we are, and we do play a significant role in supporting development. However, a player believing that the coach is responsible for their development can be a detrimental thought. What happens when they go on to work with a coach who does not favour them or does not have any new knowledge to teach them? Will the player then plateau and become frustrated as they wait for someone to teach them? Teaching a player that they are responsible for their development while still supporting them is key to ensuring a player is successful in the long term. As a modern-day player, there are many ways to develop on a day to day basis, from watching football matches at home, to starting yoga or Pilates, from learning about nutrition online, to completing extra training. There are even external staff members that can be hired such as private analysts or fitness coaches. Opportunities to take responsibility for our own development has never been so prevalent. Players that are waiting for others to develop them are losing out on crucial time.

Self-Achievement: While there are many benefits to team sports, particularly social benefits, one of the downsides is that it allows an individual to believe they will achieve based on the hard work of others. They can be a part of team achievements such as winning leagues, trophies, and tournaments without maximising their potential. Many of us as coaches won many team trophies during our youth years, yet never fulfilled anywhere close to our football potential. Did our focus on team achievements take over our focus on self-achievement? Had we spent our youth years focusing on being the best player we could be would we have achieved far more in football? This is not to say that team achievement is not an amazing aspect in football, it is to make the point that self-achievement must also be a key focus. A classic example is when we identify FA Youth Cup winning teams that had a squad full of players who only made a handful of first team appearances between them.

Creativity

Creativity has been one of the hot topics across football for decades, with the phrase being frequently used by coaches, pundits, fans, and commentators. It is often a 'creative moment' that leads to recognition from those working in football environments. The player who does things other players do not. The player who stands out in games and gains attention from other players, staff, and fans. Before defining creativity, it is important to differentiate creativity and problem solving. On courses and discussions, they are often described as the same concept. While creativity is a method of problem solving, not all problem-solving actions are creative. And not all creative moments solve problems. So, what is creativity? The Oxford Dictionary defines creativity as: "The use of skill and imagination to produce something new or to produce art"? There are many challenges with definitions such as these. The first question is, how we define the word 'new'. Does the outcome of creativity have to be new to the person who created it or the person who sees it? For example, if a youth player in Brazil scored with a rabona one-hundred years ago, and they were the first to do it, does that count as creativity? We would assume so. If a youth player from England who has never seen it before does it tomorrow, is that also creativity? The process in 'creating' the action may have been the same, but our belief of creativity would determine that it is not as creative as the player who did it one-hundred years ago. How can our perspective determine creativity if it is a process that occurs in someone's mind and body? Other definitions suggest creativity must end in something of value? If so, that would again mean we would be externally deciding on a creative process when it is an internal process in the mind. Mihaly Csikszentmihalyi in his book entitled 'Creativity' stated that, creativity is actually externally measured based on the value in the sociocultural context. The challenge with this concept, when working with players, is that their initial moments of creativity may not be valuable. It may take numerous actions that are not valuable to eventually create a valuable creative action. As coaches we must understand this to ensure we promote the behaviours when they are not valuable, to eventually gain the valuable actions of a player. For example, a young player may be challenged to create new one-vs-one skill moves over the coming weeks. The first three they create may not be effective. At this point we must still value the creativity to ensure the player continues to create. The fourth one-vs-one move they create may be the valuable one, but it does not take away from the previous three being creative. We must differentiate between creativity and value, although we want players to eventually demonstrate creative actions that bring individual and team value.

With all the different definitions and questions around creativity, I decided to define it myself. One of the key beliefs I have around creativity, is that a human cannot create something out of nothing, even though it is a popular statement. Everything created has components that stem from something previously created. A typical example I use to explain this concept is the history of the airplane. The Concorde was 'a celebration of Britain's capacity for creative invention'. Now while this may have been creativity that led the process of designing and producing the Concorde, the base of the idea was built on a normal airplane plus the utilisation of the laws of physics, two things that already existed. Before the Boeing 747, that we so frequently fly now, there were early powered steam engine planes, and before that there were gliders that had engines built on them, and before that there were normal gliders. When we look at the process from start to finish, it has been a consistent combination of ideas and concepts that have ended with the creation of a high-speed plane such as the Concorde. My definition is therefore:

"Creativity is the process of self-led connection of two concepts that have not previously been connected in the individual's mind or body"

This definition is similar to the definition of 'originality' from W.I.B Beveridge in his book 'The Art of Scientific Investigation'. "Originality often consists of linking up ideas whose connection was not previously suspected". From a football perspective, this then means that a player who creates, is a player who regularly connects different ideas, to create an outcome that they were not previously aware of. This makes it simple to classify whether an action is creative or not from an internal perspective, and furthermore makes it easier to identify the conditions that will encourage creativity and the conditions that will restrict creativity. The one challenge is that it makes it difficult to identify if an action is creative from an external perspective. Did they copy the idea, or did they combine their own ideas to create a new idea? Using my definition breaks the creative process down into two critical parts which we can influence as coaches:

1. Exposure: Expose players to a wide variety of concepts so that players have a large library of actions they can connect.

2. Connection: Create environments which increases the likeliness of players connecting ideas.

To address the first, we can use a large variety of tools to support the exposure to a variety of concepts. This can include use of video footage of other players showing a variety of actions they may not have seen, or may also involve allowing players to train with a variety of groups in the club, for them to observe other players' actions. To address the second, there are certain lessons we know from neuroscience which encourage synaptogenesis (the bridging of neurons to make new connections). One key principle is that cortisol (stress) restricts the synaptogenesis process. This indicates that when we want to promote creativity, we should restrict stress in the training environment. As well as the stress element, we must also consider training session design. How can we utilise training session principles such as 'collaborative play' to encourage freedom and limit stress and therefore see more of these creative moments that we desire?

Tips: Develop creativity within players by:

1. Increasing exposure to various players and actions
2. Limiting stress in training where creativity is the desired outcome
3. Using collaborative play to encourage the creative possibilities.
4. Limiting the use of 'normal actions' to force players to combine ideas to create new actions.

Relationships

They cannot do it alone. Relationships are a fundamental aspect to a player's success. Players will always need the help of others around them to have success. Even the best players in the world have had great relationships with those around them on the pitch. Cristiano Ronaldo formed a partnership and friendship with Marcelo on the left-hand side of Real Madrid, across nine years where they won four champions leagues titles across a four-year period. When Ronaldo left Real Madrid for Juventus, Marcelo had remarkable words to share about their relationship. "It has been ten years at your side, ten years of joy, good football, victories, defeats and wonderful moments. I've learned a lot from you". Everything must be good for you and your beautiful family". I'm going to miss our talks before the games, when you got results right and when before the finals you reassured us with your experience and the love you gave to the youngest ones. I am proud to have played with you, not because you are the best player but because of who you are" (36). These are comments about one of the best players in the world with five Ballon d'Ors, who did not have to form relationships to gain respect. There is no doubt however, that this relationship enhanced Ronaldo's threat on the left-hand side. Similar stories can be said for Lionel Messi and Dani Alves, during Pep Guardiola's reign at Barcelona. Dani Alves has since referred to Lionel Messi as his brother who he was honoured to have in his life (37). There are two key benefits from having these types of relationships within the team. We can use the following methods to best develop relationships in our environments:

1. Identify: When identifying players who are struggling with performance, can we identify if a lack of healthy on and off the pitch relationships may be contributing?

2. Support: Can we support the process of relationship building between players, particularly those who play alongside each other, such as the winger and full back examples?

3. Recruitment: When recruiting players to fit within the team, can we consider how they form relationships and the likeliness of them having healthy relationships within the team.

Preparation Factors

Lifestyle

The happiness, development and performance of athletes is significantly impacted by the lifestyle that they choose. Lifestyle can be defined as a "set of practices which an individual embraces" (38), as well as a "statement about who an individual aspires to be" (39). If lifestyle is a set of practices that define who we aspire to be, what should a player's lifestyle look like if they are aiming to achieve success? There are many aspects of a player's lifestyle that should be managed to maximise their potential. At one extreme they should be managed all day every day, as part of the twenty-four-hour professional concept, at the other end, players may focus more on the experiences outside of life more than the ones they have within football. Players who better manage these lifestyle factors are more likely to be happy, to develop, and to perform. The first step to influencing any of the lifestyle factors of players, is identifying which key factors we should be looking out for.

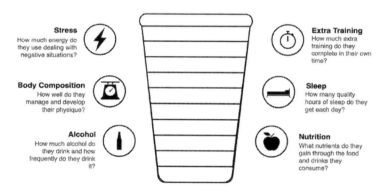

Figure 46: Key Lifestyle Factors

Extra Training: Football players rarely have a set number of hours of work per week, and the number of hours a player trains varies from club to club and week to week. A more modern approach to training, is to give a set number of working hours to players but give them freedom to use some of them how they best need them. For example, expecting players to complete six hours of work in a day, but four of them being sessions run by staff, with the other two hours being selected by the player, with options ranging from stretching, running, extra training, analysis, or extra sleep. Using a concept like this can be a great tool for working with youth players where there is limited contact time. If working with a youth age group where there is only six hours contact time per week, an expectation could be set for players to complete twelve hours per week. Within the extra six hours they can complete ball mastery, stretching, analysis of televised matches, and any other related activities. This must be monitored to manage the physical and psychological demands, but the concept can be powerful to encourage players to do extra.

Sleep: Research has demonstrated the importance of sleep for athletes in relation to a variety of factors which are critical for happiness, development, and performance. These include but are not limited to, emotional well-being, immune function, and recovery (40). Many elite clubs are utilising the advantages sleep can offer by making special sleeping arrangements for their players. Marcelo Bielsa installed beds at the training ground on arrival at Leeds United (41). Tottenham Hotspur built a lodge for players to sleep in, where each player can sleep on a mattress that is the same as the mattress they sleep on at home (42). While we will not always work in environments where we can build lodges and install beds, we can take away the message of how important sleep can be for athletes.

Nutrition: With sports science becoming more prevalent in football, the nutritional intake of players is becoming more important than ever. At the highest level of football, each player has a nutritional diet designed specifically for them, covering all their deficiencies to support overall health and performance. At other levels we can still have an influence on the nutritional intake of players. The key starting points are often water intake to manage hydration and food and supplement intake to manage energy and recovery. While everyone is unique, there are key principles that can be used across age groups and genders. Consultation with a sports scientist should be used if uncertain about nutritional advice. Research is now advancing towards periodizing nutrition towards utilising nutritional intake in relation to nutrient needs at different stages of the training programme (43). A similar process can be used to support players with utilising nutrition to enhance happiness, development, and performance.

Alcohol: With alcohol deeply embedded in many aspects of Western society, it is the most commonly used recreational drug globally, with consumption often in high volumes. The expectation of players in relation to alcohol intake varies dependent on the club, the environment, and the culture. In some clubs there is zero tolerance on alcohol, whereas with others there is complete freedom. In some clubs around the world the staff and players drink alcohol together. Research has found that alcohol has a complex relationship with recovery and sports performance, with many key variables to consider, including the timing, frequency, quantity and dosage of alcohol intake, as well as the factors that are based on the players state at the time of intake (44). Is the player injured? How fatigued are they? How hydrated are they? Understanding the complexity of alcohol and performance is key to the education process. One important factor we must always be aware of, is the potential risk of alcohol addiction and the impact this has not only on performance and development, but the long-term happiness and health of the players we work with.

Body Composition: Body composition analysis is becoming increasingly widespread in professional football as it helps to further understand the relationships between changes in body fat over time with different fitness parameters (45). Football based research has demonstrated how increased lean body mass and decreased body fat can enhance physical performance (46). If we can positively influence the body composition of our players, we have an increased chance of positively improving their development and performance. Two of the key body composition measures are often total body weight, and body fat percentages across numerous areas of the body.

Stress: Psychological life stresses have been dubbed this centuries health epidemic. There are several psychological stresses such as anxiety and depression that can have a detrimental effect on the development and performance of humans in the workplace, and this does not exclude the football industry. Stress has links to physical and mental illness, injury, growth and development, performance, and many other life and football related aspects. Throughout a player's football journey there is likely to be several stresses that they must manage, from youth players who move schools and sit exams, to senior players who go through personal relationships, marriage, divorces and many other experiences. How we support players by positively influencing and managing these situations, can significantly increase their happiness, development, and performance. The biggest challenge for us as coaches, is having enough of an influence over these factors to positively impact the players. There are four steps we can use:

1. Screening: We can use discussions, questionnaires, and technology to measure the factors
2. Educate: We can start to educate players on the benefits of maximising these factors
3. Assist: Where possible we can send players to specialists to gain further advantages using these factors
4. Monitor: Technology and daily measurements can support in flagging changes in these factors.

Periodisation

Periodisation has been a hot topic in football for years now. It can be defined as "an overall concept of training that deals with the division of the training process into specific phases" (47). There are many books, websites and articles that give periodisation plans to use within our club environments. When we approach football from a holistic perspective there are no two teams with the same requirements. This meaning taking one plan and applying it to our group of players is unlikely to guarantee long term training success. What we can take from periodisation, is the certainty that where a player is at within the training programme, will influence their level of performance, and how we periodise their training programme can either limit or maximise player performance. This is not just from an athletic perspective, although most coaches focus on this periodisation aspect. Where is the player's focus psychologically? Emotionally? Technically?

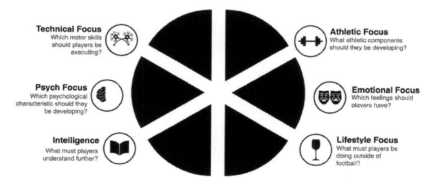

Technical Focus
Which motor skills should players be executing?

Athletic Focus
What athletic components should they be developing?

Psych Focus
Which psychological characteristic should they be developing?

Emotional Focus
Which feelings should players have?

Intelligence
What must players understand further?

Lifestyle Focus
What must players be doing outside of football?

Figure 47: Periodisation Focuses

Purpose

1. Ensure variety of focuses across the training programme
2. Limit aspects of each focus that may not be covered in the programme
3. Utilise planning to identify the moments where players must peak across all areas for performance

Coaching Role

1. Identify where individuals and the team are currently
2. Create, develop, and adapt the training programme to ensure players peak with the required attributes at the right time.

Cycles

Season Cycle (Macrocycle): The longest cycle which includes the season and all fifty-two weeks of the year

Match Block Cycle (Mesocycle): The middle cycle which contains a block of matches with a specific objective

Match Cycle (Micro-cycles): The shortest cycle which tends to be the week or days prior to a match.

Planning Micro-cycles

In different football environments there will be different amounts of time required for different focuses. Planning match block cycles and season cycles is heavily dependent on the season schedule which is unique for many coaches and clubs. However regardless of the environment, there are micro-cycle components that we should always consider. To understand these components, we should reverse engineer from what is required in the most important aspect, the match. In a development environment these components may be more individual focused, or in a performance environment they may be more team focused. Here are six key components of a micro-cycle.

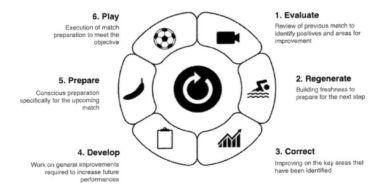

6. Play
Execution of match preparation to meet the objective

5. Prepare
Conscious preparation specifically for the upcoming match

4. Develop
Work on general improvements required to increase future performances

1. Evaluate
Review of previous match to identify positives and areas for improvement

2. Regenerate
Building freshness to prepare for the next step

3. Correct
Improving on the key areas that have been identified

Figure 48: Micro-cycle Cycle Components

1. Evaluate: *Key Principle: Reflect on the previous performance to identify areas that need to be improved.* This is the period for reflection on the previous fixture from a holistic perspective. How did the team perform physically? Where is the team psychologically? Which technical actions did the players struggle with? Questions such as these will give the answers to which corrections and preparations need to take place in the coming week.

2. Regenerate: *Key Principle: Bring staff and players back to having a balanced mind and body.* This phase is to support players returning to their balanced state, where they are as close to a state of freshness as possible within the time limit given. In some cases, this may mean rest, in other cases it may mean ice baths and recovery sessions. It can start straight after the match has finished or the next day depending on the schedule.

3. Correct: *Key Principle: After this phase players must leave the last fixture behind and move forward.* This is the last opportunity to focus on the previous match. It may be a video session or a training session depending on available time and coach preferences. This enables us to close the chapter of the last game while learning the lessons that must be taken forward. The priority is to ensure that players have let go of any emotion and stress from the previous fixture and have no questions regarding why the outcomes of the previous performance occurred. All players and staff must have clarity and understanding of what needs to be improved moving forward.

4. Develop: *Key Principle: After this phase players must be ready to move into match preparations.* The priority is to have players ready to move into the preparation phase by covering important performance aspects that the team or individuals need to improve. These aspects are not related to the opponent but are more related to the team's requirements regarding what needs to be developed. In some cases, this must be fitness through some of the physical principles, in other cases it may be regeneration due to a congested fixture period. Psychologically this is the time for players to reduce focus on external events and focus on themselves and their individual performance within the team.

5. Prepare: *Key Principle: After this phase players must be ready to perform.* This phase is closest to the match and is specifically about preparing for the opponent. The amount of time spent on this is dependent on a variety of factors such as opposition quality, time available, and personal coaching beliefs about how much focus to place on the opponent vs how much to place on our own team. For some coaches this may be a matchday minus-one session, others may use matchday minus-one and matchday minus-two. If playing against an extremely high-level opponent, it may be the whole week.

6. Play: *Key Principle: Players must give one-hundred-percent to meet the set match objective.* The most important part of any cycle. This is the starting point when designing the micro-cycle. What is going to be required within the game that needs to be developed? These aspects must be input into the programme to give the team the best chance of winning.

Priming

Priming can be defined as a technique in which the introduction of one stimulus influences how people respond to a subsequent stimulus (48). In relation to sport, the term is more frequently used to describe the activities during the 24 hour build up to competition with the objective of enhancing performance. In this case, the subsequent stimulus is the match, and the initial stimulus is the activity to enhance how a player performs during the match. What can we do in the period after matchday minus-one training up until kick off, of the match to enhance performance? Traditionally priming was left to a pre-match team talk and warm up 30 minutes before kick-off. Research has now suggested there are a lot of other activities we can execute too, that can enhance performance. The key principle to consider during this priming phase is that we want to enhance positive performance factors without inducing negative performance factors such as fatigue and stress, in order to get everyone into their optimal performance zone. Many of the factors should also be considered during half-time due to the potential change in the mind and body during the first half. Below are six of the performance factors we can affect to enhance performance:

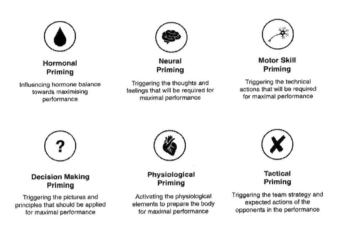

Hormonal Priming
Influencing hormone balance towards maximising performance

Neural Priming
Triggering the thoughts and feelings that will be required for maximal performance

Motor Skill Priming
Triggering the technical actions that will be required for maximal performance

Decision Making Priming
Triggering the pictures and principles that should be applied for maximal performance

Physiological Priming
Activating the physiological elements to prepare the body for maximal performance

Tactical Priming
Triggering the team strategy and expected actions of the opponents in the performance

Figure 49: Priming Components

Hormonal Priming: As discussed under behavioural endocrinology, hormones are a critical aspect of high performance. For maximal performance we want players to have the right balance in hormones that increase and performance output of the mind and the body without negative impact. Two of the key hormones which need to be managed are cortisol and testosterone. Testosterone, which has the clearest link to performance, peaks in the morning and decreases throughout the day. This meaning that performance would be at its highest in the morning and lowest in the evening. Different research projects have used a variety of strategies to impact testosterone in the morning, to boost its levels for afternoon or evening performance. These have included running sprints, cycling sprints, and weight resistance exercises. Three different research projects that have been analysed using a control group and experimental group to monitor differences in testosterone and cortisol levels in the afternoon. The control groups rested watching tv and reading newspapers, while the experimental group completed exercises from those mentioned above. In all three research papers, it was found that morning activity significantly increased hormone levels, and in most tests, also increased performance (49, 50, 51).

Key Tip: We can use a short duration high intensity morning session (6 x 40 metre sprints as an example) to minimise the decline in testosterone throughout the day without significantly increasing stress or fatigue.

Neural Priming: What thoughts and feelings can enhance player performance? Answering this question is the key to neural priming. Whatever thoughts and feelings we want players to have, we must use the twenty-four-hour period before the game to activate the neurons firing them.

For example, if we want players to feel brave, our pre-match talk, the music we play, the video we show, and the discussions we have, should be based around bravery. If we want players to think about the process and not the result, we should focus the elements we can control in the process. If we want players to relax then we should influence the factors which make players relax. The next level of application for neural priming is understanding which players need which thoughts and feelings before performance. Some players need to think about how they will feel if they lose to ensure they are focused, some may need to focus on their family to get the best from them. The Individual Zone of Optional Functioning (IZOF) model is one method of identifying and predicting performance in relation to emotional state prior to performance. It focuses heavily on anxiety as one of the key emotions that must be managed on an individual basis to maximise performance. According to research, successful performance occurs when pre-competition anxiety is near or within the individually optimal intensity zones. When pre-competition anxiety falls outside of their optimal zones, individual performance usually deteriorates (52). Neural priming methods can modify the anxiety state to nudge it closer to a player's optimal state.

Technical Priming: How many hours before the warm up should players have their last ball contacts and relative match movements. At times, a team may train in the morning on matchday minus-one, then not play until the evening on matchday. With what we know about neuroplasticity it is clear that the brain is continuously adapting to the environment and our actions; therefore, should we be activating neural pathways responsible for technical actions closer to the match? Some of these actions may be used in a warm up, however there are many that are not. Is it possible to include some of these technical actions in a morning session on the day of the game? Again, this goes back to coach and club preferences. In other individual sports we can find athletes practicing all their motor skills prior to performance. For example, boxers practice the range of moves and punches they are going to be using. A tennis player moves through the range of shots they play including backhand, forehand, serves and volleys. If a key part of the football match plan is to switch play, when should players last practice switching play before the game? Neuropriming is a term used to describe the activation of neurons prior to performance to gain a performance advantage. While there are technological approaches to neuropriming such as halo (53), we can also gain this advantage by ensuring match-relative motor skills are utilised as close to warm up and match time as possible (54, 55).

Decision-making Priming: Prior to a match how can we best trigger the processes that will have a significant impact on the decisions a player makes. One of the most important methods in achieving this is psychologically or practically activating the pictures and principles that are required for the match. This means verbally reminding them, presenting them with video, or letting the players practice them at points during the twenty-four hours prior to kick off. For example, if one of the important principles for the game involves the defensive line dropping early to prevent balls in behind, we can discuss this principle with the defenders, show it through video, or put on a light session with opportunities for players to see and react to the situation. If the attackers are likely to encounter numerous one-vs-one situations with the goalkeeper, and the principle is composure in front of goal, discussions, video, and practice can be used to trigger the picture and principles to be applied when that situation occurs.

Physiological Priming: Preparing the body for performance is the most common priming method used around the world to enhance performance. It often involves a short warm up prior to the match, but what should this look like? Should it be linked to the upcoming game, or be a routine for every match? When is the ideal time to start the warm up, and how many minutes before match time should the warm up finish? Anecdotal evidence has suggested that players warm up for between twenty to forty minutes prior to the match, however prolonged warm up routines have been found to be non-beneficial (56). Research has also indicated that the interval between warm up and kick off could negate some of the warm up outcomes such as decreased core temperature and heart rate and muscle temperature, with the values returning to their baseline (57). There are many warm up habits in relation to physiological priming that have been passed down through experience which are not necessarily supported by research. To attempt to simplify physiological priming, we should focus on key principles that research is currently suggesting, which includes utilising short intense physiological priming as close to kick off as possible, and maintaining activity and temperature where possible during any moments of rest in between breaks. Other factors to consider prior to warm up include monitoring and influencing individual factors such as diet, body temperature, and general movement.

Tactical Priming: Reminding players of what is to be expected of them and the opponents is a key component of tactical priming that is often executed through pre-match talks and video footage. The frequency and time spent on tactical priming is dependent on factors such as the emphasis we place on the opponent vs the emphasis we place on our strategy. Another key factor to consider is the amount of the time the players have had to prepare on the pitch. When playing regular games with minimal training time, tactical priming may become a more important tool than in cycles where there is only one fixture per week and many training days to prepare. Whether players have had many days or no days to prepare, tactical priming can trigger the concepts within the strategy and the pictures that the opponent is likely to create during the match.

Tips: Prime players for performance by:

1. Boosting testosterone and minimising testosterone reduction
2. Carefully managing any cortisol raising activities
3. Minimising any activities that cause fatigue
4. Activating neural pathways required for the match in the brain and the body
5. Linking the match to individual motivations
6. Activating and warming muscle groups
7. Keeping muscles warm and active post warm up routine and during breaks

Logistics

In many coaching environments we have a limited influence over a player's logistics. In academy football it is the parents who take most responsibility, and in senior football there is normally a team manager or director of football, who has the responsibility for organising the team's logistics. If we are lucky, in some environments we have some level of logistical influence. The kind of logistical decisions that influence performance mostly include travel and accommodation. What are the positive and negative outcomes regarding the different logistical options? Some of the decisions we may encounter are whether to fly or take a bus? What time to arrive at stadiums before the game? When to use hotel accommodation and when to travel on matchdays? Many of these decisions may be impacted by a wide variety of factors such as finances, club culture and player preferences. Our role as the coach is to be aware of the influence that logistics can have on players achieving holistic success, and influence logistics where possible to enhance holistic success. There are hundreds of different logistical decisions that need to be made throughout the season, with two ways to approach these decisions. The first is to have a clear set of principles and priorities that are followed. The second way is to evaluate logistical decisions on a case by case basis and decide what is best for short- and long-term performance. Below are a few typical examples that may give context to some of the potential challenges:

Match Travel: When we move towards senior football, the logistical challenges we might identify are vastly different to those we identify at youth level. A common logistical decision which varies across the world of football, is how to manage the night before training. Some countries and clubs prefer to use hotel accommodation before local games so that preparations are under control by the club. Others give players the freedom to stay at home and manage their own nutrition, sleep, and focus. In some environments players staying at home may lead to players sleeping late before a game, whereas in others, players may stay at home and prepare for the match as best as possible. The impact of poor preparation is poor performance, so we must try and influence preparations to be as beneficial as possible.

Post-Match Travel: If playing an evening match, is it best to travel back straight after the match or best to stay in a hotel for the night? If the team travels back straight away, it may limit recovery protocols such as ice baths, nutrition, and a full night's sleep. It does, however, enable players to have a full day the next day without any travel. Which is the better option? It depends on various factors that need to be evaluated. Is recovery protocol more important than players having time off to spend with family or is spending time with family more important? If evaluating on a case by case basis, then factors to consider may include, when is the next fixture? When is the next scheduled training session? When is the next break where players will have consecutive days off?

Youth Players Travel: There is often a difficult period for some youth players in their mid to late teens where they are left to travel by themselves without parents or club assistance. This means that in certain instances, players spend hours getting public transport to get to training and get home. Some players may finish school at four-pm to get to training for five-pm, train until seven-pm, then get home after eight pm and still need to eat and complete their schoolwork. After doing this three times per week, there is bound to be both psychological and physical fatigue, which has a negative impact on performance. If we understand these potential effects, we can identify players who may be going through these challenges, and in some cases, we can assist with club transport methods or adjusting training days or times.

Understanding Potential

Potential is "the possibility of something happening or being developed or used" (25). To understand potential, we must ask two key questions; what is the maximal level that a player can reach? And how close to that level are they likely to get? The maximal level they can reach is determined by the limitations they have, and time they have left to get there. For example, a goalkeeper who is twenty-one, with poor motor skills and height far under six-foot tall has two key limitations in relation to the time they have available. Height, motor skills, and the time for both to develop. These limitations dictate their ceiling of potential. In particular, the athletic aspects of the game can often be the key limitations. If we have a growth mindset, we should have high visions of what level our players can get to. We can develop a player's mindset, we can enhance their motor skills, teach them the game, and give them experiences, however we cannot turn a player who is predisposed to be short, into a player who is going to be six-feet three inches. At many academies, coaches assess the height of a goalkeeper's parents to attempt to determine their maximum height when they have fully matured. At the elite level there are biological tests that are used to identify future height. Once we have identified a player's limitations, we can then identify their ceiling which is labelled potential.

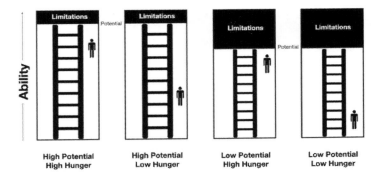

High Potential
High Hunger

High Potential
Low Hunger

Low Potential
High Hunger

Low Potential
Low Hunger

Figure 50: Ladders of Potential

1. Potential: How high is their ladder?

2. Ability: How high up their ladder will they climb? (Represented by the human icon)

Founder of Life Sports Performance, Blaine McKenna, created a template for understanding potential utilising the imagery of players working up ladders to reach their potential (58). The above figure is an adaptation of the model, to look at four types of players in relation to their potential. The message behind this illustration of potential, is that it is our limitations that dictate our potential. It is our hunger that dictates how much of our potential we utilise. Player three, who has lower potential than player two, achieves a higher level of ability due to their hunger to climb the ladder. Player one and two have the same potential, however player two has lower hunger to meet their potential so they end up far behind in terms of ability. Therefore, to identify potential we must identify limitations, but to identify who is going to meet their potential, we must identify a player's hunger to meet their potential. We may be better working with players with lower potential and higher hunger, than higher potential and lower hunger. Of course, in an ideal world, we would love a squad full of players with high potential and high hunger.

Working with Potential

Once we have identified a player's potential and likeliness to meet their potential, we must work with the players to support them in getting there. In order to best support them we must ask one key question. What are they likely to need in their journey that they are unlikely to gain without intervention? This means visualising what the player will look like when meeting their potential, then reverse engineering what the player is likely to gain without intervention, and what they are unlikely to gain without intervention. For example, if working with a player who lacks the speed to dominate their one-vs-one duels, we must identify if their athletic development will give them enough speed to meet their potential, or if they need an intervention to work on their speed during development years. Many attributes of a player's development will occur through the development process of playing regular fixtures and having regular training sessions, however some attributes may need more focus. Lionel Messi required intervention to support his growth deficit in his childhood years, which supported his journey to maximising his potential (59). This was an intervention that was necessary, as without it, it was unlikely that he would have been able to meet his potential. Analysing the performance factors is one method of identifying necessary interventions.

Understanding Form

Form is an ambiguous term used to identify how players are performing over a set period, however there is no measurable way of determining when a player is 'in form'. A goalkeeper can keep consistent clean sheets without playing well, and strikers can play well without scoring goals. If referring to the performance factors in the figure above, we can also identify reasons for why a player may be 'in form' or 'out of form'. When we tend to assess why a player is 'out of form', we often look at football factors. The challenge when only focusing on football factors, is we often miss out on all the other factors that contribute to consistent performance. The Fernando Torres story where he moved from Liverpool to Chelsea brings a classic example of our need to understand form. Torres averaged over one goal in every two games for Liverpool, but in his time at Chelsea he averaged under one goal every five games (60). Throughout his time at Chelsea the media, fans, and pundits all spoke of his 'poor run of form', often linking this to football factors. Only years later did Torres open up about his difficulty with the personalities within the Chelsea team at the time (61), and about his fear of being in certain areas under pressure (62). As coaches, are we skilled enough to identify factors such as these when our players are 'out of form', or do we keep applying pressure on them and give them extra individual training as solutions that miss the actual problem?

Utilising form is a key job for us as coaches. How enhanced would our team's happiness, development and performance be if we could get all our players in 'top form'? And what does 'top form' look like for each player? If we can identify which performance aspects are missing for a player, we can start to bring all our players closer to their 'top form'. For example, if we identify that a player is struggling with relationships within the team, it may be this aspect which will create a significant increase in performance. Understanding this becomes particularly important when arriving at a new club. It would not be difficult to find examples of us arriving at a club and judging players in the first week of training, without even seeing them in top form. In that initial moment at a club, there could be a player dealing with adversity which is limiting their training and match performance. We then end up judging them as not being 'our type of player', or believing they are 'not needed' in the team. After they move onto a new club, and we find they had ability far beyond what we believed they had at the time. This is one of the reasons why players may become surplus to requirements at one club but go on to become a great player at another club. Those initial judgements are vital to determining the success a player is going to have. Therefore, it is important that we work on getting every player on 'top form' before judging their ability.

Understanding Choking

How can we prevent our players from failing in the most important moments? Choking is a common term used by coaches and psychologists when explaining a moment where a player with the required skills has a substandard performance in high-pressure situations, or a negative experience leaving psychologically damaging effects (64). Different to form, choking is often related to a single performance or single moment within a performance, where an action or performance was significantly below expectations, based on previous observations of the player. Choking happens at all levels of sport, so it is critical for coaches and players to understand what choking is, and theories around how it happens. This allows us to create interventions and adapt coaching styles to ensure we limit the frequency of choking with our players. The two main theories of choking are:

1. Distraction Model
2. Self-Focus Model

Distraction Model

The distraction model suggests that athletes who choke are distracted by events that shift their focus from task-relevant cognitive processes, to task-irrelevant cognitive processes. This meaning, a player shifts their focus from aspects which help them achieve success with their actions, to aspects which have nothing to do with achieving success with their actions. This shift in focus then affects the player's decision-making and motor pattern processes. For example, a player who has high success of hitting the target when taking a penalty, is taking a penalty in a cup final, and as they are about to take the penalty, they start to focus on the crowd watching the game. This focus on a task-irrelevant aspect interferes with the hormonal state and neural mechanics, which then changes the execution of the penalty, with the penalty then missing the target. Examples of distractions can be put into two categories; internal distractions, and external distractions. Internal distractions may include, over reflecting on previous actions, and external distractions may include crowd pressure, or pressure from the coach shouting. There is no specific way to measure choking and be one-hundred percent sure they choked, however there are examples such as the Steven Gerrard slip at the end of the Liverpool season which is often referred to as a choking moment (65).

Self-Focus Model

The self-focus model suggests that the cause of choking is linked to anxiety and conscious attention. "Choking occurs because, when anxiety increases, the athlete allocates conscious attention to movement execution, which interferes with the automatic nature of movement execution (66). This therefore causes a decrease in motor skill performance. When a skill is learned in an instructional step by step method, through the repetition, the action becomes an automatic process, and under anxiety an athlete goes back to the step by step method, they may struggle to execute the skill. An example of this would be a player who has learnt how to defend one-vs-one with step by step details, such as speed up, slow down, set your body etc. He eventually becomes a strong one-vs-one defender using the steps, but no longer needs to think about the process. Due to a high-pressure game, anxiety kicks in, and the player tries to revert to the step by step processes. This would slow down and limit the efficiency of the one-vs-one actions, due to interference in the automatic process, and the speed of the step by step thought processes.

Interventions to Prevent choking

High Pressure Specific Training: Prior to high pressure fixtures, can we create high pressure training components to get players used to playing under pressure before the fixture comes. For example, creating scenarios in small sided games where there are consequences for the losers, and rewards for the winners, or creating rules and games to replicate a penalty shootout before a cup game. Where possible, can we add distractions to the actions to test players focus when distractions arrive.

Monitoring and Influencing Anxiety: Can we identify signs of stress and anxiety in our players? Do we know our players well enough to notice when a player's behaviour changes due to stress and anxiety? Once this has been monitored, in the immediate build up to a fixture, it is our job to ensure that players go on to the field with the right level of anxiety and arousal. Players who are extremely anxious may need words that will reduce anxiety, such as "whatever happens in the game, you are going to go on to have a fantastic career in football". As previously discussed, there are many priming methods that can be used to influence the state of players prior to performance.

Educate Players: Can we educate players on the processes of choking, so that they are aware of the importance of executing the actions with the normal processes that they would under training and previous matchday situations. This is key for players who have high anxiety, as it is a natural process for the brain to question its own decision-making under stressful circumstances. Players must know that if they follow the normal decisions and processes as usual, they will be successful.

Summary

1. Understanding performance: As coaches who expect high performance from the players we are working with, we should have a deep and wide understanding of the factors which contribute to performance, from a variety of life, preparation, football, and psychological perspective.

2. Decision-Making and Ability: A player's performance is the sum of the ability the player's body has, and the decisions they make on the pitch. Once we understand all of the factors affecting performance, it is our job to use these factors to best influence a player's ability and the decisions they make.

3. Success leaves clues: Taking time to analyse the best players in the world can give us insights into which factors may be heavily influential for the success of the players we are working with.

4. Variety of experiences: Players should experience a wide variety of experiences throughout their development journey, particularly if we are uncertain of their end destinations inside and outside of football.

5. The player's self: The player must develop an understanding and awareness of themselves which enables them to become independent, make decisions in moderation, motivate and regulate themselves, with an internal desire for success.

6. Lifestyle balance: The life of players outside of football will have a significant impact on their long development and performances. Supporting players in finding the right balance will help them achieve any long-term goals.

7. Priming and preparing for performance: In the build-up to performances, we can use a number of different activities to best prepare players' minds and bodies for maximal performance. We can also encourage players to execute these activities in their own time, outside of group priming activities.

8. Insights from understanding performance: Once we understand performance, we can build a greater understanding of performance factors such as form, potential, and choking. These factors can be critical for long term performance of players at all levels.

References

1. Barcelona Innovation Hub (2019). Applying the principles of Johan Cruyff to Data Science. Available at https://barcainnovationhub.com/applying-the-principles-of-johan-cruyff-to-data-science/ (Accessed 1 May 2020)

2. Kahneman, D. (2012). *Thinking fast and slow. Penguin Books*. UK: London

3. Peters, S. (2012). *The chimp paradox: Mind Management programme for confidence, success, and happiness. Ebury Press*. UK: London

4. Keep it on the Deck. (2017). 50 Inspirational Football Quotes. Available at http://keepitonthedeck.com/blog/2017/6/7/50-inspirational-football-quotes (Accessed 1 May 2020)

5. Njororai, W. (2014). Timing of goals scored in selected European and South American soccer leagues, FIFA and UEFA Tournaments and the critical phases of a match. *International Journal of Sports Science*, *4*(6A), 56-64.

6. Baert, S., & Amez, S. (2018). No better moment to score a goal than just before half-time? A soccer myth statistically tested. *PloS one*, *13*(3).

7. Boon, J. (2018). Mod Almighty: Ballon d'Or winner Luka Modric: the refugee whose granddad was shot dead when he was six who became a world superstar. Available at https://www.thesun.co.uk/sport/football/6730206/ballon-dor-luka-modric-croatia-granddad-shot-dead-refugee/ (Accessed 3 May 2020)

8. Saha, R (2018). Reaction of Juventus Player After Seeing 'Impossible' Ronaldo In Training. Available at https://www.blamefootball.com/2018/08/08/reaction-of-juventus-player-after-seeing-impossible-ronaldo-in-training/ (Accessed 3 May 2020)

9. All News (2014). Fabio Cannavaro: The street urchin who became a World Cup 'legend'. Available at http://worldwideallnews.blogspot.com/2014/05/fabio-cannavaro-street-urchin-who.html (Accessed 3 May 2020)

10. Owen, M (2019). *Reboot: My life, my time*. Reach plc. UK.

11. Dooley, K. (2009). The Butterfly Effect of the "Butterfly Effect". *Nonlinear dynamics, psychology, and life sciences*. 13. 279-88.

12. Sportspsychjimbo. (2013). Perfect practice makes perfect performance – Beckham. Available at https://www.youtube.com/watch?v=7LtWBjPZPVQ (Accessed 3 May 2020)

13. Hodgson, A. (2014). 'There is no pressure when you're chasing dreams' - Neymar shrugs off weight of Brazil. Available at https://www.standard.co.uk/sport/football/there-is-no-pressure-when-youre-chasing-dreams-neymar-shrugs-off-weight-of-brazil-9558402.html (Accessed 3 May 2020)

14. Ankersen, R. (2013). *The Goldmine Effect*. London: Icon Books

15. Wigmore, T (2018). Biobanding: Example of Alex Oxlade-Chamberlain shows how to solve age-old problem of football's late developers. Avaliable at https://inews.co.uk/sport/biobanding-age-group-football-rugby-james-bunce-alex-oxlade-chamberlain-214518. Accessed (3 May 2020)

16. Subramani, P. C. N., Priya, J. J. (2019). Teaching Skills for Effective Teachers.

17. Diedrichsen, J., & Kornysheva, K. (2015). Motor skill learning between selection and execution. *Trends in cognitive sciences*, *19*(4), 227-233

18. Uphill athlete. How myelination can make you a better athlete. Available at https://www.uphillathlete.com/myelination-make-you-better-athlete/ (Accessed 3 May 2020)

19. Savelsbergh, G. (2013). The effects of perception-action coupling on perceptual decision-making in a self-paced far aiming task. *Int. J. Sport Psychol*, *44*

20. Walker, M. P., Brakefield, T., Seidman, J., Morgan, A., Hobson, J. A., & Stickgold, R. (2003). Sleep and the time course of motor skill learning. *Learning & memory*, *10*(4), 275-284.

21. Davids, K., Araújo, D., Vilar, L., Renshaw, I., & Pinder, R. (2013). An ecological dynamics approach to skill acquisition: implications for development of talent in sport. *Talent Development and Excellence*, *5*(1), 21-34.

22. Craig, C., & Watson, G. (2011). An affordance-based approach to decision-making in sport: discussing a novel methodological framework. *Revista de psicología del deporte*, *20*(2), 689-708.

23. Roca, A., Ford, P. R., & Williams, A. M. (2013, May). The processes underlying" game intelligence" skills in soccer players. In *Science and Football VII: The Proceedings of the Seventh World Congress on Science and Football* (pp. 255-260). Routledge.

24. Lennartsson, J., Lidström, N., & Lindberg, C. (2015). Game intelligence in team sports. *PloS one*, *10*(5).

25. Soanes, C., & Stevenson, A. (Eds.). (2004). *Concise oxford English dictionary* (Vol. 11). Oxford: Oxford University Press.

26. Jones, E. (2020). My Life and Rugby. Pan MacMillan. UK: London

27. Phatak, A., & Gruber, M. (2019). Keep your head up—correlation between visual exploration frequency, passing percentage and turnover rate in elite football midfielders. *Sports*, *7*(6), 139.

28. Nunome, H., Drust, B., Dawson, B. (2014). *Science and Football VII: The Proceedings of the Seventh World*. Taylor & Francis. UK: London

29. Klostermann, A., & Hossner, E. J. (2018). The Quiet Eye and motor expertise: Explaining the "efficiency paradox". *Frontiers in psychology*, *9*, 104.

30. Wood, G., & Wilson, M. R. (2012). Quiet-eye training, perceived control and performing under pressure. *Psychology of Sport and Exercise*, *13*(6), 721-728.

31. Race, E. A., Shanker, S., & Wagner, A. D. (2009). Neural priming in human frontal cortex: multiple forms of learning reduce demands on the prefrontal executive system. *Journal of Cognitive Neuroscience, 21*(9), 1766-1781.

32. Duckworth, A. L. (2017). *Grit: Why passion and resilience are the secrets to success.* Ebury Publishing. UK: London

33. Larkin, P., O'Connor, D., & Williams, A. M. (2016). Does grit influence sport-specific engagement and perceptual-cognitive expertise in elite youth soccer? *Journal of Applied Sport Psychology, 28*(2), 129-138.

34. Duckworth, A. L., Peterson, C., Matthews, M. D., & Kelly, D. R. (2007). Grit: perseverance and passion for long-term goals. *Journal of personality and social psychology, 92*(6), 1087.

35. Pavliscak, P. (2019). Emotionally intelligent design: Rethinking how we create products. O'Reilly Media. US: Sebastopol.

36. Marca. (2018). Marcelo says goodbye to Ronaldo: When I retire, I'll sit at the bar and tell our stories. Available at https://www.marca.com/en/football/real-madrid/2018/07/12/5b47274222601d66468b45d6.html (Accessed 1 May 2020)

37. SL Social (2019). Dani Alves Pays Touching Tribute to His Brother Messi. Available at https://www.soccerladuma.co.za/fan-park/update/dani-alves-pays-touching-tribute-to-his-brother-messi/658447 (Accessed 1 May 2020)

38. Giddens, A. (1991). *Modernity and self-identity: Self and society in the late modern age.* Stanford university press.

39. Veal, A. J. (1993). The concept of lifestyle: a review. *Leisure Studies, 12*(4), 233-252.

40. Venter, R. (2012). Role of sleep in performance and recovery of athletes*: A review article. South African Journal for Research in Sport, Physical Education and Recreation.* 34. 167-184.

41. Miles, J. (2019). Making his marc: Leeds training ground upgrade delayed by perfectionist Bielsa complaining that light switches were 'off-centre. Available at https://www.thesun.co.uk/sport/football/8822123/leeds-training-ground-delayed-bielsa-light-switches/ (Accessed 1 May 2020)

42. Austin, S. (2018). Tottenham aiming for mammoth gains in rest and recovery. Available at https://trainingground.guru/articles/tottenham-aiming-for-mammoth-gains-in-rest-and-recovery (Accessed 1 May 2020)

43. Oliveira, C. C., Ferreira, D., Caetano, C., Granja, D., Pinto, R., Mendes, B., & Sousa, M. (2017). Nutrition and supplementation in soccer. *Sports, 5*(2), 28.

44. Barnes, M. J. (2014). Alcohol: impact on sports performance and recovery in male athletes. *Sports Medicine, 44*(7), 909-919.

45. Mills, C. D., De Ste Croix, M. B., & Cooper, S. M. (2017). The importance of measuring body composition in professional football players: A commentary. *Sport and Exercise Medicine Open Journal.*

46. Atakan, M. M., Unver, E., Demirci, N., Bulut, S., & Turnagol, H. H. (2017). Effect of body composition on fitness performance in young male football players. *Turkish Journal of Sport and Exercise*, *19*(1), 54-59.

47. Lorenz, D., & Morrison, S. (2015). Current concepts in periodization of strength and conditioning for the sports physical therapist. *International journal of sports physical therapy*, *10*(6), 734.

48. Janiszewski, C., & Wyer Jr, R. S. (2014). Content and process priming: A review. *Journal of Consumer Psychology*, *24*(1), 96-118.

49. Christian J. Cook et al. (2014). Morning based strength training improves afternoon physical performance in rugby union players., *Applied Sports Technology Exercise and Medicine Research Centre*

50. M. Russel et al. (2016). A Comparison of Different Modes of Morning Priming Exercise on Afternoon Performance. *International Journal of Sports Physiology and Performance*

51. Ekstrand, L. G., Battaglini, C. L., McMurray, R. G., & Shields, E. W. (2013). Assessing explosive power production using the backward overhead shot throw and the effects of morning resistance exercise on afternoon performance. *The Journal of Strength & Conditioning Research*, *27*(1), 101-106.

52. Hanin, Y. L. (2000). Soccer and Emotion: enhancing or impairing performance. *Soccer and science. Copenhagen, Denmark: University of Copenhagen*, *22*.

53. Halo. Available at https://www.haloneuro.com/pages/science (Accessed 4 May 2020)

54. William, Rajesh & Kirubakar, S. (2019). An innovative initiation for sports performance – neuropriming.

55. Ashford, K. J., & Jackson, R. C. (2010). Priming as a means of preventing skill failure under pressure. *Journal of Sport and Exercise Psychology*, *32*(4), 518-536.

56. Zois, J., Bishop, D., & Aughey, R. (2015). High-intensity warm ups: effects during subsequent intermittent exercise. *International Journal of Sports Physiology and Performance*, *10*(4), 498-503.

57. Crowther, R. G., Leicht, A. S., Pohlmann, J. M., & Shakespear-Druery, J. (2017). Influence of rest on players' performance and physiological responses during basketball play. *Sports*, *5*(2), 27.

58. McKenna, B. (2020) Ladder of Potential. Available at https://www.lifesportsperformance.com/experience/ (Accessed 4 May 2020)

59. Williams, G. (2018). Barcelona superstar Lionel Messi opens up about details of childhood hormone injections: 'It was a small needle; it did not hurt... I had to do it'. Available at https://www.dailymail.co.uk/sport/football/article-5523775/Barcelonas-Lionel-Messi-opens-childhood-hormone-injections.html (Accessed 3 May 2020)

60. Wikipedia (2020). Fernando Torres. Available at
https://en.wikipedia.org/wiki/Fernando_Torres (Accessed 3 May 2020)

61. Wilson, S. (2017). Fernando Torres explains why he flops at Chelsea. Available at
https://www.givemesport.com/1034502-fernando-torres-explains-why-he-flopped-at-chelsea
(Accessed 3 May 2020)

62. Lipton, M. (2012) Lost it! Torres admits 'mental block' left him too scared to shoot
Available at https://www.mirror.co.uk/sport/football/news/chelsea-striker-fernando-torres-
admits-846612 (Accessed 3 May 2020)

63. Mesagno, C., & Hill, D. M. (2013). Definition of choking in sport: re-conceptualization and
debate. *International Journal of Sport Psychology*.

64. Kaviraj, T. (2017). 10 biggest chokes in football history. Available at
https://www.sportskeeda.com/football/10-biggest-chokes-football-history/6 (Accessed 3 May
2020)

65. Gröpel, P., & Mesagno, C. (2019). Choking interventions in sports: A systematic
review. *International Review of sport and exercise psychology*, *12*(1), 176-201.

"

TRAINING SESSION
DESIGN & EXECUTION

IN THE END, IT'S ABOUT THE TEACHING, AND WHAT I ALWAYS LOVED ABOUT COACHING WAS THE PRACTICES. NOT THE GAMES, NOT THE TOURNAMENTS, NOT THE ALUMNI STUFF. BUT TEACHING THE PLAYERS DURING PRACTICE WAS WHAT COACHING WAS ALL ABOUT TO ME

John Wooden

Introduction

Objective: The objective of this chapter is to analyse a variety of principles and concepts that should be considered when designing training sessions, which can then be utilised to increase the happiness, development, and performance of all players involved.

Session design and execution are key topics which are frequently discussed by coaches around the world. Coaching sessions are our direct method of impacting individual players and the team from a variety of perspectives. This is the reason why it is so important to be purposeful with our design and execution, so that we can maximise the opportunity for impact. There is no right or wrong session template, we need the full context of every detail to design the best session. The reason why design and execution have been separated is to reflect how the greatest session design is not so great if not executed well, and the best execution is not as effective if the session design is not great. As coaches we must use both session design and execution to enhance the happiness, development, and performance of the players and the team we are working with. In this chapter there are several topics discussed, including purposeful training, reverse engineering the game, and managing coaching moments, as well as topics discussing the following principles that should be considered when designing and executing coaching sessions:

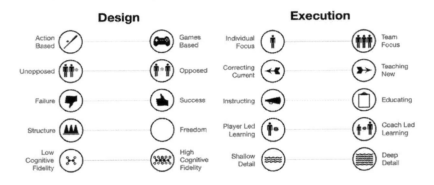

Figure 51: Session Design and Execution Principles

Purposeful Training

The internet has changed many aspects of coaching. One of the key areas that has changed significantly is the availability of session design ideas and concepts. Coaching sessions are so accessible to the public, from session plans that can be downloaded, to session videos that coaches and clubs have recorded. While this can be a huge benefit to coaching success, it can also hinder our growth. Having access to hundreds of session plans is beneficial as it can expose us to a wide variety of ideas and concepts that we can utilise in our own environments. However, one of the potential dangers to the availability of session plans is the cut and paste concept, where we find a session plan that another coach or club has used, then replicate the session for our players and team without any modification for suitability. It is quite unlikely that a session plan for another group is going to be the perfect session plan for the group we are working with. Every group of players has different needs and are at different stages of development within the topic. This means our objectives, session design, and session execution should be unique to our group. The key to purposeful training is being able to utilise ideas that are available to us, to create the best objectives and most efficiently meet those objectives and topics that we have set.

Selecting the Focuses: For some of us, there will be a training programme which dictates the focus for the session, in other environments we may choose our own focus on the day of the session. When we must choose our focus, the starting point should be, what do the players and team need from this session to best prepare them for their short-term and long-term future? If we are working with young players, we should be more heavily focused on their long-term future, whereas working with senior players requires a heavier focus on their short-term future. However, sight should never be completely lost on the opposite term. A young player still requires development of attributes that will help them in their next match, and a senior player still requires development that will make them a better player next season. Getting the balance right in relation to the environment is the first key to a successful session focus.

Objective Creation: After selecting the focus, we should then create objectives for upcoming sessions. There are many considerations which should include achieving happiness, development, and performance. Of course, in each session and each environment, one may be prioritised more than the others. Our objectives should start with; 'by the end of the session'. By starting our objective with 'by the end of the session', we have a measure as to whether the session has been successful. This makes us accountable for ensuring the objective is met. For example:

By the end of the session, all players must be able to execute the Cruyff turn using both feet, and must have experienced executing the Cruyff turn in match realistic situations.

After the session, evaluating the success of the session is a straightforward process. Can all players now execute the Cruyff turn using both feet? Did they all experience using the Cruyff turn in match realistic situations? If the answer is yes, then the session was successful. If the answer is no, then how could the session be designed or executed better next time to achieve a higher level of success. If we are having a lot of success in achieving our session objectives, the more difficult question to answer is, are we setting the best objectives? The only measure of setting the right objectives is the short-term and long-term outcomes. Are the players happy, are the players and team efficiently developing towards their potential, and are the players and team performing beyond expectations? As we become more experienced coaches, we can start to set a number of objectives for one session, which may cover a wide variety of factors, such as conditioning outcomes, psychological outcomes, plus many others. The more positive outcomes we can fulfil, the more efficient we can be in achieving success in our environments.

Reverse Engineering the Game: Our objective is ready. What is the starting point for designing the exercise we are going to use? Is it going through our session folder? Is it searching online to see what other coaches have used or can we create our own exercises? The answer will be different for many of us. Designing our own sessions may be the most time-consuming, mind-consuming, and high-risk option. However, it can certainly be the method which brings innovation to our team, the players, and the coaching industry. Fundamentally, the option we select must bring us the outcome that we are looking for. If we know our players and team well, we are in the best position to design the exercise that will most efficiently meet our objectives. If we are creating our own sessions, reverse engineering the game enables us to start with the full match and work backwards to consider what will be required in the session. Here are some factors to consider when reverse engineering the game to design a session to meet a specific objective:

1. **Actions:** What actions do the players need to repeat frequently?
2. **Location:** What area of the pitch do those actions happen?
3. **Players:** Which players will impact the decision-making and execution of those required actions?
4. **Pictures:** What scenarios need to occur within the exercise?
5. **Rules:** What limitations can support the increase of the required scenarios?
6. **Structures:** What shapes, dimensions and markings will support the increase in the required actions?

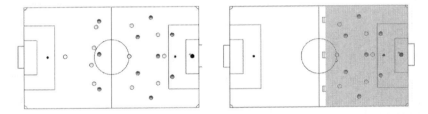

Figure 52: An Example of Reverse Engineering for Session Design

The above figure is a simple example of a full match scenario being broken down into a session. If the objective was, by the end of the session, the players and team must develop an understanding of strategies to build-up against a high press, using ball retention and combination play, this is one method of reverse engineering to design the session. The left image shows a full picture from a situation when the team is building from the back against a high press utilising a goal kick. The image on the right, highlights a key area selected in relation to some aspects of build-up play, including all the players in that selected area, with goals added to replace the attackers who would be receiving the ball in a match. Below are the details considered:

1. **Actions:** There must be a lot of receiving and passing under pressure with options to penetrate
2. **Location:** We need the full width of the pitch and enough depth for players to penetrate the first lines

3. Players: We need the first two lines of build-up, meaning defenders and midfields with opponents to match

4. Pictures: We need the team building-up to experience penetrating against a variety of high presses.

5. Rules: The team building-up scores by scoring in the mini-goals which represent attacking players receiving.

This is a very simplified example of reverse engineering to design a session, however, it is a tool that we can utilise to design our own sessions that meet our specific objectives without having to copy session plans hoping they are going to achieve what we need them to.

Action Based vs Games Based

The first scale is the action-based vs game-based session design. This refers to whether we create an exercise that forces a specific action, or we create a game which encourages those actions to be made. For example, we can set up a one-vs-one exercise where we instruct an attacking player to beat a defending player, or we can create a one-vs-one game with mini goals at each end and give points when they score after being past the opponent. Both methods create a one-vs-one practice for the players involved but each method offers different trade-offs. The decision of which to use, is dependent on the outcomes we are looking for:

Action Based	Games Based
Increased repetition of specific action	Decreased repetition of specific action
Increased control over technical detail	Decreased control over technical detail
Easier to frequently intervene and correct	Harder to frequently intervene and correct
Decreased cognitive fidelity	Increased cognitive fidelity
Decreased frequency of decision making	Increased frequency of decision making
Decreased probability of entering a state of flow	Increased probability of entering a state of flow

Figure 53: Trade Offs: Action Based vs Games Based Exercises

There are several different approaches to action based and game-based exercises, with methods of managing the trade-offs. For example, using game-based approaches, there are strategies to increase repetition, similarly there are action-based methods which increase decision-making. Therefore, the principles are on a scale, with extremities and middle grounds that can be found in between. Within the scale there are specific game-based approaches such as Teaching Games for Understanding (TGFU) and Play Practice Play. More recently there has been a digital gaming approach to coaching design and execution, which includes great tools for us to utilise.

A Digital Gaming Approach: According to research, one-hundred and sixty-four million adults in the USA play digital games (13), and ninety-one percent of children play digital games (14). Twenty years ago, children were more likely to be out playing games in the streets than playing digital games. It is clear digital gaming has a hook on a huge amount of people. Can some of the principles of digital gaming played by children and adults be applied to the coaching world? Can we consider how the 'digital gaming era' may influence the learning styles of the players we are coaching? Coaches such as Amy Price are currently leading the way using digital gaming concepts to develop coaching methodology (1). The idea behind this approach, is understanding the attributes that make gaming so appealing and enjoyable to those who play them and identifying the attributes that encourage people to become better at them and conquer them. Here are some of the gaming concepts to consider when designing coaching sessions:

1. Story: Create a story behind why the session is important.
2. Mission: Create a clear aim for the session.
3. Rules: Create clear conditions that must be stuck to in the session
4. Levels: Create levels that can make the session more difficult
5. Level Up: Create targets that can take to the next level
6. Superpowers: Offer opportunities for the players to earn tools and tips to make them more effective
7. Superheroes: Clearly state the key actions that players must be able to do to be the best in the session
8. Pause: Create opportunities for players to ask for breaks to discuss coaching points to gain success
9. Twists: Introduce changes in scenarios which force the players to adapt in the session
10. Save: Discuss key learnings with players to support them in storing what they have learnt from the session

Below is a simplification of how we can use some of the gaming related considerations in our session design and execution:

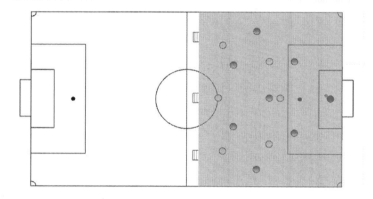

1. Story: If we build-up under pressure, we can dominate this league
2. Mission: Become masters of building up under pressure
3. Rules: Score in the mini goals to gain points
4. Levels: Extra opponents and reduced pitch size
5. Level Up: Three goals for extra opponent, six for reduced pitch
6. Superpowers: After ten passes the opponent must drop deeper
7. Superheroes: Players who can beat their opponent and penetrate
8. Pause: Three intervals for players to discuss or ask for help
9. Twists: Halfway through one team add or lose a player
10. Save: Players conclude three key learnings after the exercise

Opposed vs Unopposed

Another scale often discussed among coaches is whether exercises should be opposed or unopposed. There are numerous studies that have attempted to identify an answer to the opposed vs unopposed question. Research has demonstrated significant changes in participant's coordination when completing a basketball shot, or pass in football when opposed compared to being unopposed (2). Similarly, football specific research has suggested that kicking behaviour is specific to performance context, and some movement regulation features will not emerge unless a defender is present as a task constraint in practice (3). There are positives and negatives to both opposed and unopposed training, and the decision as to which to use again goes back to trade-offs. The decision of which to use should strictly relate to the objectives set for the session. For example, if the session objective is focused on preparing the team for an upcoming fixture, transferability may be a key principle. Therefore, opposed training would be of critical importance. On the other hand, if developing an individual's crossing, there may be times where high repetition is needed and unopposed work may be more suitable. Of course, in the middle of opposed and unopposed we can use semi-opposed training, where there can be a balance which gains some of the advantages of both ends of the scale.

Unopposed	Opposed
Increased control over motor skills used	Decreased control over motor skills used
Increased manipulation of success	Decreased manipulation of success
Increased repetition	Decreased repetition
Decreased contact injury risk	Increased contact injury risk
Decreased cognitive fidelity	Increased cognitive fidelity
Decreased frequency of decision making	Increased frequency of decision making
Decreased probability of transferability	Increased probability of transferability

Figure 54: Trade Offs: Unopposed vs Opposed Exercises

Context is needed to decide between unopposed vs opposed exercises. The only people with the full context are the coaches working with the players and the team. Being aware of both ends of the scale can enable us to find the right balance. For example, during an opposed session it may be possible to have some players working unopposed to develop the areas they are struggling with. For example, within a small sided game, if a player is struggling with receiving on their back foot, there may be an opportunity to give them some unopposed repetition on the outside of the exercise to support their motor skill execution. This is, providing the reason they are struggling is due to their myelination or neural capacity, as opposed to decision-making related aspects. Can we understand and utilise the right balance of opposed exercises and unopposed exercises based on the full context of the environment, the team, and the players we are working with?

Failure vs Success

From both a research and anecdotal perspective, there is no doubt that players and teams must experience both failure and success in their journey to make it to the highest level. Understanding this principle is key when designing and executing coaching sessions. Often due to our ego, we want our coaching sessions to look great to the parents and staff watching us, so that we can get feedback on how great we are. The challenge with this desire, is that failure never looks great to the eye, yet it is needed for the players and teams we work with. For example, a four-vs-one rondo without mistakes looks great to the eye, with a lot of quick passing and movement to retain possession for the four players. It may also be a massive confidence booster. However, if the players have achieved success, why are we not progressing to make it more challenging and forcing failure? This would mean adapting the rules of the rondo, such as reducing the size or adding an extra opponent to make it four-vs-two.

Failure	Success
Challenges players to develop	Limits opportunities to develop
Enjoyable for those with a growth mindset	Can become boring for those with a growth mindset
Decreases confidence for those who are insecure	Increases confidence for those who are insecure
Brings pressure prior to performance	Brings comfort prior to performance
Brings opportunity to increase grit	Limits opportunities to increase grit
Can put strain on group dynamics	Can support group dynamics

Figure 55: Trade Offs: Coaching for Failure vs Success

Getting the timing right for when the team and players need to feel failure, and when they need to feel success is the key. A typical example of utilising failure and success is planning a matchday plus-two session in relation to the outcome of the previous match. If the team lost and did not perform well, they may need the feeling of success to boost confidence, comfort within the environment and a boost in the dynamics between the players. If the team won the match comfortably, and there is a feeling or arrogance, a session designed to promote failure may be beneficial to bring balance back to the players and the team. A second concept to understand is that the need for failure and success can often be an individual need. While a team may feel confident, there may be individuals who are craving success and are not ready for failure. To take our coaching skill to the next level, we should be able to plan a session that forces failure for those who need failure, and success for those who need success. This may mean putting the players who need success, on a stronger team in a small sided game which will make them more likely to win, or putting the players who need failure, in a smaller sized rondo grid so they are more likely to lose possession frequently. The more we can influence the success and failure of the players and the team, the more likely we are to enhance happiness, development, and performance.

Structure vs Freedom

'Let the game be the teacher' has become a common phrase within youth development courses and structures in recent years. One of the key considerations with this point, is that the new generation of football players who no longer play football in the street, are often limited to playing within organised football structures only. With the change in technology and perceived safety of children in some locations, many young football players spend their free time at home playing gaming consoles. This has therefore limited the number of hours a player plays unorganised football without pressure and expectations. There was a belief that this loss in play may be one of the big challenges within player development, which is one of the reasons why the 'let me play' concept became so popular. There are also countries with the opposite situation, where players have limited organised football playing time, and have a lot of free football time in the streets and parks with their friends. Both bring critical benefits to the development and performance of players and teams.

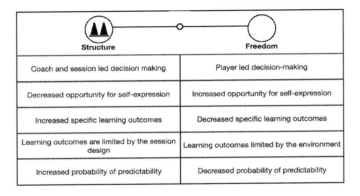

Structure	Freedom
Coach and session led decision making	Player led decision-making
Decreased opportunity for self-expression	Increased opportunity for self-expression
Increased specific learning outcomes	Decreased specific learning outcomes
Learning outcomes are limited by the session design	Learning outcomes limited by the environment
Increased probability of predictability	Decreased probability of predictability

Figure 56: Trade Offs: Session Structure vs Freedom

In an under-six environment where the focus is more weighted towards happiness and development, it may be understandable to coach for half of the session and let the players play freely for the other half of the session. The benefit of this structure may be the high amount of self-expression the players can use, and enough observation time for us as coaches to identify which individual actions players are executing well, and which actions they are struggling with. In a session close to a matchday within a senior setup there may be no time for free play, and frameworks and principles may need to be embedded using a lot of structure and interventions. This more 'robotic' model of coaching certainly has its place in increasing short-term performance. If two coaches joined two different teams and had to play a fixture against each other after just one coaching session, the coach who used a structured approach to organise the team would probably have more success than the coach who gave them the freedom to play throughout the session. In some high-pressure coaching roles, this situation is a reality. Having a minimal number of sessions to prepare a team with the key purpose of getting three points is a common situation in modern day senior football.

Low vs High Cognitive Fidelity

"Training better decision-makers requires simulations that present the user with realistic problem-solving experiences" (4). Cognitive Fidelity is a term that is used in many industries in relation to skill acquisition. In relation to coaching, cognitive fidelity is 'the level to which players are training in situations where their thoughts, feelings and actions are in line with those that will be present in the game'. This means that players are practicing utilising the same cognitive processes to experience different outcomes and therefore make better decisions. To put this more practically, a player who is practicing finishing in situations that create the same thoughts, feelings, and actions, is more likely to improve finishing in those situations. In a game, a winger is delivering crosses while running down the line with pressure from an opponent and teammate support from behind, the player should also practice with these factors during training where possible. In sports such as baseball and cricket, where players have specific roles with a limited number of decisions, cognitive fidelity is easy to maintain, as there is a more limited number of affordances to choose from. In football however, the number of potential decisions is almost infinite. Here are the some of the trade-offs when considering cognitive fidelity:

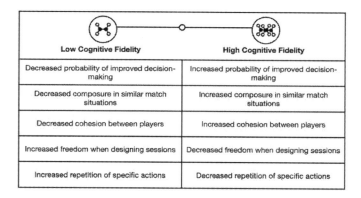

Low Cognitive Fidelity	High Cognitive Fidelity
Decreased probability of improved decision-making	Increased probability of improved decision-making
Decreased composure in similar match situations	Increased composure in similar match situations
Decreased cohesion between players	Increased cohesion between players
Increased freedom when designing sessions	Decreased freedom when designing sessions
Increased repetition of specific actions	Decreased repetition of specific actions

Figure 57: Trade Offs: Low vs High Cognitive Fidelity

If we could utilise high cognitive fidelity while meeting all of our other ideal principles such as high repetition, we would be likely to have significantly more success. However, cognitive fidelity often comes as a trade-off to some of the other principles that we wish to apply. It is not possible to have one-hundred-percent cognitive fidelity during a training session. This is because being against an unpredictable opponent in a competitive situation can already influence the cognitive processes. Though we can still utilise the attributes we can control to increase cognitive fidelity when required. The key to utilising cognitive fidelity is understanding the variety of factors in a situation that influence a player's thoughts, feelings, and actions.

1. Location: The location of the action in relation to pitch markings and the goal.
2. Teammates: The positioning, communication, strengths, and weaknesses of their teammates
3. Opponents: The positioning, actions, strengths, and weaknesses of the opposition
4. Pictures: The pictures the player can recognise before and during the decision-making process?

5. Game State: The match situation, particularly in relation to the score and time remaining

6. Pressure: The level of psychological and practical pressure felt before and during the decision-making process

Training sessions that consider these factors are more likely to be high in cognitive fidelity, meaning the decision- making processes during training are more aligned with the decision-making processes during the match. Below are some of the factors that can be considered when planning sessions to keep cognitive fidelity high. All should be considered in relation to the full match:

1. Players: How many players should be used? Which players? And how should they be utilised?

2. Layout: How big should the area size be? Should it be directional? Which markings should be used?

3. Scenarios: Which game states should be covered?

4. Freedom: What objectives should the players get? Which limitations are realistic to the full match?

This is not to say all sessions must prioritise cognitive fidelity. For example, there may be a place for restricting players to using two touch, however we must be aware that as we reduce the fidelity of the cognitive processes, we therefore reduce the probability of successful transfer to matches.

The Repetition Trade Off: The biggest loss when utilising high cognitive fidelity is the natural occurrence of lower repetition. In an eleven-vs-eleven game, many of the key football components do not have a high level of repetition. For example, a player may only head the ball a small number of times or engage in a minimal amount of one-vs-one duels. However, the cognitive fidelity in an eleven vs eleven game is one-hundred-percent, because it is the real game. In many of the typical high-repetition exercises such as players heading the ball to each other, the number of actions each player is getting is extremely high, in the hundreds potentially, however, the cognitive fidelity is minimal as the cognitive processes of heading the ball to a partner in training are nothing like those used in the game. The key is in finding the sweet spot in relation to the session objectives. Sometimes this may be at either end of the scale, and sometimes this will be somewhere in the middle. There are session objectives that will require extremely high repetition, such as players who are learning to head the ball for the first time. We may need a high repetition basic exercise where players can learn to use the right part of the head with the right technique. However, there may also be a session which requires the eleven-vs-eleven game because we want to observe or prepare the centre back to deal with long balls and make decisions based on the positioning of teammates and opponents. For example, a defender needs to experience dealing with situations where teammates are available to receive the header, teammates are unavailable to receive the header, there are options to head back to the keeper, and there are moments where the ball may need to be cleared. For these situations to occur like the game, it requires opponents playing the long ball, teammates covering and supporting, opponents applying pressure, a large pitch size, plus some pressure on the players to not allow any turnovers in possession.

Individual Focus vs Team Focus

Depending on the environment we are working in, the scale of team focus may be tipped to one side. However, as previously mentioned, this does not mean the other should be ignored or forgotten. Individuals need an element of team structure to support their brilliance, and the greatest teams need the best individuals to achieve success. If working in a development-focused environment such as youth academies, the focus should be tipped towards the individual, and less towards the team. Individual focused coaching means designing a session and executing a session with the individuals as the primary focus. For example, a finishing session with focus on developing each players motor skill execution, with interventions focused on the needs of specific individuals as opposed to generic points for improvement. At the other end of the scale would be a possession session focused on team shape and movement patterns.

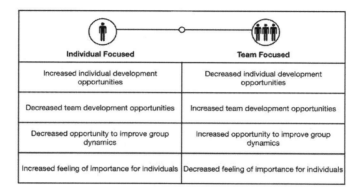

Individual Focused	Team Focused
Increased individual development opportunities	Decreased individual development opportunities
Decreased team development opportunities	Increased team development opportunities
Decreased opportunity to improve group dynamics	Increased opportunity to improve group dynamics
Increased feeling of importance for individuals	Decreased feeling of importance for individuals

Figure 58: Trade Offs: Individual vs Team Focussed

In an ideal situation, we are working alongside assistant coaches, where one coach can focus on the individuals within the team and others can look at the overall team structure and dynamics. This enables us to execute the session addressing both ends of the scale. However, we do not all have this luxury, meaning we must either attempt to focus on both within the session, or decide to focus more heavily on one than the other. When working in an environment that requires significant team and individual focus, we may periodise our focus based on the week or the phase of the season we are in. For example, during the initial weeks of pre-season our focus may be placed heavily on the individual players, ensuring they are developing to the required levels. As pre-season progresses, the focus may switch to more of a team focus to ensure the team is prepared for the season ahead. It is possible we may even start to periodise individual vs team focus throughout a week cycle. At the start and end of the week we may be focusing on correcting and preparing the team for the next match. The days in between may be used to focus on the individuals within the team to ensure they get the attention they need to be happy, to develop, and to perform at training and in the next match.

Correcting Current vs Teaching New

When should we move on from what we are currently teaching? How many of our players must be successful at playing passes to break lines before we move on to a new topic? As coaches, we are responsible for not only correcting what players can execute, but also teaching new attributes, ranging from motor skills, athletic skills, intelligence, and mindset characteristics. How long do we coach crossing and finishing before we move on to central combination play? Finding the right moments to correct current abilities and teach new abilities is a skill we should develop to maximise session outcomes.

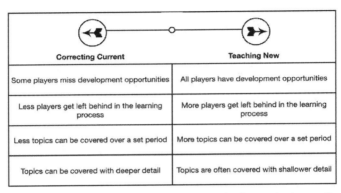

Figure 59: Trade Offs: Correcting Current vs Teaching New

One of the big questions when discussing the trade-offs of teaching new abilities and correcting current abilities; is are we catering for the best players in the group or all players in the group? Our priorities here will guide the decision of when to move on to teaching new information and abilities. There are many coaches and coach educators who speak about senior players lacking 'brilliant basics'. Is this because we move on too quickly as coaches without ensuring enough detail and repetition has been applied to what we are teaching? At one extreme we could spend a whole week teaching the Cruyff turn, ensuring every player can execute the turn effectively, with the right detail, the right speed, and in the right situations. While doing this, there are some players who will certainly be ready to move on before others. Those players ready to move on are potentially missing out on new learning opportunities, while we are focusing on helping those who are not ready to move on. How do we find the right balance between pushing players to move through the learning experiences they require, without leaving players behind? In some environments it is a strategic move to cater for the 'best players'. With the information we have around topics such as biological age and birth bias, catering for the 'best' may leave some of the players with the best potential behind. At senior level, the scale between correcting current ability and teaching new ability becomes even more important, yet even more challenging to manage. There is going to be a wide variety of standards among a group of senior players, where there are experienced professionals who do not need to correct many of their current abilities, alongside others with less experience, who need their ability corrected. For coaches working with senior players, the priority is of course going to lie with the players who are playing in the next competitive match. So, we must find the balance to meet the performance objectives, while still ensuring there are processes to work with the players who need to correct their current abilities.

Instructing vs Educating

We know decision-making is a complex task, but for the purpose of this analogy, let us imagine completing a Rubik's cube was just as difficult. The cube contains options, and each option affects the next option, and that option affects the next one, and eventually will dictate the outcome of whether it is completed or not. Now there are two key approaches to teaching someone to complete a Rubik's cube. For those who have learnt or attempted this, the concept may be more familiar. Option one is, we give them the cube and instruct them step by step on how to complete the cube. Turn this line left, turn this layer right, spin the cube around etc. If we know how to complete it, then they will probably complete it quickly. But now when we give them a new cube unsolved and leave the room, how are they ever going to solve it? They may sit for hours, days, and weeks trying to remember what they were told to do. Especially when the cube does not start off looking exactly as it did the first time. This was an instructional method of teaching, which works when the triggers are all the same and each instruction can be remembered in sequence. In relation to football, set pieces would be an example of phases that may require instructional coaching. Option two is, we teach them the rules and principles of the cross, the edges and corners, then support them in completing the cube with reminders of the rules and principles, if required. There is little argument that the outcome of this would be a slower initial completion of the cube, however, when giving them a new cube and leaving the room, there is now an increased probability that they would complete the cube by themselves. In relation to football, the fact that on a matchday we are not playing, means we must educate players so that when they step on the pitch, they are able to execute the actions and make the best decisions possible to follow the principles of the team and meet the objectives of the game. For most of the decisions made, the outcome will be based on the intelligence of the player, not the memory of instructions, making educating a stronger long-term coaching method than instructing.

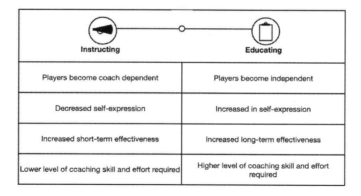

Instructing	Educating
Players become coach dependent	Players become independent
Decreased self-expression	Increased in self-expression
Increased short-term effectiveness	Increased long-term effectiveness
Lower level of coaching skill and effort required	Higher level of coaching skill and effort required

Figure 60: Trade Offs: Instructing vs Educating

If we want to step away from the idea of instructing players and really learn how to best educate players, we must delve into the world of pedagogy. Pedagogy can be explained as the theory of teaching and learning, and the understanding of how they influence each other, to offer development experiences. This meaning, understanding the teaching and learning process that can help us maximise the development experiences that our players have. Many of the principles and concepts discussed in the chapter are key pedagogical principles that are described in relation to the football environment. Using these as tools enable us to improve the learning environment to maximise learning potential.

Player Led vs Coach Led Learning

How many mistakes do we allow players to make before we step in to teach? Are we responsible for facilitating or dictating what is learnt in our coaching environments? These are questions we must ask when deciding the role, we want to play as the coach within a session. A player-led approach refers to the method of allowing the learning process to be controlled by the players, whereas a coach led approach refers to the method of dictating the learning process. At one extreme of the scale, a player led approach may allow players to control the whole session, from the topic they want to work on, to the session they want to execute. At the other extreme, there is the approach of the coach controlling the learning experience by taking full control of the session. In between there are many balances we can use to find the right approach to meet our objectives in the most suitable manner.

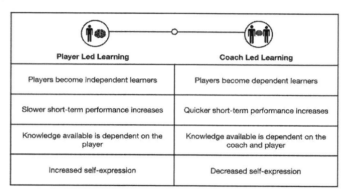

Player Led Learning	Coach Led Learning
Players become independent learners	Players become dependent learners
Slower short-term performance increases	Quicker short-term performance increases
Knowledge available is dependent on the player	Knowledge available is dependent on the coach and player
Increased self-expression	Decreased self-expression

Figure 61: *Trade Offs: Player Led vs Coach Led Learning*

Wherever we sit on the scale of player led vs coach led, there is one element that we must consider. At some point in a player's career, they are likely to have an unsupportive coach, or a coach who is busy working with other players. In these moments, the players who will achieve success, are the ones that lead themselves to developing and performing. Therefore, if we can encourage players to lead themselves, while still supporting them where needed, we have a greater chance of giving them the tools they will need in the future. When identifying the world's best players, they are not the best under one coach, or in one environment. These are players who have pushed themselves to be at the top level of football regardless of the circumstances around them. This means if we sit at the coach led end of the scale, we could potentially be failing our players. At the opposite end of the scale, leaving players to lead themselves all the time may mean we miss out on opportunities to nudge them closer to their potential. An example of finding a balance on the scale is Cristiano Ronaldo's work with Rene Meulensteen. While we are aware that Cristiano Ronaldo has put in the extra hours throughout his years as a professional, we also know that there have been moments where coaches have supported him. For example, Rene Meulensteen frequently spent hours working to get the best from him during vital years in his development. If we listen carefully to Meulensteen discuss his work with Ronaldo, he did not set goals for him and tell him what he must achieve. He guided the process and let the player decide on their own targets and areas for improvement (5). For their coach-player relationshipm that may have been the sweet spot needed to enhance Cristiano Ronaldo's development and performance. Can we consistently find the right balance for our players to ensure they lead themselves to meet their potential, but with our support as coaches to help get them there?

Shallow vs Deep Detail

One of the key attributes that is less spoken about, is the understanding of detail and being able to apply that detail in a coaching session. Every action has so many levels of detail, and the level in which we understand each action will dictate our skill to identify problems, and then apply correct solutions. When watching a full back struggle with one-vs-one defending, how many different possible problems can we identify? Do we just look at their speed, or can we identify body shape, acceleration, footwork, and other deeper details? At times there are simple challenges that players are facing, but as coaches we do not understand enough detail to identify and support them with the problem. This does not mean that we should always teach with a deep level of detail, as there are times when players use detail that we would not agree with but have success with it. How many of us would have taught Ronaldo to shoot using the 'knuckleball' technique? What we can do with our detail, is support the development of the knuckleball shot, using an understanding about the different effects we can have on the ball using different parts of our foot. When designing session plans it is rare to find sections for deep detail, yet that may be the aspect which takes a player to another level.

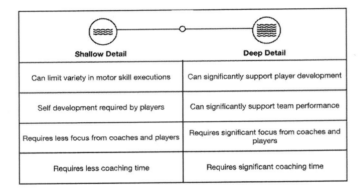

Shallow Detail	Deep Detail
Can limit variety in motor skill executions	Can significantly support player development
Self development required by players	Can significantly support team performance
Requires less focus from coaches and players	Requires significant focus from coaches and players
Requires less coaching time	Requires significant coaching time

Figure 62: Trade Offs: Shallow vs Deep Detail

As the level of competition increases, the requirements for detail will increase in order to ensure success. Similarly, the higher players want to play, the deeper the level of detail they will need to be better than their teammates and opponents. There are many ways to develop our level of detail, and the method we use will depend on how best we learn and what we have access to. One option is to brainstorm each topic before coaching it and consider all the different factors that may affect the success of the action. For example, if coaching finishing, how much detail can we brainstorm that can support a player's development of finishing. Arsenal Academy Coach Temisan Williams has a fantastic book called 'The Coach's Guide to Mind Mapping', which really helps with developing the tools to brainstorm effectively (11). Once we have gone through this process of developing deeper detail across the game of football, we will then have a catalogue of knowledge we can utilise on the coaching field. Here is an example of a brainstorm in relation to finishing:

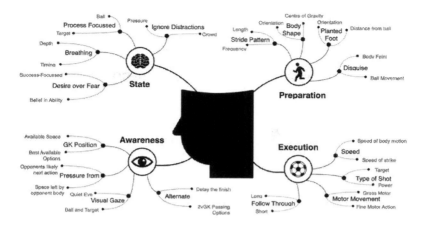

Figure 63: Example of Deep Detail

Flow State

According to Csikszentmihalyi, the concept of flow is a "state in which people are so involved in an activity that nothing else seems to matter" (6). It is described as an 'optimal experience, where we feel a sense of exhilaration and a deep sense of enjoyment where we are choosing to stretch ourselves to our limits (7). This state has also often been referred to as, 'in the zone'. Athletes, artists, religious mystics, scientists, and ordinary working people have described their most rewarding experiences with very similar words and the description did not vary much by culture, gender, age or wealth. During the 'flow experience', athletes have said they reached their optimum performance, and they do not recall how they did it. Often this happens during big occasions, and it can be one of the keys to getting our players developing and performing as close to their potential as possible. Here are eight key elements that are required to be in a state of flow:

1. **Clear Goals:** There is a clear objective to be achieved
2. **Immediate feedback:** Every action can be deemed successful or unsuccessful
3. **High Pressure and Challenge:** High pressure, high challenge, but competence that makes success possible
4. **Continuous Actions:** Continuous practical activity working towards the objective
5. **No Distractions:** Full focus must be on the current experience and meeting the objective
6. **No Fear:** The mind must be working based on desire to achieve not the fear of failure
7. **Time Distortion:** Time must become irrelevant; hours must pass by in what feels like minutes
8. **Enjoyable:** Every moment must be loved, struggle must be an exciting opportunity

If we can consider these factors when designing and executing sessions, we are far more likely to enhance happiness, development, and performance.

Memory

How do we educate and transfer our knowledge to players, ensure they remember it, and know when to use it? The brain contains billions of neurons which transfer information through impulse signals sent across connections. Our connected neurons store our thoughts and memories, some of which can be retrieved and accessed. The synapse strength determines the likeliness of the memory being retrieved again. The key to teaching is to ensure that the important messages have a strong neural network with strong synapses, to ensure they can be retrieved when required. Here are some factors to consider when educating players so that they have stronger neural networks and connections that can absorb and retrieve the information.

Educate with Variety: When educating players, it is beneficial to understand that different players will have different reactions, to different types of education methods. For example, some players can listen to a coach explaining something, and understand exactly what is being taught. Others may need to see it on a tactics board or PowerPoint presentation. Many football players may even need to figure out the lesson through the practical coaching session, with time to experiment and feel what is being taught. There has been much debate regarding learning styles and the reliability of the theory behind them. Without a definitive answer as to their reliability, the key is to cover all the different learning methods to ensure all players are given the best chance of understanding the knowledge, and recalling the knowledge when it is required

Relevance, Emotion and Meaning (REM): To create deeper learning experiences that create easier retrieval of information, there are three key areas to consider when planning the lessons. When educating players, using relevance, emotion and meaning, enhances the learning process. For example, if educating players on the technical detail when receiving in tight areas, explaining why it is important to receive in tight areas and linking it to the feeling of creating more chances and therefore winning more games, players will be more likely to take the technical detail on board.

Repetition: When information is repeatedly absorbed, the neural pathways become stronger, meaning the likelihood of retrieving the information increases. Therefore, a continuous repetition of key messages increases the likelihood of the information being stored, and players being able to recall and therefore apply the messages with greater ease and accuracy. For example, the more we repeat set piece instructions in the build-up to a game, the more likely it is that players will remember their roles.

Story Power: Can we create a story to link emotion to the importance of what is being taught? Stories are an extremely powerful way of creating REM, as they give depth, detail, and a connection to the people listening. Peter Guber, whose films have earned over $3 billion worldwide, with fifty Academy Award nominations says, the power of story, which is emotion combined with information, becomes memorable and actionable (8). The key to the story, is creating value by linking the emotion to the learning, to create a connection. For example, telling a story of being successful against all odds, and linking it to showing perseverance in a football situation, can link the emotions of grit and determination, to succeeding as an underdog or in challenging situations. This meaning, in a situation like the story told, the emotions will be activated so the brain can react in the necessary way to get the desired outcome.

Active Retrieval: After teaching a topic or discussing concepts through video analysis, it is vital to bring these scenarios to life using coaching sessions that require retrieval of the information. They are then able to link the information stored in the brain, to the real-life decision-making they must make on the pitch, making a mental memory, as a practical piece of information that they can execute in the future. For example, if we have just been discussing the principles of defending underloaded, it is then important to create a practical exercise where the player can practice using the information. Not only does it help with storage and future retrieval, but it also gives us the chance to check for understanding and make further corrections, if needed. The most powerful tool for checking if a player understands the information, is to observe real life examples of the situations where the player must implement the information.

Chunking: George A. Miller, a cognitive psychologist introduced the teaching method of 'chunking', meaning to group pieces of information together, to create one large piece of information, as opposed to scattered pieces of information (9). When teaching any topic, it is vital to break the topic down into smaller topics that are easier to learn in a short space of time. For example, to teach a player a whole game model in a day, would be extremely challenging, and would mean only certain aspects may be learnt, and a large amount of information would not be retained. Breaking it down into smaller topics such as 'build-up', then into even smaller topics such as 'build-up against a zonal high press', may achieve a higher level of learning, and allow more detail to be applied to the lesson. Similarly, when focusing on a certain topic on the coaching pitch, it enables players to store all the information in one 'memory pocket' that is connected, with all the key terminology necessary. Players need to be consciously aware of where the information must be stored, and in which situations the information needs to be retrieved. Furthermore, chunking allows clarity in coaching, as it will help define which pieces of information are relevant for the session, and which pieces of information can be saved for another chunk.

Building Group Dynamics

When planned carefully with attention to detail, training sessions can be used to enhance group dynamics. The power in building dynamics through training is that the players are not focusing on the relationship building aspect. It is subconsciously happening while they are focusing on the session activities. Below are methods we can use to build dynamics:

Contact: There are many great coaches that can be seen making regular physical contact with players during training sessions and matches. It is certainly not a coincidence. According to research, athletes speak highly of the importance of physical touch such as high fives, hugs, physical manipulation of the body, pats on the back and hand shaking (10). Actions such as these help build social well-being and trust in a working environment between people. There are several exercises that can incorporate these actions, not only between coaches and players, but between players themselves.

Pairs and groups: Most sessions will require the group to be divided into pairs or teams. In this time there are key opportunities to build relationships between players in the same unit, or players that have had previous conflict. Encouraging players to work together can enable players to find their similarities and put their differences aside. It also encourages positive communication where communication may not have existed previously.

Incorporating Staff: In some environments it is the technical team that requires relationship building, either with each other or with the players. Training sessions can be a great method to build relationships between technical team members and players. If the schedule allows a team building focus, a technical team member can be put with a group of players to compete at a task that requires positive communication.

Designating Roles: Giving out roles during training sessions also gives an opportunity to manage the hierarchy within the group. Giving players roles such as leadership based on their expertise can be a great tool. For example, asking the fittest player to lead the group during an endurance running exercise, or giving communication roles to players who struggle with building relationships in the group.

Coaching Moments

Coaching moments are strategies used at the start, during and end of training sessions to enhance the learning experience of players. Ideally the methods used should create maximal learning with minimal interruption of the overall experience. There are two approaches to coaching moments. One is planning the key moments prior to the session, and the second is identifying them as the session happens. Both approaches are useful, as there are likely to be some key moments that may require a high level of detail, which can be identified during the planning stage. Identifying moments as the session happens allows us to intervene in moments that we may not have expected to occur. Here are some aspects to consider when planning coaching moments:

Methods for Coaching Moments

There are a wide variety of methods that can be used to educate players before, during and after the session. The best methods used depend on the objective for the session and the environment we are working in. Being aware of the variety of methods we can use, gives us the opportunity to select the most suitable method for the specific moment.

Pre-Session Coaching: Educating players before the session has many benefits. It gives a reference point to use during coaching moments in the session, allowing us to refer to what was discussed before the session. It also engages players and starts activating neurons to prepare the mind and body for the actions and decisions that are going to be required. Pre-session coaching may not be necessary for all sessions, for example, when the objective is for players to psychologically relax or recover, coaching before the session may set the wrong tone. One of the biggest advantages to pre-session coaching is the ability to use video footage and tactical boards over a longer period. We can have a fifteen-minute video session before the session starts, whereas stopping mid-session for fifteen minutes is unlikely to be ideal.

Stop, Stand, Still: This is one of the most common methods of coaching. Stop, stand, still, refers to the process of stopping the whole exercise to give coaching points to the players, units, and team. The benefits of this method are that if stopped at the right time, everyone can see the exact picture and situation we are referring to, and we can also have the attention from all the players involved. The downside is that this method significantly decreases ball rolling time. In a twenty-minute session with four one-minute interventions, we lose twenty percent of the potential ball rolling time. In many circumstances we can use minutes at a time coaching without even realising. Managing the time we spend for 'stop, stand, still' interventions is critical to keeping the player's focus, and meeting the session objectives. A key aspect to this method is also to understand the two options when freezing. One option is to freeze the exercise just before the picture or moment occurs. For example, if coaching a team to prevent crosses coming into the box, we can freeze the exercise just a winger receives the ball before they cross, to paint the picture of how the defending team should deal with the situation. The second option is to freeze after the problem has occurred. This would mean freezing the exercise after a cross has been delivered to correct what happened. The advantage to stopping it before, is that everyone can see the trigger, and the action that links to the trigger. When the ball goes wide to the opponent's winger (trigger), the defensive and midfield lines must shift and force the winger inside (action). The advantage to freezing after the problem is that the players get to see why the topic is so important, and we have a chance to observe how the players deal with the situation. Both methods are beneficial when selected with the right purpose.

Continuous Coaching: If we would rather keep the exercise going to maximise ball rolling time, we can coach without stopping the session. This involves coaching individual players, units, and the team while the exercise is on. Our coaching position is key to this method. For example, if coaching an eleven-vs-eleven session, and we want to coach the defensive line, it may be best to take a position behind the defenders to continuously give them information. In this situation we can speak with one player or the unit without stopping the exercise. The advantage to this method is that the ball rolling time stays high to maximise learning outcomes. On the other hand, the situation that we want to coach often moves on, meaning we must verbally or physically make references back to the situation.

Group Discussions: Another method is to use breaks in the session to bring the group together to develop and share knowledge. This can be led by coaching staff, a specific player such as a leader, or it can be an open discussion between all players. Deciding between these options is key to the success of the intervention. If we can use player led discussions at the right time it can be a powerful tool to encourage leadership within the group. The advantage to group discussions is that there is an increased time to teach and share ideas with everyone able to pay attention. The disadvantage is that the reference of the specific moments in the game, must now be recreated on a tactics board or through physical references, unless we are fortunate to have live analysis running where video footage of the moments can be used. A great time to use group discussions is when rotating teams in an exercise, for example a small sided game with two players playing and one team resting. In the time the team is resting, a group discussion can be used to correct and improve performance when they return inside the exercise.

Exercise Adaptations: In some moments we can influence player actions with practical reactions to moments that we observe. For example, if identifying a midfielder not searching when receiving, we can step in and become an opponent to put pressure and force them to scan. Also, we can adjust the session structure or rules. For example, if a winger keeps dribbling wide, we can cut the corner of the pitch to force the winger to start dribbling inside. This method enables the game to stay flowing, with players still taking full responsibility for their decision-making and allowing us to choose other moments to coach that may be more critical to the objective of the session.

Post-Session Coaching: After a training session there is still a great opportunity to educate the players on aspects that went well and aspects that can be improved. Video can be used to support this process when available. If not, this may be more like a session debrief with references to specific points that need to be raised. If the objectives have been met, post-session coaching is not always necessary. At times it may be more important to let players finish the session with a fun activity leaving them ending the session with a positive feeling.

Selection of Coaching Moments

As well as understanding the different methods we can use, it is also important we consider which moments we should select to coach and which moments we should let go.

Exercise introduction: Often when players start a new exercise there is an initial phase at the beginning where players are adjusting to the rules and structures. In this period, mistakes are likely to be high. If these mistakes are due to developing an understanding of the session, this may not be the right moment to intervene. This slows down the process of players feeling comfortable in the exercise to then be able to focus solely on their football actions. This is one of the reasons why clubs and coaches repeat 'core sessions' throughout the season, as this initial phase of adjustment is eliminated.

Error awareness: When players make mistakes that everyone is aware of, what is our purpose in coaching the moment? For example, if a defender plays a weak back pass to the goalkeeper and the opponent scores, do we need to go in and coach this moment? All players on the pitch are aware of the error, going in to coach, reduces the ball rolling time and increases emphasis on the error. Letting the moment go is likely to allow the player to reflect on the error and correct it themselves. This allows other moments to be selected that may be more important to be corrected. We can always check the player's understanding of the error during a break or after the session.

Player personality: Once we are aware that players are all different, it is then fair to expect that players react differently to being coached in front of others. If we can identify how each player learns best and prefers to be coached, we can identify when we should and should not intervene. For example, leaders in the group may react differently to the young players in the group. If a leader makes a mistake, it may be better to deal with the mistake on a one-to-one basis either during or after the session, rather than using 'stop, stand, still' in front of everyone. A great method to develop this skill, is to ask players how they prefer to be coached and utilising that method to support them.

Frequency of Coaching Moments

How much time we spend coaching vs how much time we spend observing can be a difficult balance to get right. If we freeze a session too often or speak too frequently throughout a session, we are likely to frustrate the players and limit our observations. How many times we intervene will also dictate the ball rolling time and the focus that the players give to the session. We should aim to find the right number of interventions that optimise player learning, player focus and ball rolling time.

Duration of Coaching Moments

We frequently believe the duration of our interventions is shorter than it is. Across a variety of levels, it is common to hear our predicted ball rolling time is shorter than the real ball rolling time. Measuring our ball rolling time is a great exercise to use to get an understanding of how the duration of our interventions affect the time players actively spend participating in the exercises. When continuously coaching, how can we keep our communication shorter by using key words and phrases that players understand as opposed to using full sentences and explanations throughout an exercise.

Communication

All forms of communication such as tone, volume and body language have a significant effect on the coaching moment. How can we use communication to ensure players are engaged and clearly understand the message we are getting across, in an efficient manner? Demonstrations can support the technical education process, and buzz words that relate to principles of the game can enhance the decision-making education process. Communication has been discussed previously regarding working alongside players and staff. The following considerations can help us with using a variety of communication styles during our coaching moments.

Command: Instructing players what we want them to do in the specific situation
Refresh: Reminding players what principles or rules need to be implemented
Educate: Teach players the details around the situations such as what, how, when, why, where
Question: Asking the players to give their input into what they think regarding the topic
Demonstrate: Executing the actions that we want players to use in relation to the topic or situation.

The Punishment Problem

Punishments for performance is becoming branded as an 'old school coaching method', however, it is still very prevalent across football. Physical development is a key part of the programme in a training week and will often involve conditioning exercises at some point. When players are carrying out these physical training elements, how do we want the exercises to be viewed? Hopefully, we want them to be viewed as an opportunity to build their athletic capacity to help them improve performance and prevent injuries. However, from a psychological perspective, if conditioning exercises such as press ups and sprints are used as punishments, eventually the brain will start to associate conditioning exercises with negativity and punishment. This in turn will cause a decrease in focus in the level to which they push themselves during conditioning sessions, which is the opposite of what is required. During conditioning sessions, to significantly create a physical overload, players need to have a heavy desire to push past their normal level with intense focus, to gain the benefits of the exercises they are completing. This means players need to have a positive association with the exercises. How do we do this if we use them as punishments? The second challenge with using conditioning exercises as punishments, is that it is does not deal with the actual reason why the performance is not high. For example, in a crossing and finishing exercise, when players are unsuccessful, it may be due to a lack of focus or desire because they do not believe in the importance of perfecting the actions. It is often seen as a fun part of the session for them to enjoy. If this is the case, then the issue that needs to be dealt with, is their beliefs about the session. Punishing them is not changing their beliefs about the importance of practice, it is only changing their reaction to that individual exercise. Amanda Stanec discusses this in her blog 'Move Live Learn' where she quotes a previous colleague, Coach Rider. "Punishment via fitness and exercise shows both a lack of understanding about the efficacy of punishment and a lack of creativity regarding dissuasion. If you make the losing team do sprints, you can only justify it if their fitness kept them from success, and even then, once losing, they probably unconsciously started saving their energy for the sprints. If a kid is being disruptive in practice and you make them run, you haven't solved the problem, but rather you've just avoided dealing with it. That pretty much ensures that it will happen again" (12).

Summary

1. No right or wrong: As coaches we often argue about which session principles are correct and which are incorrect. There is no right or wrong answer without understanding the focuses and the objectives of the session.

2. Objective Efficiency: We should be setting objectives which get maximal impact from the time frame we have with the players in our environments.

3. Reverse Engineering the game: When designing sessions, our initial thoughts and pictures should start with the full match. Once considering the requirements of the full match in relation to the focus, we can then break down the picture to create the most suitable sessions.

4. Design vs Execution: Great session design can become ineffective if the execution is not great. Similarly, great execution and poor session design can also create minimal room for development and performance improvements.

5. Level of detail: There is a real deep level of detail that we can study to gain a better understanding of the topics we are working on. If we take the time to study the topic we will be in a better place to identify and support development opportunities throughout the session.

6. Design vs copying: Where possible we should take the time to design our own sessions in relation to the specific outcomes we are looking for, and specific players and teams we are working with. When this is a challenge, we should at least adapt the sessions we copy from others to suit those we are working with.

References

1. Price, A., Collins, D., Stoszkowski, J., & Pill, S. (2019). Coaching Games: Comparisons and Contrasts. *International Sport Coaching Journal*, *6*(1), 126-131.

2. Gorman, A. D., & Maloney, M. A. (2016). Representative design: Does the addition of a defender change the execution of a basketball shot? *Psychology of Sport and Exercise*, *27*, 112-119.

3. Orth, D., Davids, K., Araújo, D., Renshaw, I., & Passos, P. (2014). Effects of a defender on run-up velocity and ball speed when crossing a football. *European Journal of Sport Science*, *14*(sup1)

4. Bell, B., Szczepkowski, M., Santarelli, T., & Schlachter, J. (2005). Cognitive Fidelity as a Touchstone for On-Demand Team Training. In *Behaviour representation in modelling and simulation conference proceedings*.

5. Mulensteen, R. (2020). MPFC Youth Soccer Development Podcast | Episode 52 - René Meulensteen. Available at https://www.youtube.com/watch?v=U7kEXRvIWLY (Accessed 10 June 2020)

6. Nakamura, J., & Csikszentmihalyi, M. (2009). The concept of flow. In Snyder, C. R., & Lopez, S. J. (Ed.). Oxford handbook of positive psychology. Oxford University Press, USA, 89-105

7. Csikszentmihalyi, M. (2014). Toward a psychology of optimal experience. In *Flow and the foundations of positive psychology* (pp. 209-226). Springer, Dordrecht.

8. Van Gorp, T., & Adams, E. (2012). *Design for emotion*. Elsevier.

9. Xu, F. (2016). Short-term working memory and chunking in SLA. *Theory and Practice in Language Studies*, *6*(1), 119-126.

10. Kerr, G. A., Stirling, A. E., Heron, A. L., MacPherson, E. A., & Banwell, J. M. (2015). The Importance of Touch in Sport: Athletes' and Coaches' Reflections. *Int'l J. Soc. Sci. Stud.*, *3*, 56.

11. Gervis, M., & Williams, T. (2017). *The Coach's Guide to Mind Mapping: The Fundamental Tools to Become an Expert Coach and Maximize Your Players' Performance*. Meyer & Meyer Sport.

12. Stanec, A. (2013). Punishing with exercises. Available at http://movelivelearn.com/20130530punishing-with-exercise-tres-uncool/ (Accessed 8 June 2020)

13. Entertainment software association (2019). 2019 Essential Facts About the Computer and Video Game Industry. Available at https://www.theesa.com/esa-research/2019-essential-facts-about-the-computer-and-video-game-industry/ (Accessed 1 June 2020)

14. Reisinger, D. (2011). 91 percent of kids are gamers, research says. Available at https://www.cnet.com/news/91-percent-of-kids-are-gamers-research-says/ (Accessed 2 June 2020)